W9-BDB-830

CANADIAN PACIFIC

SUSAN GOLDENBERG

CANADIAN PACIFIC

A Portrait of Power

FACTS ON FILE METHUEN

New York   Toronto London

Copyright © 1983 by Susan Goldenberg

All rights reserved. No part of this publication may
be reproduced, stored in a retrieval system or transmitted
in any form or by any means, electronic, mechanical,
photocopying, recording or otherwise, without the prior
written permission of the Publisher.

Published in Canada by Methuen Publications, 2330 Midland
Avenue, Agincourt, Ontario M1S 1P7, and simultaneously in
the United States of America by Facts on File, Inc.,
460 Park Avenue South, New York 10016.

Canadian Cataloguing in Publication Data

Goldenberg, Susan, 1944–
Canadian Pacific: a portrait of power

ISBN 0-458-96740-8
1. Canadian Pacific Limited—History. I. Title.
HD9505.C3G64   1983   338.7'613805'0971   C83-098926-9

Library of Congress Cataloguing in Publication Data

Goldenberg, Susan.
Canadian Pacific.

1. Canadian Pacific Limited. I. Title.
HD2756.2.C2G64   1983   338.8'8971   83-8922
ISBN 0-87196-904-1

Excerpts from *The Foundations of Its Future* by Stephen
Leacock are reprinted with permission from Joseph E.
Seagram Company. The advertisement, *Henry, A Second
Class Citizen*, is reproduced with the permission of Great
Lakes Forest Products Ltd.

Printed and bound in Canada by John Deyell Company

1   2   3   4   5   83   88   87   86   85   84

To My Parents

Contents

Acknowledgments

On December 2, 1981, I wrote Canadian Pacific requesting interviews with senior executives for this book, explaining that it would deal with the diversification that makes CP a microcosm of Canada's economic growth.

My letter was referred to Mr. Robert Rice, CP's general manager of public relations. On February 16, 1982, I met with Mr. Rice at his Montreal office, following nine long-distance calls in an effort to arrange a meeting. Such waits are not unusual for journalists wanting to do in-depth interviews with senior CP executives. Mr. Rice told me that CP once kept *Business Week* waiting two years for an interview.

We had lunch and Mr. Rice gave me some written material already available in libraries. I also got to see the Royal York Hotel and CP's freight routing center, both of which are tours open to the public. But requests for more substantive information were stonewalled.

At our February 16 meeting, Mr. Rice said CP's senior executives would not be available for interviews until perhaps late 1982 or 1983, but that I could see CP's operations. Subsequently, he wrote on February 24, 1982: "It would be helpful if you took the time to develop a detailed outline of the contents. . . .I feel it is necessary to have such an outline so that we can move ahead in a planned and coordinated manner. I am informing the senior officers of Canadian Pacific and its subsidiaries of our discussions and telling them that your process of research will be coordinated by me."

Since this book was not commissioned by CP and my publisher was satisfied with the outline I had given him, I did not provide Mr. Rice with the material he demanded. In addition, because this is an independent book, I viewed the setting up of appointments at CP's subsidiaries as my responsibility and wrote them directly. I also wrote CP's senior officers that if they did not want to talk about the company's performance before 1983, they might at least be willing to discuss human interest material. Subsequently, Mr. Rice informed me that he was telling the subsidiaries not to show me their operations, even though tours of many are given to schoolchildren and other members of the public.

Mr. Rice's prohibition did not turn out to be a handicap. Executives at the subsidiaries did speak to me, despite Mr. Rice's edict, and I did see their operations, traveling across the country to do so, even up to a lead and zinc mine in the Arctic opened by a CP subsidiary in 1981. I also wrote on the mine for *The Dallas Morning News*, for which I was then Toronto correspondent. Although Mr. Rice retracted his promise to arrange for me to see the Rogers Pass in the Rockies, that Pass can be seen by anyone who takes the Via Rail transcontinental train that goes through it—which was what I did.

I would like to thank those CP executives and other staff at the subsidiaries who were most gracious to me. I would also like to express my appreciation to those former CP employees who gave generously of their time. As I interviewed several hundred people in Canada and the United States for this book, including government and union officials, investment analysts, CP directors, friends and colleagues of CP executives, competitors, lawyers, and environmentalists, it is not possible to list each person by name, but I do thank all of them for how very helpful they were.

However, I would single out, in alphabetical order, the following people for special thanks: Donald Armstrong, McGill University Professor; John Arnett, former press aide to British Columbia Premier William Bennett; Albert Ashforth, former

Toronto-Dominion Bank President; Robert Bandeen, Crown Life Insurance Chairman and former Canadian National President; Premier William Bennett; Terrance Salman, Vancouver investment analyst; and Rod Sykes, former Mayor of Calgary.

In addition, I am grateful to Keith Knowlton; John McKellar; and Jim and Tom Yarmon.

And, of course, my very special thanks to Methuen Publications.

S.G.
July 1983

1

Windsor Station

The hub of the Canadian Pacific empire is rambling Windsor Station in Montreal. Its limestone exterior, turrets, and towers prompted rival Canadian National Railway's executives to nickname it Windsor Castle. The name was actually derived from one of the surrounding streets, which was later renamed Peel Street.

The station, completed in 1889, four years after the last spike was driven by CP on its transcontinental railway, is eerily quiet these days. Most passenger rail traffic in Montreal goes to Central Station below the Queen Elizabeth Hotel.

Above the station, CP's headquarters have just been brought into the twentieth century through a gradual modernization program. Ceilings were lowered, softer recessed lighting installed, and a women's washroom finally put on the second level of the four-storey building—previously, female employees had to take either the one elevator or climb the stairs to the third or fourth floor. The carved mantels, expensive furniture, and fireplaces in the upper echelon's offices have been retained. But the long, oval boardroom table, made of teak wood from the East, where CP steamships used to pick up exotic goods, has been replaced with a rectangular table, with leather chairs and blotters in CP's traditional color of blue. The corridor of senior executives' offices has been dubbed "Peacock Alley" by other staff.

These are not the only signs of CP's recognition of late twentieth-century realities. Canadian Pacific Enterprises—CP's twenty-one-year-old offspring through which it has diversified

1

into a sprawling collection of businesses including steel, mining, hotels, oil and gas, bake mixes, fertilizers, insurance, and pulp and paper—used to be headquartered across the street from CP in the company's Place du Canada. But in 1982, CPE, which now accounts for about 60 percent of total CP income, moved west to Calgary. It is now in the octagon-shaped PanCanadian Plaza, head office of CPE's oil and gas subsidiary, PanCanadian Petroleum Ltd.

The shift brought CPE to where Robert Campbell is located. Campbell, who is the chairman of PanCanadian, is also vice-chairman and chief executive officer at CPE and heir apparent to CPE Chairman Ian Sinclair, who moved from Montreal to Toronto to be nearer, according to the company, Canada's financial and investment community.

"CPE's move to Calgary has placed it nearer the head offices of Cominco and PanCanadian, its prime sources of revenue, cash flow, and earnings," says Terrance Salman, vice-president for western Canada of Nesbitt, Thomson Securities Ltd. and a longtime CP watcher and admirer (his ties with CP are so close that he was one of the seconders of corporate motions at CPE's annual meeting). "The move also astutely recognizes the growing importance of Calgary as the financial center of western Canada. The twenty-first century belongs to western Canada and CP has made a major step to be part of that."

Shifting its corporate staff was not an exorbitant proposition because CPE is headed by a lean staff of about two dozen people, including an acquisitions group and a team of economists, supported by a treasury department of about fifty in Toronto.

Between them, CP and CPE have become an industrial colossus, a portrait of the corporate power that Canada is so eagerly pursuing in order to become a major player on the world economic scene. The CP empire epitomizes both the size and multinational scope that Canadian firms are seeking and gradually attaining and provides a portrait of the social, ethical, and environmental issues facing the modern corporation.

However, it is revenue that has given this colossus its power, and not profit margin (net income as a percentage of revenue). Its profit margin has often been less than that of many smaller Canadian companies. So big has CP become, that its 1982 revenue of $12.3 billion from its massive total of 160 major segments, plus its majority or minority interest in another 112 smaller firms,* was equivalent to the gross national product of New Zealand and twelve times that of Jamaica. It is larger in terms of sales than such American corporate giants as Union Carbide, Xerox, and Westinghouse Electric. If it were so inclined, CP could use its revenue to buy the combined assets of General Motors of Canada, Imperial Oil, and Simpsons-Sears. If it were ranked in the annual list of the top five hundred U.S. corporations compiled by *Fortune* magazine, it would be in the upper strata, ranking thirtieth.

Two CP subsidiaries alone, Cominco and AMCA International Ltd. (engineering materials and services) own a total of close to seventy companies—Cominco owns thirty and AMCA, thirty-nine. These two companies by themselves, out of CP's huge family tree, have more subsidiaries than the fifty-six owned by CP's government-owned rival, Canadian National.

One CP subsidiary—CP Rail—has revenue of more than $2 billion. Three subsidiaries—AMCA International, Canadian International Paper, and Cominco—have revenue exceeding $1 billion. And four—CP Air, Algoma Steel, Maple Leaf Mills, and PanCanadian Petroleum—generate between $500 million and $1 billion. From 1970 to 1980 the success of these and the dozens of other CP companies helped CP's assets rise sixfold and its profit expand twentyfold.

It should be kept in mind that the buying value of the dollar has fallen by about 60 percent since 1970. Also, because CP is involved in most sectors of the economy, its results in 1981, and especially in 1982, reflect a battering by the recession and drag down the comparison with a decade ago. In 1982, CP's profit of $188.3 million was just slightly more than the profit in 1974 ($181.3 million), although it was up fourfold over 1972's $44.7 million. But while the profit comparison was nothing to brag about in 1982, CP's revenue still was up a respectable six times over what it was in 1972, and its assets had quadrupled during that period.

---

*See Appendix, Table 3.

CP has reached the pinnacle among Canadian companies in terms of revenue, even though most of the firms it owns are not the largest in their field, despite their massive size. This keeps CP safe from government anti-trust suits. CP Rail is outranked in revenue by CN. CP Air is second in revenue in the airline industry, after Air Canada. Stelco and Dofasco are in the top two spots in Canada's steel industry, while the CP-owned Algoma Steel Corporation is in the third. Although Cominco Ltd., CP's oldest non-transportation business, is Canada's largest lead and zinc producer, among mineral producers generally it is surpassed in revenue by Noranda Mines and Inco.

The largest CP pulp and paper company, Canadian International Paper Inc., is fourth in revenue in its field, outranked by MacMillan Bloedel Ltd., Domtar Inc., and Consolidated-Bathurst Inc. And although Marathon Realty Ltd., CP's real estate arm, has the largest land holdings in Canada, it still ranks only eighth in dollar value of assets among Canada's leading publicly owned real estate companies. PanCanadian Petroleum Ltd., which ranks seventh in proven reserves of oil in Canada's oil and gas industry, is twelfth in its field in revenue.

In terms of assets, CP ranks first among private enterprises in Canada, with $17.3 billion in 1982, although two government-owned utilities, Hydro-Québec and Ontario Hydro, have assets that are several billion dollars bigger.

CP's ups and downs affect thousands of Canadians directly and indirectly. CP is Canada's largest private sector employer with 127,000 employees. Many are the third or fourth generation of their family to work for CP. In many cities, CP is either the largest, or one of the largest employers, with its industries having originally attracted people to these communities. When CP plants shut down or cancel expansion, the crippling effect spreads far, pinching the shopping power of employees for food, clothes, and housing. Conversely, plant expansion, new facilities, and new product lines by CP can inject millions of dollars into the economy.

Thousands of Canadians' investment hopes are also pinned on CP, whether they are among its 62,000 shareholders or whether some of their company pension contributions are invested in CP through insurance companies.

The current national economic nightmare has presented CP with perhaps the most difficult challenge in its history. Previously, the company had to solve the problem of how to grow. In the 1880s, it built its railway largely through what seemed impassable terrain. In the 1960s, it was a pioneer in Canada's corporate world in diversifying both geographically and in product line. The diversification steered the company away from its original emphasis on people-oriented businesses to industries that lack direct public contact. But growth was a far more pleasant challenge than the present dilemma of how to cope with the worst economic times since the 1930s.

Size does not mean impregnable strength. Just because CP is big does not mean it is immune to economic hurricanes. Rather, CP is a certain victim because its involvement in natural resources leaves it exposed to the battering such businesses experience in a recession when both domestic and export sales sag. During the 1982 recession, CP's net income fell to $188 million from $485.6 million a year earlier. The $300 million drop is equivalent to two and a half times the assets of American Motors (Canada) Inc. CP could survive such an astounding decline in profits because its cash flow and working capital are still in good enough shape for daily operations. But the decline meant that CP could not plan as aggressive a campaign of expansion and acquisitions as it might otherwise have done. The downward spiral continued into 1983, with CP's first-half results down $49.7 million from a year earlier.

Because the economy as a whole is hurting, CP's management has escaped being blamed for the company's troubles. But the recession is not wholly responsible. CP's management has made some major errors in judgment. Topping the list is the 1981 purchase by CP of Canadian International Paper, probably one of the biggest corporate mistakes in recent years by a Canadian company. The takeover of CIP raised investment analysts' eyebrows because CIP's equipment was outdated and pulp and paper sales were sliding in a dried-up market. Their doubts were justified. CIP was largely responsible for Canadian Pacific Enterprises' profit falling to $150 million in 1982 from $405 million in 1981. CIP had a $101.8 million loss in 1982.

CP's management was also overly optimistic in its forecasts of shipping and air traffic, ordering what turned out to be too many ships and planes. There are doubts, too, whether the multi-billion-dollar renovation of the company's railway in western Canada will pay off, because it is pegged to increased demand for exports of Canadian coal at a time when world demand for coal by steelmakers is much lower than anticipated.

The managers who made these decisions, however, will not have to deal with the fallout. The next few years will see new management installed at the helm of CP, with both CP Chairman Frederick Burbidge and CPE Chairman Ian Sinclair slated to retire. Sinclair turns seventy in December 1983, the mandatory retirement age for CP directors. He stepped down as CP's chairman at the age of sixty-eight. If Burbidge follows Sinclair's pattern, he will not remain as CP's chairman past the age of sixty-eight, which he will reach in 1986.

Thus, as CP heads into its second century, it is at an important crossroads in its history. The quiet of Windsor Station reflects the drifting away of the threads of CP's power held in Montreal. Instead, the future thrust of the company has shifted into the hands of executives in Toronto, Calgary, and the United States. There is a sense of anticipation among executives as they count the months until Sinclair and Burbidge leave, making way for a management shuffle affecting the many who want to be at the top. At the same time, close to 25 percent of the directors at CP companies are nearing mandatory retirement age. Together, the new executives and directors will determine what direction CP will take in the last decades of this century.

CP also must wrestle with whether it always wants to be in industries that rise and fall with the economy and that are so dependent on heavy spending, or whether it should branch into more recession-proof, high technology industries along the lines of its present data switching networks. Because CP has both contributed to and reflected Canada's evolution from a hewer of wood and drawer of water to a major player on the international scene, its decisions will point the way that industrial Canada is headed.

2

The Executive Suite

To climb the corporate ladder at CP, it helps to be the latest in a long line of family members who have worked for the company. One senior CP executive remembers being hugged by a longtime employee as part of the corporate family when he learned the newcomer's grandfather had worked for CP. It also helps to be from the West, work long hours, and be bright.

It is a special advantage to come from Winnipeg, where William Van Horne, who supervised the construction of the Canadian Pacific Railway and later became the company's second president, was originally based as general manager. Members of the "Manitoba Mafia" include Ian Sinclair, Frederick Burbidge, John Stenason (former CPE president), James McDonald (vice-president of industrial relations), John Anderson (vice-president of personnel), and John Sutherland (president of CNCP Telecommunications).

Although not from Manitoba, Norris Crump, nicknamed "Buck," who started the diversification of CP from a transportation company to a resources and transportation conglomerate, was also from the West. Crump generally gave the impression of being gruff, crusty, and tough, as well as dynamic, but his close friends regard him as being humorous and thoughtful.

One person who befriended him was Albert Ashforth, who met Crump more than forty years ago when Ashforth was manager of the King and Yonge Streets branch of the Toronto Dominion Bank and Crump was a general superintendent at CP based in Toronto. Although Ashforth was twelve years older than Crump, the two became friends, and in 1959 Ashforth,

then president of the Toronto Dominion Bank and head of the
Canadian Chamber of Commerce, introduced Crump as the
Chamber's guest with a poem Ashforth had written in his honor.
Ashforth kept the poem and proudly wrote it out for me just
after his eighty-ninth birthday, on which, he said, Crump had
remembered to phone and congratulate him.

It's certainly nice and must be fine
To be President of any line
Which owns hotels, caboose and car—
Provided it's the CPR.

It must be great to have a line
Which always leaves and arrives on time,
No problems then, as you can see
To this young man of destiny.

The Frenchmen like this guy too
This guy who runs the big Choo Choo,
He takes their money without pain
This guy who runs the big too too train.

They like to think he's for Quebec
Or Montreal, so what the heck,
Where big moguls sit around and chat,
The reason why they're all so fat!

But Frenchmen join with English, too
To pay respects to this guy, who
Speaks sense with humor, always good,
He puts you in a lovely mood.

So to our speaker from afar
Who loves life—and a big cigar
We're gathered here to hear you speak,
So please get up upon your feet.

Please tell us true, the reason why
You're so alert and always spry,
And tell us all, please, why you are
Known as Mister CPR.

Ashforth, Crump, and about eight others still meet on a regular basis for lunch in the private dining room of the Royal Bank in Calgary, where Ashforth's son is a top executive. Crump moved to Calgary after retiring from CP in 1972. The group swaps stories and a cigar-smoking Crump "cross-examines people in a funny, provoking way," Ashforth says. "One of his favorite jokes is to cross examine Red Dutton, a former hockey player who later headed the National Hockey League [from 1943 to 1946] and his own construction firm, about the number of horses Dutton actually used on a construction job for the CPR more than forty years ago."

Ashforth also praises Crump for his "keen mind, never forgetting his friends, and remembering the first names of fellow workmen and the fellow who parks his car at the Palliser Hotel in Calgary." Still active in his eighties, Crump is given an office on loan at CP's Palliser Square quarters for when he is downtown on business.

Crump was born into a CPR family on July 30, 1904, in Revelstoke, British Columbia. His father was a rail section hand who was later promoted to divisional superintendent. Crump dropped out of grade nine in 1920 to work as a laborer for the CPR and then became an apprentice, finishing grade school at night classes. The railway sent him on a scholarship to study mechanical engineering at Purdue University in Indiana.

He returned to the CPR in 1929 and was laid off for six months at the start of the Depression. Subsequently, he slowly worked his way up from night foreman to shop foreman, master mechanic, chief draftsman, and superintendent of the rail car department at Winnipeg. He broke into the corporate executive ranks in 1943 as general superintendent for Toronto.

Crump became CP's president at the age of fifty-one in 1955, and brought major changes to the company. He replaced steam locomotives with diesel engines, on which he had written his thesis at Purdue. The changeover prompted bitter strikes by the rail unions that were finally halted only by parliamentary legislation in 1957 and 1958. It was also under Crump that CP began to diversify out of the transportation business. By the time Crump retired in 1972, CP had moved into oil and gas (PanCanadian Petroleum) and real estate (Marathon), had separated its hotel (CP Hotels) from its rail operations, and had established Fording Coal, CanPac Minerals, and Canadian Pacific Consulting Services, which operates internationally.

The impact on CP's assets was dramatic. They rose from $2.1 billion in 1955, when Crump became president, to $3.9 billion on his retirement, an increase that pales only in comparison to CP's growth over the decade of the seventies when its assets, fattened by the purchase of Maple Leaf Mills and Canadian International Paper, have soared to $17.3 billion.

Crump also left the legacy of a chief executive staying on past normal retirement age. He remained until he was sixty-eight, which has been topped by Ian Sinclair, who will be seventy on December 27, 1983.

Today many Canadians would associate "Sinclair" with "CP" as immediately as they would "saucer" to "cup." But although Sinclair played an active role in diversifying CP during Crump's presidency, he was not the only crown prince in line for Crump's job. According to former CP executives, Sinclair was jockeying for the job against Robert Emerson, who was two years older than Sinclair. Emerson, like Crump, was a railway engineer and had climbed up through the ranks. His grandfather had been a locomotive engineer for the company and his father, a ticket agent. Both Emerson and Sinclair first held the vice-presidencies of various departments and then received the general title of vice-president. This appointment, based in Montreal, signifies that the individual will become president of CP some day.

Crump apparently favored Emerson, who became president from October 1964 until his death in March 1966, just seventeen months later, at the age of fifty-five. Alone at home, since his wife was away, he died in his garage and was not found until fourteen hours later. According to the Montreal General Hospital's postmortem report, he died from a "sudden coronary occlusion" and "a very high level (89 percent) of carbon monoxide in the blood."

Emerson is described by a former CP colleague as "a very lonely man, with few friends, and of whom people were afraid. But although he was supposed to dislike those who answered him back, I found he respected you if you spoke back to him. Even though he was a dedicated railroader, he was open to the concept of diversifying." A March 15, 1966 *Montreal Gazette* editorial on Emerson praised his brief presidency for "showing great competence and assurance in bringing the company more and more into modern conditions and adjustments."

Emerson was succeeded by Sinclair, who had joined CP in 1942 at the age of twenty-nine as an assistant solicitor following his graduation in economics and law from the University of Manitoba and a brief stint practicing law at a Winnipeg firm. His legal background, combined with his pugilistic style, made Sinclair an asset in CP's regular appearances before federal government commissions on rail rates. Since he did not rise through the railway departments at CP, Sinclair was unsentimental about the railway and eager to expand the company into new directions.

"Ian Sinclair has played a major role in continuing and strengthening the diversification of Canadian Pacific, which had begun under the chairmanship of Mr. Crump," says Allard Jiskoot, a director of CP since 1964 and chairman of Pierson, Heldring & Pierson of the Netherlands, a firm that has been one of CP's investment dealers dating back to 1883. "He has also played a major role in the internationalization of CP's activities through Canadian Pacific Enterprises. His great strength is his great view as an entrepreneur, his immense knowledge of financial and legal matters, both national and international, and his vision and conviction in which direction Canadian Pacific should be developed."

Tall, at six feet, one inch, and heavy set, at about 240 pounds, Sinclair has the appearance of a bouncer, or the cartoon character the "Incredible Hulk," although some might argue that Sinclair has not made a career of fighting wrongdoing as the Hulk did. The business world and the press have nicknamed him

"Big Julie," after the character in Damon Runyon's stories on crap games. The comparison was made because, like the fictional Big Julie, Sinclair has had a pretty good track record in gambling on big deals, with the notable recent exceptions of MacMillan Bloedel and Hobart Corporation of Ohio.

Although he is no longer badgering witnesses at commission hearings, Sinclair retains the mannerisms of a tough courtroom lawyer. When making a speech, he constantly takes his hands in and out of his pockets and continues to stare down opponents with his unblinking, chilly blue eyes. By contrast, another favorite tactic is to try to disarm people by calling himself "just a country boy from Manitoba," even though he was actually born and raised in the city of Winnipeg.

As a shrewd lawyer gathers small, telling details to buttress his case, Sinclair has a reputation for delving into the smallest aspects of CP's subsidiaries on his frequent inspection trips. "He will ask pilots about the inner workings of planes and stewardesses about their jobs, unlike many senior executives who rarely speak to the operations people," says Terrance Salman. "He knows the names of chefs, maître d's, and managers at CP's hotels by memory."

Yet, Sinclair can be bull-headed in labor relations to the point where he has created a crisis after other CP executives have smoothed out a difficult situation. This happened, for example, in 1973 at CP Air. "Sinclair and Yves Pratte, then head of Air Canada, had made a pact that they would not pay baggage handlers more than a certain amount and the baggage handlers requested $40 more a month," recalls Ralph Steeves, head of the Vancouver local of the International Association of Machinists and Aerospace Workers union (IAM) that deals with CP Air. "CP Air agreed to the handlers' demand and the deal was at the handshake stage when Sinclair canceled it. As a result, there was a nine-week strike which was settled with the acceptance of the handlers' original demand."

However, there apparently is still a soft spot to Ian David Sinclair. One example of its existence surfaced at CPE's 1982 annual meeting when CPE's new chief executive officer, Robert Campbell, said that "the accomplishments of CP Enterprises over the past twenty years are as much his achievements as they are the Corporation's." Campbell's praise of Sinclair, followed by thirty seconds of applause by shareholders, caused Sinclair to flush and smile happily like a youngster with a good report card. "You and the rest of the fellows will make the company better and I'll be happy about that," Sinclair replied.

The most common words that business associates use to describe Sinclair are "brilliant," "overwhelming," and "domineering." Because of his larger-than-life appearance and personality, plus his forceful, ruthless, steamroller tactics and his obvious enjoyment of power and leadership, acquaintances regard Sinclair like an intriguing and educational tourist site of which they would not necessarily like to see any other examples. "Being with Sinclair for thirty minutes is like studying business, economics, and people at university for half a year," says Donald Curtis, a former president of CP Hotels.

Despite his brilliance and despite CP's home base being in Montreal, Sinclair never learned French. During the exodus of head offices from Montreal in the late 1970s, occasioned by the election of the Parti Québécois, Sinclair was on the board of Sun Life Assurance when it voted to move its top executives to Toronto. At one time, Sinclair threatened to do the same with CP. He also said that the official language at CP's head office would be English. This prompted *Le Devoir*, in an April 1979 editorial, to label Sinclair a "reactionary" who wanted to move CP for "political motives and nothing more." These days, both English and French are used at CP's headquarters.

There is no doubt that Sinclair loves his job and happily spends long hours, including Saturdays, at work. "He has boundless energy, expected you to stay up until late at night discussing business, arrive at the office the next day at 6:00 A.M., and be cheerful both times," says Rod Sykes, who was assistant general manager of Marathon Realty in its early days, before becoming mayor of Calgary.

The same work ethic and devotion to the company is expected of other CP executives, especially if they want to get ahead. "Sinclair once told me that 'we own you twenty-four hours a day,'" says a former executive who recalls being transferred from Montreal to Calgary on one day's notice.

Despite his domineering personality, Sinclair does not like to

be surrounded by "yes men" and is capable of delegating authority to others. Sykes recalls asking Sinclair, after his Marathon
appointment, how much authority he would have. "He told me
as much as I could take and hold onto and that if I got ship-
wrecked, to send out a distress call," Sykes says. "As long as the
problems were not due to stupidity or happened too frequently,
the head office would salvage you."

One instance when Sykes showed his independence occurred
in the 1960s when he raised the rent from $900 a year to
$20,000 on cp land leased for a printing plant by Calgarian Max
Bell, owner of the *Calgary Albertan* and then one of cp's largest
shareholders. "I went to see Bell who was sitting in the dark
except for a small lamp on his desk," Sykes says. "He wanted to
buy the property and I said it was not for sale. He then pointed
out he was a cp director and a major shareholder and I told him
my position was in the best interests of the shareholders. A few
weeks later, Sinclair told me Bell had told the board of directors
that my stand was what the company needed."

cp welcomes intelligence and dedication in its employees, but
under Crump and Sinclair, and to a lesser extent under Sinclair's
successor, Frederick Burbidge, it has not encouraged familiarity.
Instead, cp is run on a formal, almost military scale. There is no
open door policy. Secretaries and their bosses call one another
Mister, Mrs. or Miss, followed by their surnames, and junior
executives address their superiors the same way.

"There is a paternal approach mixed with authoritarianism,"
says an ex-employee. "There was a feeling of being in the
military, with the use of first names not happening automatically,
no matter how long you had known someone." Says Robert
Bandeen, formerly Sinclair's counterpart at cn, "You had the
feeling, until recently, that people lined up outside the doors at cp
for inspection. There was no nonsense. Everybody knew their
rank and the guy above was God."

Sinclair, like Crump, chaired both cp and cpe. But in 1981,
with cp having more than tripled in terms of asset value since
Sinclair became chairman in 1972 and having bought or started
more than eight new companies, the task became too big even
for him. Sinclair decided to hand over the chairmanship of cp to
its then president, Frederick Burbidge, and remain as chairman

and chief executive officer of Canadian Pacific Enterprises, the expansionary side of the business. A year later, in 1982, Sinclair relinquished the position of chief executive officer at CPE to Vice-Chairman Robert Campbell.

It took Sinclair twenty-four years to rise through the ranks to become head of CP and, because CP is the country's largest private enterprise, the most powerful man in the Canadian business world. But as Sinclair said throughout the years, "The closer you are to the top, the closer you are to the door." As Sinclair neared the exit from CP, the power he relished so much began to ebb. When I telephoned CP's public relations office in Toronto in May 1982 to doublecheck the change in titles, a public relations officer said, "Sinclair is chairman at CPE, but the top man now is Campbell." *Sic transit gloria.*

Another telling symbol of Sinclair's slippage was his spot's dropping from page 1 in the 1981 edition of *Who's Who in Canada* to page 25 in the 1982 edition. *Who's Who* lists whom it regards as the top people first, rather than alphabetically. Whether it was due to Sinclair's getting upset at the demotion or *Who's Who* having a change of heart, Sinclair climbed back to page 7 in the 1983 edition.

While Sinclair was president of CP for twelve years and chairman for nine, Frederick Burbidge, who was president for nine years, will have a shorter term as chairman because he attained the job when he was already sixty-two. Normal retirement age at CP is sixty-five, and Burbidge celebrated his sixty-fifth birthday on September 30, 1983. Although both Crump and Sinclair stayed on as CP's chairman until they were sixty-eight, the spring 1984 CP annual meeting, covering fiscal year 1983, could be a logical time for Burbidge, who will then be just short of his sixty-sixth birthday, to be replaced.

A likely candidate to take over the position is CP's biggest shareholder, Paul Desmarais. Desmarais, the head of Power Corporation, has been on CP's board since 1982 and is several years younger than Burbidge. He turned fifty-six in January 1983, so that even if Burbidge were to carry on for a few years, Desmarais would still be young enough to succeed Burbidge as chairman.

However, Desmarais and CP executives have different personal and business styles, and it remains to be seen whether they are complementary or discordant. Desmarais is an entrepreneur who developed Power Corporation in the space of thirty years from a struggling bus company into a major holding company. He lives opulently and is accustomed to making most decisions without consultation. By contrast, CP executives live unostentatiously and, as managers rather than owners, are drilled in the company philosophy of being team players. If Desmarais becomes chairman, it is conceivable he would bring in his own management team and thereby stifle the ambitions of many longtime CP executives who thought their lengthy climb to the top depended largely on the deaths or retirements of those ahead of them.

If Desmarais is not appointed chairman, the normal line of succession would place CP President William Stinson, who will be fifty-three in October 1986, next in line for the chairmanship. If he becomes chairman in 1986, Stinson would be one of the youngest CP executives to achieve the office.

It is unlikely that Robert Campbell, Sinclair's successor as chairman of Canadian Pacific Enterprises, would become CP's chairman instead of Stinson, although he could conceivably get the job for a few years. Campbell, a former top Home Oil executive, was handpicked in 1971 by Sinclair to head PanCanadian Petroleum, the only success story for CP during the 1982 economic slump. However, Campbell's selection is iffy because he will be sixty-five in 1986. Moreover, he seems to like living in Calgary. Stuart Eagles, CPE's president, is another possible contender. Eagles will be fifty-seven in September 1986.

Like Sinclair, Burbidge was born in Winnipeg and attended the University of Manitoba's law school. Burbidge, however, came from a more well-to-do family. His father was a leading Winnipeg lawyer, while Sinclair's father had been a railway brakeman. Burbidge, called "Bud" by his associates, followed Sinclair's path through CP. Sinclair started as an assistant solicitor in CP's law department in Winnipeg in 1942; Burbidge joined in 1947. Sinclair became a solicitor at the Montreal office in 1946; Burbidge in 1957. Sinclair became assistant to the general counsel in Montreal in 1951; Burbidge in 1960. Then, their paths diverged, with Sinclair becoming an overall vice-president of the company, after only one year as vice-president, law, and Burbidge working his way through vice-presidencies in administration and in marketing and sales.

The two men also differ strongly in appearance and, on the surface, in personality. In contrast to the heavy set, still mostly dark-haired Sinclair, Burbidge is slim and white-haired. Associates describe Burbidge as very bright, soft-spoken, less outgoing than the extroverted Sinclair, considerate, and better at interpersonal relationships than Sinclair, who according to colleagues, cared more about achieving his goal than people's feelings. Despite their apparent differences in temperament, "they seemed to have worked out an accommodation, while working together in the law department, and respected each other for their respective strengths," says former CN President Robert Bandeen, a longtime acquaintance of Burbidge.

Still, if actions do indeed speak more loudly than words, CP's May 1982 annual meeting demonstrated that Sinclair and Burbidge were not bosom buddies. When a shareholder got up at the end of the meeting to praise Sinclair extravagantly and the audience applauded warmly, Burbidge, his face flushed red, did not clap.

Burbidge's outside activities include being a member of the Montreal citizens' advisory board of The Salvation Army, the main purpose of which is to raise funds for building projects. Such boards are located in each major Canadian city and have blue ribbon membership from Canada's top corporations that helps open doors in fund-raising campaigns. The sixteen-member Montreal board also includes Arnold Steinberg, president of Steinberg Inc., Claude Taylor, president of Air Canada, John Cole, vice-chairman of Wood Gundy, and Michel Belanger, head of the National Bank of Canada. The executive secretary of the board, Major Gilbert Fowler, praises Burbidge as "quiet and very clever, with a keen knowledge of community events."

Burbidge is not always genial, however. He can be testy, brusque, and sarcastic, as evidenced at CP's 1982 annual meeting in an exchange with M.J. (James) Fielding, representing one of CP's largest shareholdings. The Fieldings, one of the leading families in Sudbury, Ontario, own 66.18 percent of the non-cumulative preference stock of CP, which they started buying in the 1950s. The stock is mainly held through Alexander Centre Industries, started in 1935 by Clifford Alexander Fielding and now run by a committee of himself, his forty-five-year-old son, James, chairman of the company, and thirty-eight-year-old daughter, Brenda Wallace, also a Sudbury resident. Alexander Centre Industries, like CP, is a conglomerate, although its interests are primarily in construction and real estate in northern Ontario. Despite the family being large shareholders, a Fielding has not been invited to sit on CP's board since Clifford Fielding resigned in protest over a stock conversion plan more than a decade ago.

James Fielding is, on the surface, an amiable, small-town personality, but he got the last word against Burbidge at the annual meeting.

Fielding: Could a breakdown of the votes by shareholders be provided?
Burbidge: They won't be tabulated until after the meeting.
Fielding: I was under the impression they could be made available at the meeting.
Burbidge: They will be ready at the end of the meeting.
Fielding: I would prefer them during the meeting, if possible.
Burbidge: The votes during this meeting have been by a show of hand and I have no idea, for example, if you held up your hand.
Fielding: No, I didn't hold up my hand.

Fielding won out, with Burbidge providing the figures during the meeting. As Fielding said, the Fieldings had not voted in favor of management. James Fielding says he asked for a breakdown of the votes to clarify that not all of CP's shareholders supported the board. On the one hand, he smilingly describes the dialogue with Burbidge as "heated," and on the other, he carefully says that "Burbidge was very cooperative and attempted to answer to the best of his ability. He didn't evade the question." But Burbidge must have realized how testy he sounded, because when Fielding asked a similar question at the 1983 annual meeting, Burbidge answered more politely.

In the tradition of having either lawyers or railway men as presidents of CP, Burbidge was succeeded in that position by

William Stinson, whose father had been a claims agent for CP Rail. Stinson, a Torontonian by birth, is remembered by Brock MacMurray, the headmaster at the prestigious University of Toronto Schools when Stinson attended, as "quite bright, very pleasant, and a good cross-country runner." Stinson later studied business administration at the University of Western Ontario and joined CP immediately after graduating. He rose rapidly through the ranks at CP, becoming president in May 1981 when he was only forty-seven. Previously, he had been vice-president in charge of operations and maintenance and executive vice-president at CP Rail.

Dour-looking, with receding dark hair, Stinson is described as always having an "air of gloom" by R.J. Cranch, national secretary-treasurer of the Canadian division of the Brotherhood of Railway, Airline and Steamship Clerks, Freight Handlers, Express and Station Employees (BRAC). Cranch became acquainted with Stinson during labor negotiations. "If you get a smile from Stinson, you're lucky," Cranch says. "By contrast, Burbidge is more homespun and smiles and jokes. Stinson is hard-nosed but fair, capable, dedicated, and straightforward."

Over at CPE, Sinclair's successor as chief executive officer, Robert Campbell, has not spent his entire career at CP. A lawyer, Campbell previously worked at Shell Canada and Home Oil, where he rose to executive vice-president. Campbell met Sinclair in the 1960s when both served on the board of Trans Canada Pipelines. Sinclair asked Campbell to become chairman of Pan-Canadian Petroleum in 1971.

Campbell is the only top executive at this company, which likes to regard itself as a Canadian institution, who was not born in Canada. He was born in Nebraska, moved to Canada in 1955, and became a Canadian citizen in 1967, Canada's centennial year. The bald, bespectacled Campbell is described by Tom Sindlinger, both a former PanCanadian employee and a former member of the Alberta Legislature, as "politically astute, well-prepared, and capable of long-term, forward thinking. He exudes an aura of calmness, but small signs, like the muscles tightening around his eyes and fidgeting in his pockets, show a lot is going on beneath the surface."

Starting in 1970, Campbell served four terms of three years

each on the board of the Bank of Canada. He resigned in 1982 because of the time consumed by his three positions as vice-chairman and chief executive officer of CPE and chairman of PanCanadian.

CPE's president, until his July 1983 resignation, was Walter John Stenason (fifty-three on September 24, 1983), a native of Winnipeg like Burbidge and Sinclair. Like Stinson, John Stenason has a background in economics, reflecting the trend in CP's executive circles towards number crunchers. Stenason took his undergraduate degree in economics on a CP scholarship to Montreal's McGill University, from which CP likes to recruit employees. Subsequently, Stenason obtained a Ph.D. in economics from Harvard University.

The Harvard connection has lasted throughout Stenason's career, and so has his dry, academic personality that is the antithesis of the dynamic Sinclair. He coauthored *The Economics of Competition in the Transportation Industry* with John Meyer, a professor of transportation, logistics, and distribution at Harvard's graduate school of business. The book was published by Harvard University Press. Meyer, who became vice-chairman of Union Pacific Corporation in 1981, a major American rail company, is on the board of CP's subsidiary, AMCA International.

After graduating, Stenason joined CP's research department. That department is not solely for economic research. It is also a training and selection base for potential CP executives as well as the source of ideas and studies for expansion by CP.

Stenason distinguished himself by pioneering the use of computer economic models at CP in preparing the company's presentation on costing for the 1958–59 MacPherson Royal Commission on rail rates. Stenason, and his counterpart at CN, Robert Bandeen, singled out grain rates as being the biggest burden carried by the railways. The railways were bound by the 1897 Crow's Nest Pass rate agreement keeping grain rates at 0.5 cents a ton. Their findings prompted the government to establish a number of compensatory financial subsidies from which CP and CN have benefited mightily over the years.* "Stenason is

---

*See Chapter 8.

extremely bright, hard-driving, and hard-working," Bandeen says. Stenason's work brought him to the attention of Ian Sinclair, who was CP's legal counsel on the commission.

In 1969, Stenason became vice-president, transport and ships, and is credited for being receptive to new shipping concepts. "We wanted to ship forest products by containerization, rather than in rolls of paper and newsprint which suffered up to a 30 percent damage rate," says Sam Salmon, now corporate traffic manager, marine and distribution, at Domtar. Containerization involves shipping products in standard-size containers, which can be easily transferred from truck to rail to boat, eliminating the prior procedure of loading and unloading individual items.

"Other shipping lines that we approached were unenthused," Salmon continues. "One day, I bumped into Stenason at Ben's Delicatessen in Montreal and explained the idea to him over lunch. He accepted the idea enthusiastically and gave us carte blanche to proceed."

Stenason is further described by Donald Armstrong, a McGill University business administration professor who is a consultant to CP, as being "warm, friendly, unassuming" and very conscious of profit margins, even on the home front. "He used to get competitive bids from his three sons on cutting their lawn," Armstrong says.

Stenason's resignation did not come as a surprise to investment analysts who follow CPE. They had noted that while he got along well enough with Sinclair, he had lost out on the chairmanship of CPE, despite being in line as its president, to Campbell, who was parachuted in from a CPE subsidiary. Still, Stenason, who has set up a management consultant business in Calgary, will do consulting work for CPE, making his parting seem amicable to the business world.

Stuart Eagles, Stenason's successor, is another longtime CP employee, having worked his way up over thirty-four years from CP's statistical department to president of Marathon Realty. Between 1964 and 1968, in the early days of CPE, he was assistant to the two presidents of the company during that period—Crump and F.V. Stone. Investment analysts say that Campbell and Eagles share both a broad-based background, rather than one rooted only in their respective business experience in oil and real estate, and a conservative approach that is suited to the current economic climate. During the decade that Eagles headed Marathon, the firm did not have the outstanding return on assets that analysts expected in view of its vast land holdings, but it held up better than other flashier, more expansionary Canadian developers during the 1982 recession.

The selection of Campbell and Eagles also indicates the areas of business where CPE will likely be looking for growth. "Oil and gas was a major contributor to CPE's profit and dividends before oil prices dropped and the prices are expected to improve by 1984," says Robert Tang, the New York-based CP analyst for the investment house of McLeod Young Weir Ltd. "The real estate element may also rebound depending on interest rates. The backgrounds of Campbell and Eagles show that CPE will be placing a fair bit of emphasis on its land holdings." Eagles and Campbell should be thankful that the first executives at CP in the 1880s insisted that the government give the company twenty-five million acres in return for its building a cross-country railway.

Although each head of CP has been important in its development, it is the company that gives them their importance and not the reverse. Just who is up and coming at CP is not always obvious, even to CP executives, who sometimes do not know if a promotion is a move upwards or sideways. CP has able presidents at its subsidiaries, as well as a number of youthful high achievers at head office. Among those being followed with interest by CP watchers are Cominco's fifty-two-year-old chairman, Norman Anderson, and forty-eight-year-old president, William Wilson; fifty-year-old Robert DeMone, president of Maple Leaf Mills and formerly vice-president, finance and accounting, at Canadian Pacific Enterprises and president of Canadian Pacific Securities Ltd.; forty-eight-year-old Ronald Riley, corporate vice-president at Canadian Pacific Ltd.; thirty-nine-year-old Berj Zafirian, treasurer at CPE and former president of Canadian Pacific Securities; forty-seven-year-old D'Alton Coleman, vice-president, eastern region, CP Rail; and forty-nine-year-old Glen Thomas, president of Canadian Pacific Consulting Services.

D'Alton Coleman was in the limelight briefly in 1982, doing

the mud-slinging for CP against Toronto Mayor Art Eggleton in the dispute between CP and the city over CP's demolishing a west end Toronto railway station without notice. Coleman charged that Eggleton had asked CP to delay tearing down the station until after the November civic election. Eggleton denied the charge and Coleman, just as quickly as he had become available to the media, became incommunicado.

Although CP's management became legendary for the autocratic style of Crump and Sinclair, it is unlikely that the executives now working their way up through the company will achieve the same public recognition. Even now, company executives, including Sinclair, stress that management is decentralized, with subsidiaries given autonomy. For all the power that Crump and Sinclair wielded, they were still only, as Sinclair has said, "managers of other people's assets" rather than entrepreneurs. No CP executive owns more than three-tenths of 1 percent of shares of CP or its subsidiaries. They were not gambling their own money when they expanded CP.

Today's complex business world of takeovers, acquisitions, and international competition requires executives with a global perspective. Already, CP's top management has changed from primarily railwaymen to lawyers, to business administration graduates, and economists. And not only the professions have changed. Today's senior executives at CP tend to be colorless, low key, and little known compared with Crump and Sinclair.

There are also signs that CP may be starting to think its inbred system of hiring several generations of families and having its employees work their way up through the ranks results in tired blood. Outsiders like Robert Campbell are already being parachuted into senior positions. When CP Air's Ian Gray, who took early retirement at age sixty-three in 1983, relinquished the post of president in 1982 while remaining as chairman, the presidency was bestowed upon a former Pan American executive, rather than one of the longtime CP Air employees.

Their personalities may be low profile, but CP executives' spectacular salaries are high profile indeed, making them among the highest paid executives in Canada.

Until recently, CP kept its top salaries secret, but because its shares were traded in the United States, it was subject to that country's corporate disclosure rules of informing shareholders about executives' salaries. In 1977, the *Vancouver Sun* applied to the U.S. Securities and Exchange Commission to make the salaries public under the United States' Freedom of Information Act. CP argued that the confidentiality it had previously been granted by the SEC before the Freedom of Information Act was introduced should be maintained since disclosure would harm its competitive ability and help those in Canada who wanted the company nationalized.

However, the SEC ruled that "CP's position on this issue is grounded upon political and social factors, rather than business or economic considerations." The SEC also rejected as "wholly irrelevant" CP's argument that since executive salaries are treated on a confidential basis in Canada, they should get the same treatment in the United States. The commission shot down a CP claim that since its major competitor, Canadian National Railways, was not required to disclose the salaries of its senior officials, CP should not have to do so either. The SEC said this argument was "particularly inappropriate, because in June 1977 CN voluntarily disclosed such information in connection with the filing of a registration statement" with the SEC. CP appealed this ruling to the United States District Court of Appeals in Washington, but withdrew its motion two months before the court's decision was scheduled. That left the way clear for access to CP's executive salaries.

Another reason behind the company's foot dragging, besides those presented to the SEC, soon became evident. In 1977, wage increases for CP's bosses had exceeded the federal government's Anti-Inflation Board guidelines. In that year, Ian Sinclair's salary was raised to $330,450 for an increase of $3,650, ahead of the AIB's ceiling of $2,400 on annual increases. Sinclair was not the only executive whose salary increase exceeded the guideline. Frederick Burbidge, then CP president, got a hike of $3,250 and Keith Campbell, a vice-president, received $3,550 more.

CP was not breaking the law. Several loopholes in the AIB did allow larger increases. Still, the latitude they granted themselves did not apply to those less fortunate in 1982 when Sinclair, as head of a businessmen's committee supporting the federal government's 6 and 5 percent wage guidelines, eagerly accepted this ceiling for CP Rail employees, although he felt even this was too much for ordinary workers, despite the high cost of living. Before the guidelines, CN, CP, and the railway unions had agreed to a 21 percent increase over two years, with 12 percent the first year and 9 percent the following year. Cutting the wage increases in half for its thirty thousand rail workers would provide CP with a $39 million savings based on the average 1981 salary of Canadian rail workers of $21,821.

Notwithstanding this substantial saving, Sinclair did not forget that he felt the "six and five" increases were too high. In July 1983, Sinclair and his committee proposed that wage increases in general be cut back even further to 4 and 3 percent or below the 5 percent plus rate of inflation. Based on the average 1982 salary in Canada of $20,729.28 for industrial workers, Sinclair's advocated rollback of two more percentage points to 4 percent would reduce CP's wage payments to its 127,000 workers by a whopping $52 million, the equivalent of two and a half times the preliminary work in 1983 on the company's Rogers Pass railway improvements in British Columbia. On the same basis, the individual worker would be hard hit, losing $414.59 in salary— the cost of either one year's travel to and from work on public transit in Toronto or a modest vacation.

What was good enough for the railway unions, however, was not good enough for the executive suite. In 1982, Burbidge's salary, directors' fees, and bonuses totaled $531,417, up 16.5 percent over 1981, and Stinson's earnings rose 35.6 percent to $319,621. The exception was Sinclair, whose reduced workload was reflected in his earnings dropping by 51.1 percent to $271,484, although his pension and supplementary allowance brought his total package to $556,985, or slightly more than Burbidge's total.

CP's stonewalling the SEC in divulging its executives' salaries duplicated its defensive attitude in a statement to the federal government's Royal Commission on Corporate Concentration, which examined large companies such as CP. A histograph presented by CP showed that while real after-tax income for tradesmen and middle management rose substantially between

1925 and 1975, senior management was making two-thirds of what it had fifty years previously. The difference stemmed from companies paying more benefits and higher wages to blue-collar workers and middle management, while senior executives no longer got such free perks as servants, food, and transportation.

"I remember talking to Ian Sinclair about this in CP's boardroom and pointing to the portraits of his predecessors on the walls and saying his real after-tax income was less than theirs and his telling me that on an hourly basis, his income was way down because he worked from waking up until he went to bed," Donald Armstrong says. Still, even if he actually always worked sixteen hours a day, five days a week, Sinclair was not making a puny salary. In 1976, the year of the Corporate Concentration Commission, his annual salary of $326,800 would have come to $78 an hour for a sixteen-hour day.

Generous salaries are only part of the financial pie for top CP executives. In 1978, when Sinclair reached the normal retirement age of sixty-five, he started receiving an annual pension of $203,929. As of the end of 1982, Burbidge, who turned sixty-five in September 1983, became eligible for an annual pension of $278,419. On retirement, CPE's Robert Campbell is to receive two-thirds of his average monthly salary in the preceding five years, minus benefits received from PanCanadian and his pension benefits from Home Oil. In 1982, Campbell's average monthly salary was $18,055.59.

Sinclair gets even further frosting on top of the layers of salary and pension. As of July 1, 1980, employees who stay on after sixty-five are eligible for a supplementary allowance of 1 percent of their monthly basic pension multiplied by the number of months they defer their retirement. Sinclair was the first, and for two years the only senior CP executive to qualify for this fringe benefit to which both CP and CPE contribute. As of December 31, 1981, Sinclair's annual supplementary allowance was $81,752, considerably more than many executives make in salary alone.

Sinclair is able to earn even more through outside consultant work. In July 1983, it was announced that he would be paid $90 an hour to ensure that the Toronto Transit Commission does not overpay its sole supplier of new subway cars and streetcars. Not a bad assignment for someone who pulled his company out of rail passenger services.

Sinclair, Burbidge, and Campbell could, however, complain that they are underpaid. Despite CP being Canada's largest company, with so many divisions spread through many countries, they make less than executives at smaller Canadian companies. The chairman and chief shareholder of Seagram's, Edgar Bronfman, is the top earner, making more than $1 million, although Seagram ranks only thirty-fourth in revenue among Canadian companies. A.E. Downing, an executive vice-president at Hiram Walker Resources Ltd., twentieth in revenue, makes $70,000 more in total compensation than Burbidge. Like CP's executives, Hiram Walker's are also hired help and not major shareholders. Still, with unemployment at peak levels in Canada, it is hard to work up too much sympathy for CP's executives.

Although CP is generous with executive salaries, it is extraordinarily cost conscious in corporate expenses. Despite the geographical spread of CP's empire, there is no corporate jet and executives travel by commercial aircraft instead. CP Air's Ian Gray even flew Air Canada when he found its schedule more convenient. However, executives do not necessarily fly economy. Terrance Salman of Nesbitt Thomson, who was formerly at the investment dealer's Montreal office, recalls Ian Sinclair once ribbing an executive from the investment house of Wood Gundy for being given an economy ticket by his firm. "So the Wood Gundy man changed his ticket to first class," Salman says. Part of the reason behind Sinclair's jibe may have been that his son, Robert, is a vice-president and director of Wood Gundy and that firm has often been the lead underwriter in the issue of new CP and CPE shares.

Nonetheless, life at CP is usually budget class. When a long-time employee retires from CP, nothing special is done. For example, when a forty-year employee of CP's corporate public relations department retired in 1981, the department took him for lunch. Instead of the standard business practice of charging up the lunch, each employee paid his or her own way and they all chipped in for the guest of honor.

There are no big Christmas bashes, summer picnics, or golf outings. CP used to own a golf club in the exclusive Montreal district of Westmount, but sold it when the upkeep became too expensive. Donald Armstrong recalls a meeting at Windsor Station: "We worked through lunch and a secretary brought us sandwiches and milk. Afterwards, she said, 'That'll be about two dollars each,' and all of us, including the CP guys, paid."

Expense accounts are carefully examined, and Armstrong remembers "one executive who went to Japan, where you are expected to entertain royally, sweated blood when he turned in his bills amounting to thousands of dollars to CP's accountants. He was not questioned."

CP's biggest party for its employees was in 1981 when it celebrated its centennial. The festivities were held at Windsor Station, where CP employees and their families ate ten thousand hot dogs and seven thousand bags of potato chips. Company executives debated whether to give coins or certificates as mementos and finally settled on T shirts inscribed "100 CP Rail" that served the dual purpose of advertising the historic event.

The tight lid on executive spending reflects the unostentatious way in which CP's senior executives live and dress, despite their high salaries. "Buck" Crump used to drive a small Buick and have a ham sandwich and coffee for lunch in his office. And whereas early CP executives lived in a grand manner in large homes and spacious summer estates, today's style is low key and low profile. Until Sinclair moved to Oakville, one of Canada's two wealthiest communities in terms of average income, he lived for decades on a quiet west Montreal street in a three-storey, red brick house with a white sunporch at the front and black shutters on the windows. The house had a small front and backyard and was protected by a burglar alarm system.

Sinclair was unlisted in the Montreal telephone book, but Frederick Burbidge and CPE's John Stenason, before he moved to Calgary, were both listed. Both men lived simply on the south side of the St. Lawrence River, within five minutes' driving distance of each other. Burbidge has a cottage, and Sinclair had one, in the Eastern Townships region outside Montreal, while

Stenason had a farm. In Calgary, Robert Campbell lives equally unpretentiously in a medium-sized house, with a basketball hoop on the garage for his children, on the city's south side. For relaxation, he has a ranch outside the city.

The winner of the jockeying in CP's executive suite to succeed Sinclair and Burbidge will be in charge of a much different company than it was when those two men took over. Over the past decade, the company has grown from a largely Canadian-based corporation involved in many areas of the economy to a multinational conglomerate involved in nearly all areas of the economy. And whoever they are, the successors will not hold all the reins of power. The sheer size of CP means that today no one person can run the whole show.

· 3 ·

The Boardroom

Annual meetings are usually deadly dull affairs at which prese-
lected members of the audience second motions, nobody asks
questions, and the whole routine is over in an hour or less. CP's
annual meetings used to fit this pattern, but recently they have
become battlefields. The reason is that CP has denied one of its
two largest shareholders a board seat, while giving two seats to
its other large shareholder. The clash between CP and the rejected board suitor, the Quebec government-owned Caisse de
dépôt et placement du Québec, raises a number of issues affecting Canadian business life today—the concern among businessmen over how much the government should be involved in
private enterprise, the conflict between Ottawa and the separatist Quebec government over economic power, and the clash
between the Establishment of English Canada, represented by
CP, and the up and coming French Canadian business community.

The annual meetings could become even more acrimonious if
a group of Saskatchewan farmers achieves its recently announced goal of acquiring a bloc of at least two thousand shares,
the minimum required for a seat on CP's board. The farmers,
supporters of the artificially low rail shipping rate for grain that
is being increased in 1983, would probably find themselves
barred from the board because they also represent a view hostile
to the CP way of business life.

When a company like CP is the largest in a country, with an
influential stake in nearly all economic sectors, who controls it is
of vital interest not only to management and shareholders, but

also to all Canadians. Until 1981, CP's management firmly held the reins of power because even though no senior executive owned more than three-tenths of 1 percent of the company's shares, public ownership was so widespread that no outsider had control either. But in 1981 and 1982, Paul Desmarais gained control of 11.1 percent of CP through direct and indirect purchases by his Power Corporation. In 1983, Power slightly increased its holdings to 11.73 percent of CP's shares. Power also owns 1.02 percent of Canadian Pacific Enterprises, 3.49 percent of Algoma Steel, 5.45 percent of AMCA, 4.61 percent of Cominco, 2.54 percent of Vestgron Mines, a Cominco subsidiary, and 6.49 percent of Great Lakes Forest Products, giving it a foothold in most of CP's major divisions.

Desmarais' acquisition of a stake in CP did not come as a shock to Canada's investment community. While studying commerce at the University of Ottawa, Desmarais had written a paper on how CP could be taken over, and for more than a decade there had been frequent rumors that Power wanted to gain control of CP. Also, there were already interesting ties between CP and Power. Claude Pratte, who is on the executive committee of CP's board, was also on Power's board, as was Earle McLaughlin, another CP executive committee member. Both resigned from Power's board after Desmarais bought into CP. In addition, Arthur Mauro, executive vice-president of the Desmarais-controlled Investors Group, is on the board of CP Hotels.

Under the terms of a December 15, 1981 agreement between Desmarais and CP, Desmarais agreed to limit his purchases of CP stock to 15 percent until December 31, 1991. Despite the long wait, Desmarais would then be only sixty-four, which means that he would still have many years in which to increase his investment in CP. Provision was made, though, for Desmarais to acquire more than 15 percent of CP's voting shares if a takeover bid for CP were made by another firm or if another shareholder acquired more than 10 percent. CP also received the right of first refusal on any shares Desmarais might decide to sell.

Before the pact was reached, Desmarais had expressed interest in acquiring 20 percent of CP. The significance of that percentage is that it is the usual point at which a shareholder can participate in a company's profits in proportion to the amount of ownership. However, Power executives have said the company will still be able to use this equity accounting method despite having less than 20 percent because Power will be exerting "significant influence" on CP through Desmarais' membership on CP's board.

At its May 1982 annual meeting, CP's board was increased in size by one member to a total of twenty-three to allow for the inclusion of Desmarais, who was given a warm greeting at the meeting by other shareholders. His introduction triggered longer, more enthusiastic applause than that received by many CP executives. Desmarais also became a member of the board's inner circle executive committee, a powerful influence in policy making.

Desmarais' interest in CP is less than the single largest shareholding in many other Canadian conglomerates. For example, 20 percent of The Molson Companies is owned by one shareholder; 46.69 percent of Imasco Ltd. is owned by one shareholder; and 37.2 percent of the common shares and 59.6 percent of the preferred of Noranda Mines Ltd. are owned by Brascade Resources Inc., in which the Caisse de dépôt et placement du Québec, also a major CP shareholder, is a co-owner with Brascan Ltd.

Nevertheless, the size of CP and Power raises the question of how much concentration of corporate power should be allowed. Desmarais and CP are in many of the same fields and control leading companies in those fields. In pulp and paper, Desmarais has a 40 percent interest in Consolidated-Bathurst; CP owns Great Lakes Forest Products, Pacific Forest Products, and CIP. In insurance, Desmarais controls Great West Life Assurance, Canada's third largest life insurer; CP owns Château Insurance, which deals in all types of insurance except life and annuities. All told, CP and Power together have a controlling or large-scale investment in close to two hundred Canadian companies.

Even if the two giants do not amalgamate companies in the same field, and even if there is no collusion in pricing, should there be such close ties between giant corporations? Should one person, be it Paul Desmarais or anyone else, have so much economic power? Do such ties leave control of the economy and its future in too few hands? Could the situation encourage nationalization by the government?

CP's other major shareholder is the eighteen-year-old Caisse de dépôt et placement du Québec, a Quebec government agency that invests Quebeckers' pension funds. By 1982, the Caisse owned 9.97 percent of CP. Its $258 million CP investment accounted for 7.4 percent of the Caisse's $3.5 billion stock and corporate bond portfolio, Canada's largest capital pool that also includes major investments in such other big companies as Canada's five biggest banks, Alcan Aluminium, Bell Canada, and several oil, food, publishing, and department store companies. The Caisse administers assets of $16 billion, larger than the $12 billion of the better-known Alberta Heritage Savings Trust Fund and larger than the assets of such financial institutions as Royal Trustco, Canada Permanent Mortgage Corp., the Continental Bank of Canada, and Montreal Trust, which is controlled by Desmarais. The Caisse is the only provincial public pension fund that buys shares.

In the United States, several major pension funds larger than the Caisse have kept their holdings in major companies to a maximum of about 5 percent and do not request board seats. The Caisse has requested a seat at CP, but in vain. Moreover, CP is not alone in refusing the agency a place on its board. Alcan and Dominion Textile Inc., in which the Caisse also has substantial shareholdings, have also rejected a request for board representation.

The Caisse's size aroused grumbling among the chieftains of corporate Canada about how much the government should be involved in private enterprise. It also raised the specter of a potential clash between the federal and Quebec governments, since the Caisse, a provincial government agency, owns a substantial portion of several federally incorporated companies besides CP. Furthermore, the Caisse's 9.97 percent ownership of CP (shaved slightly to 9.92 percent in 1983) brought it close to the 10 percent trigger in the CP-Desmarais agreement that would allow Desmarais to go beyond his 15 percent ownership before 1991.

While CP's board was enlarged to make room for Desmarais and another Power executive, Caisse Chairman Jean Campeau was refused a seat on what he termed "the passkey to the English Canadian corporate establishment." But since CP's board does include several Quebeckers, it would appear that the rejection of Campeau was based on CP's traditional dislike of government intrusion into its private turf, unless it is to CP's benefit. The Caisse's board is appointed by the Quebec government and critics say the government pulls the Caisse's strings, a charge vehemently denied by Campeau.

The issue, though, was not merely economics. Underlying it was the traditional conflict between the long entrenched English-speaking corporate establishment, epitomized by CP, and the up and coming French-speaking financial community, represented by the Caisse, which wants entry to the other side's Club. This wrangling on the business front was paralleled by the rancor between the federalist Trudeau government, supported by CP, and the separatist government of René Lévesque. Ottawa viewed the Caisse's investment in CP as an intrusion by Quebec into the federally regulated area of transportation; Quebec felt that Ottawa was once again protecting the English establishment.

CP's Burbidge skillfully played on this political jousting for power: "CP was deliberately created as a private company by the federal government and now a province that wants to separate from the rest of Canada is buying into a company that was meant to bind the country together."

All these potential conflicts were reaching the boiling point in November 1982 when the federal government introduced legislation restricting provincial ownership of transportation companies. The bill, called the Corporate Shareholding Limitation Act, prohibits the provinces from owning more than 10 percent of transportation companies and pipelines involved in interprovincial and international trade. It blocked the Caisse from buying more of CP, which it had wanted to do, and also blocked it from investing in Dart Containerline Ltd., a major shipping firm with which CP has formed a quasi partnership in overseas shipping.

Despite the uproar over this federally imposed limitation on corporate ownership, the restrictions were not the first of their type. The Bank Act sets a general 10 percent ceiling on any one holding in a major Canadian chartered bank, and under Canadian law only 10 percent of a pension fund can be invested in real estate. Limiting provincial ownership of national transportation and pipeline companies is also in the federal interest because it ensures the federal government's retaining control over interprovincial transportation, as called for under both the 1867 British North America Act and the 1982 Constitution Act. This, in turn, makes certain the smooth flow of interprovincial commerce.

But angry Quebec government officials charged that the federal legislation was a payoff to Ian Sinclair in return for his spearheading a group of business executives in support of the Liberals' "six and five" wage restraint program. Jacques Parizeau, Quebec's finance minister, said the legislation "protects the traditional Canadian establishment from Caisse incursions and even succeeds in giving this establishment means to allow it to disqualify present investments made in good faith by the Caisse."

Sinclair furiously rejected Parizeau's charges of political patronage:

Transportation has always been a factor in Canadian life and a factor in which all parts of the country felt they had a stake. I'm sure the federal government felt it absolutely essential that the railroad not be controlled by any provincial government or any emanation of a provincial government because by definition, provincial governments represent regional interests.

The full meaning of this statement came to light a few weeks later when CP Chairman Burbidge appeared before a parliamentary committee hearing on the legislation. He said that CP had requested Prime Minister Pierre Trudeau in March 1982 for legislative limitations on ownership of transportation companies by provinces. The request followed the Caisse's increasing its CP holdings in March by two percentage points.

The timing of the legislation was marvelously convenient for CP. It parroted CP executives' oft-expressed view that the government should stay out of business and kept future control of CP in the friendly hands of Desmarais, while at the same time preventing him from getting more of the company. Desmarais, also an ardent free enterpriser, having built Power on his own into a multimillion-dollar empire, had expressed his opposition to the Caisse's growing investment in the private sector. Besides, with the strong possibility of becoming CP's chairman soon and the close approach of 1991 when he can buy more of the company, Desmarais could afford to be sanguine.

The uneasy relationship between CP and the Caisse broke into open fireworks during the 1983 annual meeting. At the end of his conventional state of the company address, Burbidge made a stinging attack on the Caisse's investment in CP: "Quebec is interfering in companies where it has acquired an equity position, not openly through legislation but imperceptibly by the use of economic power—through a telephone call to its stockbroker. If this goes unchecked, it will result in provincialization of a national undertaking by a government dedicated to separation."

In return, the Caisse's representative at the meeting said it was withholding its 7.1 million voting shares from all resolutions at the meeting. If a shareholder is dissatisfied with management, the most drastic step he can take is to sell his stock. The Caisse refrained from doing this, but in announcing its abstention it showed both that it was only a passive investor, since it had no board seats, and that it was protesting Burbidge's comments.

This move highlights a significant aspect of CP's being incorporated under the Railway Act rather than the Business Corporations Act. Under the Business Corporations Act, shareholders can specify whether they are voting for or against management or withholding their votes as a milder form of disapproval. Thus, the battle lines are clear from the start if there is a proxy fight. By contrast, there are fewer choices under the Railway Act. If shareholders give their proxies to management, it means they are in support. If they don't, it means they are in disagreement, but the only way the public knows they have withheld their votes is if one of the dissenters gets up, as James Fielding did two years in a row, and requests a breakdown of the voting. In 1983, the votes withheld by the Fieldings and the Caisse totaled eleven million shares, or about one-seventh of the seventy-six million CP voting shares.

The furor over how much of CP any one individual or group should own raises questions from all directions. Should Canada's largest company be substantially owned by one person? Is it fair for CP to make an exception for Paul Desmarais, while applying a different set of rules to the Caisse? What rationale can a federal government that owns a railway and an airline, and has nationalized oil companies, give for restricting provincial investment in certain industries? How far should the federal government go to protect a large, hardly defenseless company like CP? Will it set a precedent for other national companies to run to Ottawa for help, thus possibly eroding provincial jurisdiction? What is the difference between the Caisse owning part of a company involved in interprovincial transportation and the province of Alberta owning Pacific Western Airlines, which already flies across much of Canada and is pushing the federal government to allow it entry into more markets? How much of the business sector in general, not just companies involved in interprovincial and international trade, should be owned by governments, especially in view of increasing government investment in private enterprise? Isn't there something ironic in the private sector appealing to the federal government for legislative protection when it keeps saying government should stay out of business and there should be fewer government regulations? Finally, what investment opportunities will be left for the Caisse in view of the Corporate Shareholding Limitation Act providing a loophole for any company not wanting the Caisse as an investor? Such a firm could buy a small interprovincial transportation company and thus prevent the Caisse from obtaining more than 10 percent of the present company.

CP's board contains the corporate blue bloods of Canada's banking, legal, and business circles. They, in turn, sit on the boards of more than two hundred of Canada's biggest companies, once again demonstrating the incestuous relationship among the boards of directors in Canada's business world. Despite the large number of directors making it possible, there are no women on the boards of any CP companies, and CP has deflected questions at its annual meetings as to when it would admit women directors. CP's senior management is also primarily a man's world, although the comptroller is female. It took her forty years to rise to that post.

CP, CPE, and their subsidiaries all make a point of having a mixture of inside and outside directors on their boards of directors. All together, 160 people are on the boards of CP companies, with many serving on more than one board.

Seven of CP's twenty-three directors are on CPE's board. They are Sinclair, Burbidge, Stinson, and Campbell from CP, plus Earle McLaughlin, former chairman of the Royal Bank of Canada, Paul Paré, chairman of Imasco Ltd., and Ray Wolfe, chairman and president of The Oshawa Group Ltd.

Directors at CPE, which is governed by the Canadian Business Corporations Act, serve one-year terms, whereas CP Ltd.'s directors serve four years on a rotating basis, in accordance with the regulations of the Railway Act under which CP was incorporated. CP is now studying the legal ramifications of switching to the jurisdiction of the Canadian Business Corporations Act, although no rapid decision is expected.

There is only a faint sprinkling of politicians on CP boards. Most directors instead are bankers, lawyers, or businessmen. The lone politicians are Senator Willie Adams, who is on the board of Panarctic Oils Ltd., in which CP holds a 16.75 percent interest, former Alberta Energy Minister Mervin Leitch (on the board of CPE), and former Liberal Finance Minister John Turner (CP and Marathon). McMillan Binch, the Toronto law firm of which Turner is now a partner, was paid $268,335 in legal fees by CP in 1981. According to CP's 1982 information statement to shareholders, no payment was made to McMillan Binch in 1982.

While there are only three people with political backgrounds on CP-related boards now, the company did once hire a politician to head the non-transportation side of the business. Former Manitoba Premier (1958–1967) and now Senator Duff Roblin was president of Canadian Pacific Investments (now CPE) from 1968 until 1974. Former CP executives say Roblin was selected as a "figurehead" to give the company status in its early days.

On the Canadian front, CP's directorships are most closely tied to the Bank of Montreal and the Royal Bank of Canada. CP's association with the Bank of Montreal dates back to its first president, George Stephen, who was president of the Bank of Montreal from 1876 to 1881, but nowadays the ties are stronger with the Royal Bank in terms of the number of directors. William Moodie, president of CPE from 1974 to 1979, was recruited from the Royal Bank where he had worked nearly forty years and had become senior vice-president and general manager.

The CP ties to Canada's banks are extensive. Ian Sinclair is honorary vice-president and director of the Royal Bank and serves on the board's management development and compensation committee. In turn, Royal Bank President Jock Finlayson is on CP's board, and former Chairman Earle McLaughlin is is on the boards of both CP and CPE. Frederick Burbidge is on the board of the Bank of Montreal, and the bank's chairman, William Mulholland, is on CP's. Other CP executives are on the boards of different financial institutions. CPE's chief executive officer, Robert Campbell, sits on Crown Trust's board, John Stenason, CPE's former president, is on Canada Trust's board, and Cominco Chairman Norman Anderson is on the board at Toronto Dominion. Royal Trustco Chairman Kenneth White is on the boards of CP and Great Lakes Forest Products, and William Wilson, Cominco's president, is on Royal Trustco's board.

Indirectly, CP has further links to the banks with outsider board members who serve both on CP companies' and the banks' boards. In this category are Montreal lawyers Neil Phillips, of Phillips and Vineberg, who is on the boards of CPE and the Royal Bank, and Claude Pratte of Letourneau and Stein, who is on the boards of CP, CIP, and the Royal Bank. Paul Paré, chairman of Imasco Ltd., is also on the boards of both CIP and the Royal Bank. Lucien Rolland, president of Rolland Inc., a Montreal-based paper products firm, is on the boards of CP and the Bank of Montreal.

CP also maintains ties with the European financial community through two blue-blood directors from overseas: Lord Henry Polwarth, former governor of the Bank of Scotland and the tenth lord in his family since 1690, and Allard Jiskoot, chairman of the Netherlands investment banking firm of Pierson, Heldring & Pierson, which was founded by his grandfather. In 1883, two years after CP was incorporated, Pierson, which then operated under the name of Adolph Boissevain & Co., introduced $4 million worth of CP shares on the Amsterdam Stock Exchange. Between 1975 and 1981, Pierson participated in more than $200 million worth of new securities issued by CP. Through the Dutch company, CP has ties with the Rothschild banking fortune; the Rothschild family controls Pierson, Heldring & Pierson.

Besides the banks, another major meeting ground between CP directors is Sun Life Assurance, the largest life insurer in Canada. Sun Life's chairman, Thomas Galt, is on the boards of CP and the Bank of Montreal, and Ian Sinclair is on Sun Life's board. But the interlocking relationship stretches even further. Angus Mac-Naughton, president and co-chief executive officer of Genstar Corporation—the real estate, construction, and financial services conglomerate—is on the boards of CPE, Sun Life and Dart Containerline Ltd., with which CP established a joint shipping service to Europe in 1981. Imasco's Paul Paré is also on Sun Life's board, as is Lord Polwarth.

In addition to its close links with Power, CP also has an indirect connection with another major Canadian holding company, Argus Corporation, which Desmarais once tried to take over. CP's vice-president, corporate development, Ronald Riley, is the son of the late Margaret Black Riley (an aunt of Conrad Black, the current head of Argus) and is a director of three Conrad Black-controlled companies: Argus, Dominion Stores, and Hollinger Argus.

CP officers and directors also meet through appointments to the boards of other companies. For example, IBM Canada's board includes CP Air's Ian Gray, Paul Paré of Imasco, and Toronto lawyer John Geller, of Campbell, Godfrey and Lewis, who is on the board of three CP companies—Algoma Steel, CP Air, and Maple Leaf Mills. Claude Pratte, who is on CP's board, runs into Maple Leaf Mills Chairman Robert Dale at board meetings of National Life Assurance. Further illustrating the far-reaching web of directorships in Canada are John Taylor, president of Simpsons-Sears, who is on the boards of CP Hotels and Rio Algom Ltd., and Rio Algom's chairman, Robert Armstrong, who is on the boards of Marathon and Algoma.

There is also an extensive interlocking relationship among CP's insider directors. This not only applies to Burbidge, Stinson,

Sinclair, and Campbell, who are on the boards of the subsidiaries of CP and CPE, but also to the heads and senior executives of the subsidiaries. Russell Allison, executive vice-president of CP Rail, is on the boards of Algoma and CP Hotels. James Bromley, vice-president, Pacific region, CP Rail, is on Pacific Forest Products' board. J.P.T. (Paul) Clough, vice-president of finance and accounting at CP, is on the boards of CP, CNCP Telecommunications, and Canadian Pacific Consulting Services. John MacNamara, chairman of Algoma, is on the boards of CPE and AMCA International, of which Algoma owns 42.7 percent. Paul Nepveu, chairman of CIP Inc. and former CPE vice-chairman, is on the boards of CPE, Algoma, Canadian Pacific Securities, Cominco, and PanCanadian. And L.M. Riopel, general manager, development, at CPE is on the boards of Fording Coal and Canadian Pacific Consulting Services.

In addition to sitting on many of the same boards, CP directors see one another at exclusive men's clubs to which they belong. Sinclair and Desmarais, for example, both belong to Ottawa's Rideau Club and Montreal's Mount Royal. Some seem to collect company boards, clubs, and community organizations like trophies. There is, for example, Thomas Bata, chairman of Bata Industries, and a member of the boards of IBM Canada and CP Air, plus eight clubs, one university board (Trent University), two bi-national chambers of commerce, and a handful of public affairs groups, including the Canadian Institute of International Affairs.

Or, there is Paul Desmarais, whose club memberships run the gamut from the Mount Royal and Rideau to New York's "21," the Bath and Tennis in Palm Beach, and the Eldorado Country in Palm Desert. In addition, he is on a dozen business organizations, including the blue ribbon Business Council on National Issues and the egghead Hudson Institute.

Eighty-one of CP's directors are from eastern Canada, sixty-three from western Canada, twelve from the United States, three from Europe, and one from Bermuda—Albert Joplin, president of Bermuda-based CP Ships. Retirement age for CP Ltd. and CPE directors is seventy, but this restriction does not apply to its other companies. The ages of eighty-one of the one hundred and sixty directors are given in *Who's Who*: three are already in their seventies and forty-three in their sixties, which means there will be a major change in the lineup during this decade.

As the changeover occurs, CP's board and annual meetings are bound to become even more tense than they have been in the early eighties. At a time when CP should have unity of purpose in planning its future economic direction, dissension among the key shareholders is growing with no effort by the company to pacify it.

· 4 ·

More Than a Railway

Canadian Pacific looks like a conglomerate and acts like a conglomerate, but refuses to call itself by that name. Conglomerates have been defined as having at least $1 billion in sales and as being diversified into at least three unrelated or little related fields. Each division, while large, may not be the dominant one in its industry. They are usually multinational and are organized into profit centers with a small head office of experts in law, finance, public relations, personnel, and corporate development. The parent company acts as a banker, when required, for the subsidiaries, and the whole works is headed by executives who want to build empires and know where opportunities lie. Frederick Burbidge has frequently expressed this belief, saying that CP "made its own luck by being receptive to change and alert to new opportunities."

Conglomerates are willing to play a corporate version of Monopoly, buying promising ventures, dumping losers, and moving into unrelated areas, mainly through acquisitions and mergers. Buying existing companies saves time and money and enables faster entry into a new market than through internal development.

Profits and cash flow are siphoned from relatively slow-growing businesses to acquire more dynamic ones. Such purchases have been possible at bargain basement prices in recent years because of the depressed stock exchange prices of most firms. Conglomerates do not necessarily own 100 percent of a company, but rather the controlling interest, and unlike most pre-World War II companies, are prepared to finance their purchases through multiple issues of long-term debt and additional issues of capital stock. Owning under 100 percent allows parent companies to control more assets and companies than if they bought outright.

The reluctance of CP and other conglomerates to admit they are conglomerates is due to the word's conjuring up the impression of too much economic decision making and power in too few hands. So conglomerates like CP prefer to label their widespread empires with the more euphemistic term of diversification. A study on CP conducted by Nesbitt Thomson Securities at the request of the 1975–76 Royal Commission on Corporate Concentration unhesitatingly called CP a conglomerate. In their testimony to the commission, however, CP executives said the term was inaccurate because CP "has branched out into related activities" that "have grown. . .out of its original railway and resource position."

But CP fits all the criteria of a conglomerate. It has well over $1 billion in sales and is involved in ten industrial categories ranging from transportation to natural resources, real estate, and financial services. It has facilities in more than a dozen countries, operates on the profit center principle, has its own financing arm, and has growth-hungry executives. Its head office also has the largest in-house legal department among publicly owned corporations in Canada. Furthermore, reflecting the tendency of conglomerates not to control the individual industries in which they are involved, most of CP's non-transportation subsidiaries are not the largest in their respective fields, although they are usually in the top five. The exception is Cominco Ltd., Canada's top lead and zinc producer.

As a multinational conglomerate, CP runs hotels in the United States, West Germany, and Israel, as well as a flight kitchen in Mexico City. Maple Leaf Mills, whose product lines range from drink crystals to pastry mixes, flour, cereals, and pet foods, operates in the Barbados and St. Vincent. PanCanadian Petroleum is exploring in the North Sea off the coast of Great Britain and in the China Sea. Cominco has mining operations in Australia, India, Spain, Greenland, and Ireland. Canadian Pacific Consulting Services supplies transportation expertise to more than fifty countries.

AMCA International, the construction products and engineering services firm, of which CP owns 52 percent through its two subsidiaries of Algoma Steel and Canadian Pacific Enterprises, is itself a multinational conglomerate. Besides its original business of structural steel fabrication (begun in 1882, one year after CP's formation), AMCA now also produces oil drilling and food packaging equipment, helicopter parts, and paper mill machinery. The company is the world's largest manufacturer of cranes, food and beverage processing and packaging equipment, vehicular tunnel tubes, compaction equipment, and offshore mooring systems for the transfer of liquid and slurried bulk cargo.

AMCA has also spread geographically, with facilities now in seven countries and exports to one hundred nations. AMCA has predicted that its diversification will boost its sales to $5 billion by 1990, compared with $1.5 billion in 1981 and $237 million in 1972. According to its recent annual reports, its philosophy is pure conglomerate strategy: "Straddle a number of industries and markets. . . . Avoid the instability and unfavorable consequences invariably associated with single industry/nation identification."

Among conglomerates, CP has more foreign-share ownership than most of its Canadian counterparts. This may be partly due to CP being listed on the New York, Amsterdam, and London stock markets, whereas many other Canadian conglomerates are only traded in Canada. CP is 28.04 percent foreign owned, compared with Molsons, which is 3 percent, and Noranda Mines, 4 percent. Of that 28.04 percent, 18.31 percent is held in the United States and 3.59 percent in Britain. Foreign ownership has decreased considerably from 1955 when it totaled 90 percent, although management control was in Montreal.

Among railway companies generally, CP has been a leader in diversifying. Railroad companies in the United States have been latecomers to the diversification trend and derive much less of their revenue from non-rail activities than CP does. Only 17 percent of CP's revenue comes from CP Rail. By contrast, at CSX Corporation, the largest diversified railroad company in the United States, 85 percent of its revenue comes from rail. CSX used to own some Florida newspapers, is still in coal development, and also owns the world's largest fleet of corporate aircraft plus the well-known Greenbrier Resort in West Virginia.

The elimination of federal government restrictions barring railroads from offering full-scale trucking service and the recent spate of railroad mergers in the United States, giving the companies more financial muscle, are expected to lead to more non-rail transportation activities by the American lines. Through starting truck and barge service, the U.S. railroads will be able to meet different freight needs of customers, just as CP and CN already do. And, following the lucrative pattern of CP and CN, as well as European railroads such as British Rail, the American lines are expected to turn their land holdings into real estate developments.

The American lines have a long way to go to catch up with CP. With the twenty-five million acres it was granted by the government to build its railway in the last century, CP was perched on its future and could easily diversify, beginning by developing the mineral, oil and gas, and forest wealth of its huge land grant.

From the beginning, Canadian Pacific has been much more than a railway. Supplementary provisions in the 1881 parliamentary Act that incorporated CP allowed it to become involved in telecommunications, shipping, and port facilities. CP steamships brought tea and silk from the Orient to Canada's west coast as early as 1886, providing freight for CP's eastbound trains. Previously, the trains were filled with settlers going west, but had little return traffic. The telecommunications business developed when CP extended its telegraph service from train dispatching to the settlers. Another logical evolution was the construction of hotels to feed and shelter the homesteaders as they moved west. The oldest of CP's early hotels that is still in business is the ever-popular Banff Springs Hotel, opened in 1888, just three years after CP's transcontinental trains began operation.

Although CP did not start its major push into non-transportation activities until the 1960s, in 1897 it acquired a smelter at Trail in British Columbia, which formed the nucleus of Cominco, and in 1958, on land it had obtained free from the government as an incentive to build the railway, CP moved into oil and gas with the establishment of Canadian Pacific Oil & Gas (now PanCanadian Petroleum).

While CP had begun edging into non-transportation businesses, the official move in this direction came only in 1962. On July 9 of that year, Canadian Pacific Investments (now CPE) was incorporated by CP "as an investment and stock company." CP's 1962 annual report further explained that the new company would concentrate on natural resource companies. Like the railway, natural resources are basic and essential to the economy and have an existing demand, rather than one which has to be created, as is the case with high technology.

In a September 29, 1962 interview in the *Financial Post*, Norris Crump was quoted as saying that CPI was just an "internal bookkeeping procedure" and was not a prelude to CP's "spinning off its non-transportation holdings." Crump said there were no plans to issue CPI shares to either existing CP shareholders or the public, and further told the paper that "CPI will be limited to holding shares and other securities of companies in which CP has an interest, particularly those companies carrying on the development of natural resources."

It soon became apparent, however, that CP had much more planned for CPI than Crump indicated. In 1963, the company signaled its new direction by changing its slogan from "the world's most complete transportation system" to "diversification is the key to Canadian Pacific's progress." Then, in 1967, CPI went public with the sale of $100 million in convertible preferred shares, the largest public financing to that date in Canada.

Going public provided seed money for further development of CPI and its subsidiaries. More favorable terms could be obtained from lending institutions because the rate of return on natural resources, until the recent recession, was higher than on rail and air transportation. Also, the establishment of separate corporate entities, rather than simply divisions, meant each could raise money on its own, lifting the onus from the parent company. "The splitting of Canadian Pacific Enterprises from CP enabled the raising of capital against the interesting part of the company without CP's losing its control," says Professor Donald Thompson of York University, who coauthored a study on conglomerate mergers for the Royal Commission on Corporate Concentration.

Diversification had another plus for CP in addition to the

potential for growth in new businesses. It also made it possible for CP to head off criticism that it was enormously profitable at a time when it was pressing for railway freight rate increases. Splitting off the more profitable non-transportation businesses made it possible for the transportation side to argue, without critics pointing to its previously bulging balance sheet, that the railway needed higher rates. The company could also cite its slim transportation financial results whenever unions sought higher wages.

Both Crump and Ian Sinclair came to regard CP's transportation core as deadweight—the industry is highly regulated, which keeps returns low, earnings are extremely cyclical, and the huge fixed assets require large amounts of debt both to build and maintain.

Today, the child is almost bigger than the parent. On average, 60 percent of CP's net income now comes from CPE. The rapid growth elicited some self-congratulation by CP executives on CPE's twentieth anniversary in 1982. Chairman Ian Sinclair boasted at CPE's annual meeting in Calgary:

In Calgary parlance, the Corporation was born of good stock and the bloodline has continually been improved during the last twenty years. . . .

Sir Francis Bacon said, "A wise man will make more opportunities than he finds." This has been the key to Enterprises' success. The Corporation inherited a base from its pioneering parent—a base rich in opportunities which continue to be developed. The individuals associated with Enterprises have made much of their inheritance, and they have found and made opportunities farther afield.

Although Enterprises (as CP executives refer to CPE) has grown so big, a reverse takeover in which it would buy parent CP is considered unlikely. Not only would it cost a bundle to buy CP in the best of times, but Enterprises is stuck with hefty interest payments on its 1981 purchase of CIP Inc. Moreover, CIP's weak performance has had a dampening impact on Enterprises' overall balance sheet.

Investment analysts also consider it improbable that CP would decrease its interest in Enterprises from the current 70 percent.

As evidence, they point to CP's purchase in November 1982 of 70 percent of a new share offering by Enterprises. If CP had not participated, its interest in Enterprises would have fallen by about five percentage points, and this might have encouraged a takeover bid for Enterprises. Moreover, the November 1982 offer, unlike two previous ones in 1980 and 1981, was below the book value of the stock, making it a relative bargain for CP, which had not bought in those preceding years.

In spinning its web, CP has been part of the trend towards conglomerates over the last two decades that *Fortune* magazine has called "the most portentous business phenomenon of the post World War II era." CP's evolution into a conglomerate started in the same decade that saw the development of such American conglomerates as International Telephone and Telegraph (telecommunications, hotels, financial services, natural resources), Borg-Warner (air conditioning equipment, chemicals, financial services, transportation equipment), W.R. Grace & Co. (automotive parts, home improvement centers, book distribution, oil and gas), and Litton Industries (business and marine products, and electronics).

In 1975, according to the Royal Commission on Corporate Concentration in Canada, there were more than thirty conglomerates in Canada among the top two hundred publicly held non-financial firms. Since then the list has grown. Besides CP, the list includes Canada Development Corporation (oil and gas, petrochemicals, and medical research), Jannock (electrical transformers, bricks, sugar refining), The Molson Companies (beer, lumber stores, specialty chemicals), Genstar (real estate, marine services, construction, financial services), Imasco (cigarettes, drugstores, sporting goods), and Noranda Mines (minerals, oil and gas, forest products, wire goods).

So far, this corporate concentration has not led to any government prohibitions or prosecutions of takeovers or of conglomerate mergers, because it has not been proved that trade practices after such actions were anti-competitive. On the other hand, the government could be said to have a weak-kneed reputation in cracking down on anti-trust behavior; it has never successfully prosecuted a company under the Combines Investigation Act for lessening competition. Besides, CP and its fellow conglomerates have never been caught in dirty tricks such as those that ITT, the world's largest conglomerate, allegedly pulled. (Allegations against ITT include plotting in 1970 to stop the election of Marxist Salvadore Allende in Chile and bribing Nixon Administration officials to obtain a favorable anti-trust ruling.) Nor, despite their autocratic ways, have CP's senior executives inspired the fear and loathing that ITT executives had for its longtime chief executive, Harold Geneen, who held the post from 1956 until 1977. His browbeating was so rough that executives were known to faint or become blind drunk after a meeting with him. And, unlike Geneen's corporate collectomania, which resulted in ITT's acquiring a jumble of companies often on a Geneen whim, CP's acquisition strategy has been more logical and its procedures have been financially conservative.

Unless a conglomerate owns 100 percent of a successful subsidiary, it cannot shift the cash flow from that subsidiary to the parent holding company for use by a less successful subsidiary. But even with those subsidiaries that it wholly owns, CP does not dip into their cash flow. "Ian Sinclair felt that if cash flow were taken away, subsidiaries could say that their problems were due to the parent company's doing this," says Terrance Salman of Nesbitt Thomson.

In lieu of draining off cash flow, a conglomerate can force its subsidiaries to pay dividends so high that they bleed the subsidiaries. Most CP subsidiaries pay out a higher percentage of their earnings in dividends to their shareholders (of which CP is the largest) than competitive firms do, but the difference is usually not that great. For example, PanCanadian pays out a higher percentage of its earnings in dividends (55.2 percent in 1981 and 41.4 percent in 1980) than Exxon-controlled Imperial Oil (47.3 percent in 1981, 29.5 percent in 1980).

One subsidiary that does pay out an inordinately high proportion of its earnings in dividends is Pine Point Mines Ltd., a lead and zinc mine in the Northwest Territories that is 69 percent owned by CP's minerals arm, Cominco. In many years Pine Point's dividends have exceeded its net income, and these dividends have largely helped underwrite Cominco's geographical expansion.

In daily administrative procedures, though, the subsidiaries have considerable autonomy. Each has its own public relations department, and not all of them use the same auditor as CP and CPE. CP was one of Price, Waterhouse's first Canadian clients following the opening of the firm's first office in Montreal in 1907. CP signed up with Price, Waterhouse in 1908, largely because of the accounting firm's work for railroad companies in the United States. While CP Air, Marathon, and PanCanadian are audited by Price, Waterhouse, Algoma Steel's accountant is Peat, Marwick, Mitchell & Co., AMCA uses Arthur Young & Co., and Cominco and Great Lakes Forest Products both use Thorne Riddell.

The companies also employ different advertising agencies. According to *Marketing* magazine, CPE and its subsidiary companies were Canada's nineteenth largest advertiser in 1982, spending $11.5 million. Their expenditures were lower than those of such firms as Procter & Gamble, General Motors, and The Molson Companies, but higher than Coca-Cola's.

CP leaves daily management to its subsidiaries, while providing them with assistance in financing and long-range planning. Canadian Pacific Securities, a wholly owned CPE subsidiary, raises money through bank loans, short-term promissory notes, and medium- and long-term debt to provide financing for all CPE's subsidiaries. CPE monitors the debt to equity ratios of these companies and steps in when the ratios are worrisome. Several of the larger companies, such as Algoma Steel, Great Lakes Forest Products, and AMCA International, are also partly publicly owned, enabling these firms to increase equity through their own share splits or rights issues, as well.

The decentralized structure also has the advantage of each business operating as a separate profit center. This system allows greater objectivity in decision making, because it isolates the corporate planning function from any single line of business. Each division, therefore, is under pressure to be more efficient and achieve better financial results. Their results can also be measured more readily against those of competitors, enabling speedier remedial action.

Although each division has its own public relations and legal staff, they are backed up by a large department in Montreal, which charges the divisions for its work. There is a staff of one hundred PR employees in Montreal, more than the seventy-member PR staff of Prime Minister Pierre Trudeau. CP's PR department includes four photographers and two people familiar with printing techniques for when the department farms out work. Company speech writers tape the thoughts of CP executives so that the speeches will contain the flavor of each person's way of expressing himself. Until the late 1970s, when the operation became too expensive to run, the department also used to sell souvenirs from CP's early days to railway buffs. The items included old timetables, place mats, posters, coffee sets, and silverware at prices ranging from fifty cents for a timetable to two hundred dollars for a five-piece silver-plated coffee set.

CP also has the largest in-house law department among major Canadian corporations. According to the 1981 *Canadian Law List*, CP had forty-six lawyers on staff as compared with thirty-four at CN, thirty-three at Bell Canada, seventeen at Imperial Oil, eleven at IBM Canada, eight at the Royal Bank, and four at Stelco. In addition, the subsidiaries have their own in-house lawyers. Cominco has the most, with fourteen on staff. CP's law department is headed by Donald Maxwell, vice-president and general counsel, who has impressive credentials. He joined CP in 1973 after twenty-two years with the federal Department of Justice, where he was deputy minister from 1967 until 1973.

CP has elected to stay in conventional, well-established industries that, except when the economy goes haywire everywhere, provide stability and are counter-cyclical to one another. Another successful Canadian conglomerate, The Molson Companies, anchored by the brewery firm that is more than a century older than CP, has taken a more daring, far-ranging approach into advanced technology and consumer goods. Close to half of Molson's revenue now comes from its non-beer businesses. The opposite paths of CP and Molson's provide an interesting contrast in how conglomerates develop.

CP spun off the strands of its empire from its existing land core, and in its acquisitions it has been primarily a buyer, not a seller. Molson's had to build itself into a conglomerate entirely through acquisitions because it lacked a basket of potential riches. It has been as much a seller as a buyer of companies while searching for the right mix. It has also moved into high technology, investing in a venture fund backing research in biogenetics. So far, CP has avoided high technology industries, although its investment in CNCP Telecommunications is taking it in that direction.

CP's main contacts with the public today are CP Air, CP Hotels, Marathon Realty's shopping centers and office towers, the bake mixes and pet foods made by Maple Leaf Mills, and hotel china made by Syracuse China. PanCanadian has no gasoline stations, and CP does not make such consumer items as tobacco, health care products, liquor, automobiles, farm machinery, or food service equipment, although it would have entered the latter field if it had acquired Hobart, a leading kitchen appliance manufacturer, in 1981.

Molson's, well known to consumers through its strong-selling beers, did not begin its diversification until 1966 when it bought a small furniture business. In 1968, Molson's merged with Anthes Imperial Ltd., which made oil pumps, scaffolding, and boilers. Shortly afterwards, most of the Anthes' companies were sold because Molson's discovered they lacked sufficient potential.

Molson's next ventured into consumer products through the acquisition of Aikenhead Hardware, Beaver Lumber, and Willson Office Specialty, an office supplies firm. These were followed by the purchase of Diversey Corporation, a specialty chemicals producer with operations in forty countries. Diversey has done well, but Aikenhead has not been expanded. Beaver has been scaled down, and Willson was recently sold, both because of a bout of over-expansion. Unlike CP, where each new step had a link to previous expansion and could benefit from that experience, Molson's suffered from rushing into areas that seemed similar to selling beer but were not.

"The marketing of beer and lumber are not the same," says Dan Pleshoyano, formerly senior vice-president, planning and development, at The Molson Companies, where he whipped the company's diversification program into shape. He is now president of Molson Breweries. "Beer is sold by establishing images and doing this is a long, meticulous job. It can take years to introduce a new product. But in retailing, the process must be instantaneous. Also, there are very small margins in retailing and the slightest inefficiency makes a tremendous difference."

As a result, Molson's decided to place more emphasis on Diversey, where the distribution system of servicing accounts is similar to the marketing of beer. In addition, the chemical specialty business has big potential in its more than one thousand products, including water treatment, for which there is great demand in the Middle East and Third World countries.

Judging CPE's and Molson's success as conglomerates by their bottom line, Molson's is the winner despite its more ad hoc approach to diversification. In 1982, Molson's profit margin was twice that of CPE and its return on investment was five times greater.

The major attraction of conglomerates to their executives is that one part can offset seasonal and cyclical fluctuations in other parts. But what has been painfully realized by CP and other conglomerates in the last few years is that during a recession all the spokes in the corporate wheel can be rattled simultaneously.

Unfortunately in a resource-based conglomerate like CP, the weaker components of the empire are often the major employers in their communities, and when they suffer, the communities are also in trouble. In the recent recession, this happened in both Sault Ste. Marie, Ontario, where Algoma Steel, CPE's subsidiary, is the largest employer, and in Trail, British Columbia, where Cominco is the top employer. The distress resulted from the downturn in demand for steel, lead, and zinc.

When there is full employment, Algoma has 12,000 workers. In the summer of 1982, as the steel market caved in, Algoma laid off 4,500, equivalent to 10 percent of the Soo area's work force of 40,000. Of the 4,500, 2,650 worked in the mills and the remainder were office workers. The layoffs were the largest made by Algoma in thirty years.

The layoffs battered both the relief fund of Local 2251 of the United Steelworkers' Union and the Soo's economy. By September 1982, Local 2251's $3 million supplementary unemployment benefit fund, which had taken sixteen years to accumulate, had been wiped out. The fund had provided laid off workers with sixty dollars a week. To avoid another two thousand

layoffs, a work-sharing program was established in which employees worked four days a week and collected unemployment
insurance on the fifth. What made the situation worse was that
the overall slump in the economy meant that there were no
alternative employment opportunities for Algoma workers in
forestry and manufacturing activities in the area.

Algoma's problems seeped into Sault Ste. Marie's economy,
with the city having the highest jobless rate in Canada. The local
newspaper, the *Sault Ste. Marie Star*, had no employment opportunity advertisements during this period, and bankruptcy trustees reported that personal bankruptcies were up by almost 75
percent due to the layoffs, the high inflation rate, and overall
economic weakness. Fourteen small manufacturers in the area
went out of business during 1982.

In the Trail area, where Cominco accounts for three-quarters
of all jobs, the community's outlook rises and falls with that of
the company. In good times, Cominco's miners have traditionally spent part of their paychecks on a second car, snowmobile,
or power boat. The mine has been the major employer in Trail
for several generations of the families living there, and not only
the miners, but also retired Cominco employees and Trail's
merchants depend on Cominco for their livelihood. But, in 1982
and 1983 Cominco was in its worst slump since the 1930s.

Trail is where Cominco has the smelter and refining operations
for its two biggest lead and zinc mines in Canada, the Sullivan
Mine, located at Kimberley, near Trail, and Pine Point in the
Northwest Territories. Of Cominco's total full-strength employment of 12,600, one-fourth worked at the Trail smelter. In
1982, with lead and zinc demand way down and prices falling to
forty-year lows, Cominco stunned the community by permanently laying off 765 workers, equivalent to 21 percent of the
smelter's employees. Overall, Canada's mining industry laid off
8,500 of its 130,000 employees through 1982 and early 1983, or
6.6 percent of the total, a lower percentage than at Trail.

Laid off workers at Trail were even less fortunate than those at
Algoma because they had no supplementary unemployment
benefits package, nor was the union prepared to accept a work
sharing program. The union found new jobs for several dozen
people, but their task was made more difficult by the sharp

downturn suffered in British Columbia's major industry, forestry, which might otherwise have provided alternative employment. The workers' troubles also affected Trail's economy, with housing prices depressed, apartment vacancy rates way up, and several real estate firms going out of business.

CP's size and diversification enabled it to ride out the recession, although it did not escape being badly bruised. But while as a conglomerate it could rely on its stronger diversified businesses to cushion the impact of the slump suffered by others in the CP family, industrial communities like Trail and Sault Ste. Marie could not look elsewhere for relief.

· 5 ·

The Acquisition Spree

In its first ninety years, CP grew through making different uses of its original land grant and the rich resources under this land. But in the 1970s, with this growth tactic at maturity, CP started to look outside for expansion. It began to make acquisitions, slowly at first, then speeding up with a rash of purchases beginning in 1980.

At first, CP tended to buy companies in even-numbered years and digest them in odd-numbered ones. Algoma Steel and Great Lakes Forest Products were bought in 1974, Baker Commodities (an agriproducts firm) in 1976, Syracuse China in 1978, and Maple Leaf Mills in 1980. When it deviated from this pattern, its good luck streak ended. In late 1978 through early 1979, CP was unsuccessful in its bid for MacMillan Bloedel, and in 1981, it was thwarted in its bid for Hobart Corporation, an American kitchen appliance manufacturer. Its purchase of Canadian International Paper, also in 1981, turned out to be a blight on its balance sheet.

While friendly takeovers are much preferred by bidders, CP has not hesitated to fight tooth and nail in acquisition battles. Sometimes it wins, as with Algoma Steel; sometimes it loses, as with Hobart and MacMillan Bloedel. The Algoma Steel purchase is regarded by the investment community as a case study of how Ian Sinclair's stubborn, skillful, juggernaut style works.

CP's initial 25 percent stake in Algoma was acquired from a major West German corporation, Mannesmann AG. In typical fashion, Sinclair's terms were tough. Although most of the deal was in short-term notes, he refused to pay interest on them. He also insisted on paying in dollars, rather than Deutsche marks, at a time when the mark was rising in value. Sinclair also prefers negotiating on his opponent's turf because he believes that makes the other person relaxed to the point where he may make a mistake. True to this belief, the final negotiations over Algoma were at Mannesmann's headquarters in Düsseldorf. Sinclair won. CP paid a low markup on Algoma's shares of only $1$1/8$ over its price on the Toronto Stock Exchange. CP's only concession was in agreeing that half the notes would be in marks. Algoma turned out to be a nifty acquisition. Between 1974 and 1982, its profit margins have been among the highest in the steel industry.

The success of the Algoma acquisition has been offset by other CP takeovers that have created discontent, or have been stymied either by takeover candidates who fight back or the local government. One example of the first category is Corenco Corporation of Boston, an old-line company that recycles animal waste products into fats and proteins. Corenco was purchased in 1979 by California-based Baker Commodities, the rendering firm that CP had bought in 1976, its first acquisition in the United States. Baker had a blemished history. The rendering industry is one in which there have been many anti-trust cases in the United States, and in 1974 the Justice Department slapped an anti-trust consent decree on Baker for its 1970 purchase of a West Coast firm, California Rendering. Baker was ordered to sell it.

When Baker bought Corenco, Corenco's executives were less than thrilled, and clashes over the company's operational thrust quickly developed. As one former executive says, "CP wanted to run the place as a plant, rather than invest in its future." Corenco's executives were also unhappy with management at CPE's U.S. headquarters in Syracuse headed by Robert Theis, formerly a group general manager at ITT.

"While CP's operations are decentralized and conducted in a highly ethical, straightforward, conservative way, ITT has had a long string of legal and other problems in their operations and conducts business in a different style," the ex-Corenco executive says. In any event, all the senior Corenco executives were either forced out or, seeing the handwriting on the wall, quit.

Generous financial termination settlements, coupled with

agreements that former executives would not talk, kept the Corenco situation under wraps. But CP's attempt to buy MacMillan
Bloedel, Canada's largest forestry products firm, was a front
page embarrassment for CP and for Ian Sinclair, until then a
legendary negotiator. With hindsight, CP may well be relieved
that it did not succeed in acquiring the company in view of its
recent financial performance—MacMillan Bloedel's net income
dropped from $154.9 million in 1979 to $3.3 million in 1981,
and it registered a $93.3 million loss in 1982.

CP's interest in MacMillan Bloedel dated back only to 1963
when the then one-year-old Canadian Pacific Investments
bought shares as part of its investment portfolio. But CP's
interest in British Columbia's forest industry dated back to 1905
when CP bought the Esquimalt and Nanaimo Railway on Vancouver Island from the Dunsmuir coal family. (James Dunsmuir
had been a British Columbia premier.)

When the E and N was built in 1883, it received two million
acres of timber and coal-rich land that made up one-fourth of the
entire island. This grant was as controversial as the twenty-five
million acres CP received as an incentive to build its railway.
Indicative of the hostile sentiment towards the E and N was an
April 5, 1897 speech in the House of Commons by William
McInnes, a Liberal member of Parliament from Nanaimo: "Of
all parts of British Columbia, that section has progressed the
least, and there is no explanation for this except that the E and N
holds the land as a monopoly, and will only alienate it on
conditions which are very unfavourable to settlers. Not only is
there an enormous land monopoly established, but with the
grant of land goes all the base minerals."

CP eventually sold most of E and N's land to settlers, but
300,000 acres are still owned by CP's fully owned subsidiary,
Pacific Forest Products Ltd. This is a treasure trove in an age
when most forestry companies log on Crown-owned land under
licenses of specified duration. About 95 percent of British Columbia's forests are Crown owned.

CP, which owned 13.4 percent of MacMillan Bloedel as part
of its investment portfolio, never made a secret of its interest in
acquiring the company. Indeed, Sinclair unhesitatingly said in a
February 1976 interview in *Business Week* that "we might take

over MacMillan Bloedel some day." That day arrived during the 1978 Christmas season when CP made its move.

The battle for the forestry giant started when Domtar Ltd. of Montreal, in a surprise move, bid for control of MacMillan Bloedel, which countered the next day by seeking to take over Domtar. Then CP entered the picture with its own takeover bid.

If it had succeeded, CP—already the province's biggest employer—would have become even more powerful. At this time CP was the biggest landowner in Vancouver, as well as the owner of Vancouver-based CP Air, Cominco, the province's leading minerals producer, Fording Coal, a major southeastern coal producer, and Pacific Forest, the second largest forestry landowner in the province, ranking only after MacMillan Bloedel.

Because of the amount of power the takeover would give CP and because he had not been given the usual courtesy of advance knowledge of its intentions, British Columbia Premier William Bennett was both concerned and infuriated. The politically astute Bennett also recognized the situation as a golden opportunity to make political points because of the widespread dislike of CP in western Canada. Bennett, who had been on Christmas holidays at home in Kelowna, flew to Victoria and called a press conference. He told reporters that "British Columbia is not for sale," a stance that made him the cover story in *Maclean*'s, which called him, in a phrase that politicians' press agents dream of, "the man who won't sell out."

Keeping in mind Ian Sinclair's rabid dislike of the media and publicity, Bennett put him on the defensive by conducting the battle in the glare of publicity to which a premier is accustomed. He called Sinclair and the heads of MacMillan Bloedel and Domtar to a series of individual meetings in his Robson Square office in Vancouver. Although the meetings could just as easily have been in Bennett's Legislative Building office in Victoria, that locale would not have permitted the showdowns to be as much of a media event. Even Sinclair recognized the showdown for what it was. Although glowering in typical fashion and giving monosyllabic answers, if any, to reporters, Sinclair obligingly stopped for a Canadian Broadcasting Corporation cameraman who was filming while walking backwards and fell off a sidewalk curb.

"Those meetings got the most media attention of any event during my time with the premier," says Bennett's former press secretary, John Arnett, now an executive with the province's Urban Transit Authority. "It was viewed as David versus Goliath . . . at last somebody was standing up to CP. There was a great feeling of support, even in the media. For B.C.'ers, who historically hated CP, it was an uplifting experience because the general feeling was that Sinclair felt bigger than anybody and that no premier was going to tell him what to do."

Arnett says that Bennett has the same steely qualities as Sinclair. "Bennett rejoices in being taken on. He cannot be intimidated. He likes to win, whether in politics or tennis. He wouldn't go skiing with me because I was a better skier. In addition, Bennett's background is in business, so he understood Sinclair very well."

Nevertheless, while Bennett gave an outward impression of icy control, the confrontation was a tense occasion for him, which he took out on his staff afterwards in a rare outburst of anger for letting the press near his office. Arnett recalls:

On the plane trip from Victoria, he seemed totally determined. The flare-up stemmed from the crowd of reporters pressing forward from the outer hallway, where they normally wait, into the inner area where they could hear the raised voices. I had to stand in front of the door to keep the media from getting any closer.

The premier and Sinclair were sitting at a small conference table near the windows, which had had the drapes pulled across so people outside could not see what was happening, but they could see the reporters in the foyer outside the office. Afterwards, Bennett bawled us out for letting the reporters get in the restricted area. His face was contorted in rage, but then he turned around a moment later with a beatific smile. I found the sudden change amazing. On the return flight, Bennett was introspective most of the time and he never talked about it again.

Bennett had a trump card in dealing with CP. A 1978 provincial Forest Act had given the government the power to cancel any timber rights agreement between the government and a company if, without the forestry ministry's consent, another firm bought 50 percent or more of that company, or if that company merged with another. That placed CP in a no-win situation. The legislation meant the government could remove 80 percent of MacMillan Bloedel's timber cut.

Just what went on during the meeting has never been divulged publicly, but afterwards, CP, Domtar, and MacMillan Bloedel all dropped their respective bids. CP later sold its MacMillan Bloedel shares to the Bennett-created British Columbia Resources Investment Corporation at a profit. In retrospect, Bennett says his main concern was that "no single company should have too large a share of the forest industry." He calls the Robson Square meeting with Sinclair "straightforward," and emphasizes that "*I* never raised my voice."

Looking back, Bennett likes to give a dispassionate, almost Olympian impression of the showdown. "I found Mr. Sinclair delightful, very dynamic, and naturally gregarious—the type you would expect to run the CPR. I told Mr. Sinclair that 'On 99 percent of the things you do, we agree with you, but here is our policy on this matter.'" However, as he said goodbye to me, Bennett allowed a gleeful crack in his facade of the incident's being just an everyday occurrence. "I guess our little deal with CP is part of folklore today," he laughed.

Over the two years following the MacMillan Bloedel defeat, CP made three major takeover bids. Two acquisitions from U.S. firms were successful, both involving the acquisition of Canadian-based companies. Maple Leaf Mills, one of Canada's largest agribusinesses, was bought from Norin Corporation of Florida in 1980, and the following year Canadian International Paper was purchased from International Paper Company of New York for $1.1 billion, making it that year's sixteenth biggest deal in terms of price, according to a survey by *Fortune* magazine.

The Maple Leaf Mills takeover was a good example of how a chief executive officer cannot always predict the future. In 1974, in an interview in *Executive* magazine, Maple Leaf's president, Robert Dale, who is now its chairman, was asked if he "didn't have any urge to become part of somebody else's conglomerate." Dale replied: "I don't think that many companies do. We feel we are strong enough to stand on our own two feet and have our own long-range plans for company expansion. So, no, we certainly don't relish the idea of being part of somebody else's conglomerate. Our feeling now is that we have the type of stability we need to expand in the future."

The third major takeover bid was for Hobart Corporation of Ohio, and in this case, CPE's $380 million bid ($32.50 a share) crashed. CPE did not realize the depth of hostility in the United States towards Canadian takeovers of American firms during the early 1980s. Not that CPE was alone in its misreading of the climate; other Canadian firms made the same error. During the same period, for example, Seagram's was foiled both in its bid for Conoco, a large oil company, and for St. Joe Minerals.

The situation had its ironic side in that it reversed the usual pattern of Canadian anger over American takeovers of Canadian firms. What particularly irked the Americans was what they perceived as the roadblock of Canada's Foreign Investment Review Agency; there was no similar protection in the United States. This climate made it possible for Hobart, which was opposed to the takeover, to stave off CPE through appeals ranging up to the United States Senate until it found a "white knight" bidder. Hobart's counter-attack of fighting CPE through the media, the courts, and Congress is a case study of how American firms held off the Canadians during their 1980–81 takeover drive south.

In a takeover fight, a white knight is a company that is more to the liking of the target company or one willing to pay more. Riding to the rescue of Hobart was Dart and Kraft Inc. of Illinois, formed in 1980 through the merger of Kraft Foods and Dart Industries, the producer of Tupperware plastic products and West Bend appliances. Dart and Kraft's president, Warren Batts, knew Hobart's president, David Meeker, from when Batts had been president of Mead Corporation, located in Dayton, near Hobart's home base of Troy, Ohio. CPE had been prepared to offer a maximum of $35 a share; even at $32.50, its offer was generous because Hobart had been trading at only $23.50 on the New York Stock Exchange. Dart and Kraft bought Hobart for $40 a share.

Hobart was a tempting takeover candidate on several grounds. It had built up a high-quality reputation since its establishment in 1897. Furthermore, as an internal CPE memorandum on the proposed acquisition said, it had "good growth prospects," "fit" with another CPE company, Syracuse China, which supplies tableware to institutions and hotels, and was "counter-cyclical" to other CPE businesses.

Hobart's plants in Australia, Brazil, West Germany, France, and the United Kingdom would also enhance CPE's international thrust. Overseas businesses in 1979 accounted for 27.4 percent of Hobart's $700 million sales. In addition, it would allow CPE to establish food services equipment as a seventh core area of business, to encompass both Hobart and Syracuse. CPE calculated that in the first five years of owning Hobart, it could derive an average of as much as $47.3 million in net income from Hobart. In the fifth year, it calculated Hobart could contribute $65.7 million in net income, which would have made it one of the top earners at CPE, ahead of minerals, real estate, agriproducts, and forest products.

Hobart had other pluses, too. Its long-term debt had declined every year since 1975 and its earnings had increased throughout the 1970s; its shares were undervalued, and less than 3 percent of its stock was owned by management, making it vulnerable to a takeover. Furthermore, Hobart was well established in Canada, with a branch plant at Owen Sound, Ontario.

Another clincher was that the proposal was brought to CPE by First Boston Corporation, a New York investment banker with a good track record in corporate matchmaking. Among its successes was the March 1981 sale of Bache Group Inc., a securities firm, to Prudential Insurance Co. of America. It had also helped DuPont accomplish the biggest takeover of all time, the 1981 purchase of Conoco for $7.8 billion (U.S.).

As it had done with MacMillan Bloedel, CPE bid for Hobart during the Christmas season. In his testimony to a February 16, 1981 United States Senate judiciary committee hearing, which fell on the one hundredth birthday of CP's founding, Hobart President David Meeker outlined the sequence of events:

Late Friday afternoon, December 12, 1980, Canadian Pacific's attack began. Mr. Robert Theis of Syracuse China—later to be identified as a subsidiary of Canadian Pacific—called for me and, in my absence from town, Hobart's vice-president of marketing for commercial equipment returned the call. Mr. Theis' message was clear: I was to call immediately, as it was extremely urgent that a meeting be set up for the next day or the day after.

I returned that call that evening, and thus became embroiled in a situation which can only be described as unbelievable, or at least unbelievable to a simple businessman who just believes in defending his country, paying his taxes, and operating an orderly business.

Over the next 24 hours I was alternately praised and chided, propositioned, then threatened. The message of Friday evening was conciliatory—indeed even friendly—with the initial comment to me being the desire to discuss a "friendly merger."

A few moments later I was told that Canadian Pacific had received the authorization of its board of directors to acquire Hobart, that tender arrangements were underway, and that if my answer at the Saturday or Sunday meeting was no, the tender would proceed promptly. I was asked to reflect upon this proposal, taking as much time as I wanted—so long as I would respond and meet with them no later than the next day or the day after. It was also suggested that a willingness to engage in such blitzkrieg negotiations would result in the possibility of an attractive employment arrangement for me.

After two later calls from the president of Canadian Pacific Enterprises Ltd. of Montreal, Mr. John Stenason, I declined the invitation to participate in these hasty "negotiations," particularly with the suggestion of some personal benefit to me, and I indicated that any such meeting would have to be preceded by authority and directions from Hobart's board of directors.

Also, I indicated that if they had an offer to make for a transaction of this magnitude and importance, they surely had it in writing and, if sent to me, I would see that such an offer was promptly reviewed by our board, with immediate response to Canadian Pacific. My refusal to capitulate erased Canadian Pacific's earlier facade of congeniality, and a hostile tender offer was again threatened.

It is now my belief that the urgency of Canadian Pacific's demand to meet, and its timing of the offer to coincide with the Christmas season, was to stampede Hobart's shareholders into accepting what has been determined to be an inadequate offer. This became abundantly clear in some of the recent testimony before the Ohio Division of Securities by officers of Canadian Pacific, who admitted that Hobart had been under consideration as a possible target for over a year and that the timing was carefully orchestrated with their counsel and investment bankers so as to effect a maximum of surprise and confusion at the Christmas holiday season.

Meeker quickly showed himself to be an adversary capable of fighting CP. He attacked on the legal and political fronts, using every possible avenue to stall CP until a white knight could be found. First, he took Hobart's case before the Ohio Securities Commission, arguing that CPE had not provided sufficient information about itself or its offer. CPE successfully countered Hobart's arguments. Next, Hobart asked the federal district court to grant a preliminary injunction against CPE, hired a public relations firm that specialized in gunning down takeovers of American firms by Canadians, and took its case to Congress, where Meeker complained of unfair encroachment by Canadian companies. Many of Meeker's arguments were nitpicking and specious, but they bought him precious time.

The public relations expertise was provided by Hill and Knowlton Inc., the world's largest public relations company and a subsidiary of the mammoth J. Walter Thompson advertising agency. Hill and Knowlton's senior vice-president, Tony File, to whom Hobart was assigned, advised his client to launch a media blitz and buttonhole members of Congress as well as Canadian diplomats in the United States. Meeker took the advice to heart, issuing a shower of press releases, a departure for his low-profile firm, and even voicing his criticisms to Peter Towe, then Canadian ambassador to Washington.

Meeker had excellent political connections. He was chief fund raiser in Ohio for President Ronald Reagan, and with the support of Ohio Senator Howard Metzenbaum, Meeker got Hobart's case heard by the Senate judiciary committee on February 16, 1981.

Each side was backed by heavyweight talent. Meeker was accompanied by a former Internal Revenue Service commissioner and by a former chairman of the Securities and Exchange Commission. CPE astutely hired as its lawyer former Attorney General William Saxbe, a native of Ohio.

The committee had no power over individual takeovers, but

the one-day hearing yielded Hobart further publicity and gave Meeker another opportunity to take potshots at the Canadian corporate invaders:

Without question, Canadian law and governmental policy would prohibit this very transaction in reverse, and certainly with all of the questionable matters relating to tax avoidance, securities law violations, and potentially reduced employment. We strongly believe in the free trade and investment among nations. However, should Congress permit American companies to stand vulnerable to the sort of raid now underway by Canadian Pacific, reaching out from all of the protections of fortress-Canada?

Can we sit by and watch foreign takeovers, which are financed through the improper manipulation of our treaties and tax laws, and which threaten the integrity of our markets and the opportunities for our independent businesses to compete, without any legislative challenge? And should we not expect timely, forceful implementation by our courts and Government agencies of the applicable laws already in effect?

All of these things lead to a diminution of American control over U.S. industry, to a loss of jobs and their companion tax revenue, and to a lessening of our Nation's overall economic well-being.

Meeker's tax law comments referred to CPE's plans for Hobart to be a subsidiary of its Netherlands holding company, Canellus International N.V., which already owns CPE's other American businesses, including Corenco, Syracuse China, and Baker Commodities. The significance of this arrangement is that when dividends are sent back to the parent company, CPE does not pay the 15 percent withholding tax called for under the U.S.-Canada tax treaty. Instead, only 5 percent is paid, because that is the amount of taxes on dividends due if an American company pays them to a Dutch company. This tax dodge is used by many American companies as well as by Canadian real estate companies with American subsidiaries, so CPE is by no means unique.

Despite all of Meeker's energetic efforts, Hobart would have been bought by CPE if Dart and Kraft had not made its counterbid. That is often the fate of less fortunate, widely held companies, and the takeover fever of the late 1970s prompted some of these companies, unlike Hobart, to buy back their shares in order to avoid being bought by strangers.

Losing a takeover bid can be very costly, as CPE found out. Its legal bills topped $3 million. But while CPE lost Hobart, it gained a public relations counsel. CP hired Tony File of Hill and Knowlton to, as he says, "provide general counseling on the American view of what's happening." File deals with Barry Scott, CP's public relations vice-president, and has high praise for CP's PR operation. "It's one of the better ones that I've come across in twenty years in the business. It's good in its knowledge of what is going on and their ability to do quality work. They're so good, that after a month of advising them, I told them I wasn't sure what I could do for them." Still, in the case of Hobart, CP's best was not good enough.

Even when CP has won a takeover bid, it has sometimes been the loser, either because it has bought a troubled company, as happened with Canadian International Paper (CIP), or a company in a troubled industry, such as Giddings and Lewis Inc., a major firm in the shaky machine tool industry.

CPE, like other acquisitors, follows today's legal, but cruel, takeover tactic of having its target pay for its own takeover, which can weaken the previously sturdy balance sheet of the acquired company. Such was the case with CPE's 1981 purchase of Canadian International Paper for $1.1 billion (U.S.). CIP, which had under $200 million in debt when it was bought, wound up with $850 million more debt because of the way CPE structured the deal. CPE acquired CIP by using a shell company, Portemiac Paper Corporation, to borrow $850 million. CPE paid the remaining $250 million itself. After CIP was purchased, it was merged with Portemiac and automatically inherited the $850 million debt.

CPE's snaring of CIP was regarded by investment analysts as more of a victory for its former owner, International Paper, than for CPE. Not only did it get a good price, but it was also able to pull out of Canada at a time when American firms and money were fleeing the country in the wake of the Trudeau government's National Energy Program, announced in October 1981.

Additionally, 80 percent of International Paper's Canadian mill capacity was in Quebec, where French-speaking separatism was a further worry to investors.

For CPE, CIP has been bad news. Its 1982 losses of $101.8 million were largely responsible for CP and CPE reducing dividends to their shareholders in the fall of 1982. Nor are the forestry industry and CIP expected to recover until 1985.

"It would have been better for CPE to have sat on the $1.1 billion than buy CIP, because its purchase price was enormously inflated in view of the serious trouble the forest products industry is in," says Laird Grantham, a forest industry analyst at the investment dealer firm of Walwyn, Stodgell Ltd. of Toronto. "It might have been more beneficial to shareholders if the company had bought the remaining 45.7 percent public ownership of another, more successful pulp and paper subsidiary, Great Lakes Forest Products, or the 12.9 percent outstanding share ownership of its oil and gas subsidiary, PanCanadian Petroleum."

There are similar doubts about the wisdom of AMCA's $262.5 million (U.S.) takeover in 1982 of Giddings and Lewis Inc. of Wisconsin, the fourth largest American machine tool manufacturer with 1981 sales of $393 million. AMCA executives regarded the purchase as a natural offshoot of its existing construction and engineering business, but the acquisition occurred during a downturn in the machine tool industry and fast recovery is not expected. Moreover, competition from overseas machine tool makers is increasing. Imports into the United States from Japan, as well as from West Germany and Britain, have grown to 40 percent of the American market, compared with 10 percent five years ago. Furthermore, the machine tool industry generally lags by up to a year behind economic recovery because it can take a year between when a customer orders a machine tool and when it receives the tool and pays for it. As well, the machine tool industry's fortunes rise and fall with the market for automobiles and the car industry has been in a slump. Although there is a potentially strong market because two-thirds of the machine tools in the United States are more than ten years old, investment analysts are doubtful that manufacturers will retool before they recover more from the recession.

With CP's acquisitions strategy less than a glowing success in recent years, partly because of the poor economy and partly due to its own blunders, the company faces a major challenge in the pursuit of growth. Either it must make better purchases or it must concentrate on expanding its existing empire.

· 6 ·

Unbeloved

"Are you going to call your book *CP: good guys or bad guys?*"
former Vancouver Mayor Jack Volrich asked, after talking about
several instances in which he tangled politically with CP.
Volrich's question reflects the controversy that has swirled
around CP in its more than a century in business. The nub of the
controversy is the thesis that CP's growth has been largely due
either to its getting a free ride from the government at the
expense of taxpayers, or to its juggernaut tactics in takeover bids
of other companies. Politicians, businessmen, and consumers
who have battled CP also criticize company executives for being
arrogant and highhanded.

Such views reflect intense dislike for CP, especially in western
Canada where most of its early growth occurred. The classic CPR
joke is the one about the western farmer who returned home one
afternoon to discover that a hailstorm had destroyed his wheat
crop, his farmhouse had been struck by lightning, and his wife
had run off with the hired man. The farmer raised his eyes
heavenward, shook his fist angrily, and yelled, "Goddamn the
CPR!"

The joke is echoed in actuality. On its centennial, CP was
wished "an unhappy one hundredth birthday" by Les Benjamin,
a Saskatchewan New Democratic member of the Legislature
opposed to CP's pressing for the then eighty-four-year-old half
cent a ton per mile rail freight rate on grain to be lifted. And
Volrich says CP is "historically disliked in Vancouver because it is
the biggest landlord and this automatically gives it a certain
negative image. The company is viewed as doing things auto-

71

cratically and lacking concern for the environment. For example, their western headquarters at Granville Square is too big a building for the city's waterfront because it obliterates the view."

British Columbia Premier William Bennett has a more philosophical attitude:

I am not one of those who feel CP stole the country. It was very important for the building of Canada. In fact, my great, great grandfather worked on the construction of the railway. Who but an adventurous company would have built a railway in the middle of nowhere? They got huge tracts of land in return for taking big risks. But with these grants went the responsibility for maintaining consistent rail service.

CP's record is mixed with its sometimes acting in its own self-interest and sometimes responding with sensitivity to the community, such as its recent swap of land in Vancouver with the Province, for an urban development project called B.C. Place, at a very fair price.

The free ride argument about CP's development dates back to when the company was incorporated on February 16, 1881, to build a transcontinental railway. It received rail lines already built or under construction, a $25 million cash subsidy, and a land grant of twenty-five million acres. Construction of the railway helped spur settlement of western Canada by immigrants who then bought land from CP.

As economist and humorist Stephen Leacock wrote in *The Foundations of Its Future*, a 1941 history of Canada privately published by the House of Seagram:

It consisted of a half-made railroad which had fallen back into the possession of a group of Dutch bondholders, to whom it owed over $20,000,000, and into the occupation of vast annual flocks of grasshoppers which were eating everything in the country except the iron rails. The Canadian group bought out the Dutch, it is often said, for a song, yet it was a song that touched the highest note the Bank of Montreal could sing ($6,780,000). Then the grasshoppers went away, and in their place came immigrants, settlers, goods and chattels and more and more settlers—till the Canadian syndicate hardly knew what to do with their money. A shrewd associate said to Sir John A. Macdonald, "Take their money while they still have it."

When the railway was started, Calgary was not yet on the map; it had only a few shacks. Rather than move the railway line, the CPR decided to move the whole community about a mile. Since then, the debate over CP's lands has continued to flare because the railway continues to be either the largest or one of the largest landowners in most Canadian cities. The core of the argument is that while CP did Canada great good in building its railway, it has been a bad urban citizen.

Two of the noisiest battles between CP and municipal authorities occurred in Calgary and Vancouver. A third, involving one hundred and ninety acres in Winnipeg, is still unresolved after more than fifty years of discussion. And a fourth, involving a proposed redevelopment in downtown Toronto by CP and Canadian National, was in limbo for more than a decade. *

In Calgary, the debate revolved over one hundred acres downtown where Palliser Square, CP's headquarters in the city, is now located. Rod Sykes, who was in charge of real estate development in Calgary for CP before he became the city's mayor in 1969 and active in the Social Credit Party, recounts the struggle in the 1950s to develop the office and retail complex:

Calgary's then mayor, Harry Hays, was highly critical of CP for mismanaging its land in Calgary. He said it was a blight in the fastest growing city in Canada. Moreover, city officials were angry because CP paid no taxes on the land since it was exempted by its original land grant. A perpetual tax exemption, such as CP had, can lead to abuse because if one does not have to pay for the land, then they don't have to do anything and can ignore the municipality. When the land is used for other than railway purposes, it is taxed, however.

Hays' criticisms were taken personally by Norris Crump, then CP's president, who had worked in Calgary, and were meant to be taken personally. I had been sent from Montreal to get Hays off Crump's

_____

* See Chapter 13.

back. But when I was introduced at a press conference by Hays, instead of giving the usual corporate response of promising to study the matter, I agreed with him that the lands were shockingly mismanaged. If I had hedged, I might have been executed and sunk without a trace in Montreal. But by the time I returned to Montreal, the company was thoroughly committed to the area's redevelopment.

However, Hays' successor as mayor, Grant MacEwan, hated the CPR and tried to get extra payments for the city, which resulted in Crump's canceling the whole thing after three years of non-stop work.

Eventually, the project was resumed and Sykes faced a fresh problem of how to make it financially viable. "No lender wanted to become involved in providing mortgage money for buildings in such a rundown area and it was also hard to get tenants." So CP proposed building an observation tower as a landmark for Calgary, an idea suggested by the president of Husky Oil when he was having dinner with CP executives.

Husky and Canadian Pacific Oil and Gas (PanCanadian) had been negotiating with one another, and each thought they were going to buy the other. Neither did, but it was agreed to build the tower, originally called the Husky Tower, on the former site of the rail station, which was a way of getting rid of the station.

During Canada's centennial, the province planned to build a carillon tower in Edmonton as its centenary project. That was the year the Husky Tower was scheduled to open. I phoned Premier Manning, and he said there was no point spending taxpayers' money on what private enterprise could do and that took care of the threat of a competitive tower.

In 1969, Sykes won the first of his four terms as mayor of Calgary and promptly bit the hand that had fed him.

Pioneer railway hotels, such as CP's Palliser in Calgary, were tax exempt, but when I became mayor, I decided to tax it. Some people at CP have still not forgiven me. As mayor, I felt the Palliser was competing at an advantage and I asked the company to surrender its exemption. I was dealing with my former bosses and they would stall and delay meetings. Finally, I said that if they would not negotiate an agreement, I would get the Alberta Legislature to override it.

CP executives told me this would fail because Premier Peter Lougheed had assured Ian Sinclair that such legislation would not pass. The bill was referred to the private bills committee where it could have died, but I waited until Merv Leitch, then attorney general and later energy minister, was out of the province and managed to get the bill out of committee and voted on in the Legislature, which passed it unanimously. Lougheed also voted for the bill's passage.

Although Sykes is proud of the precedent he set, he says that in retrospect he "did not want to win that way." Apparently, Ian Sinclair was unhappy, too. Sinclair had bet Sykes a bottle of whisky that Sykes would lose, but Sykes never received it after winning.

Sykes is only one of several mayors in Canada who have taken on CP, an experience that most find memorable, albeit unpleasant. "It's impossible to negotiate with either CP or CN because their view is that their way is the way it's going to be and they are here forever and you are just a puny politician," says former Toronto Mayor John Sewell, who fought both companies over their proposed Metro Centre in the late 1960s.

Like Sewell, Jack Volrich was elected on an anti-development platform. He attributes much of his early success in political life to a 1967 battle with CP's real estate division, Marathon Realty, over a Marathon proposed shopping center:

CP had deliberately kept thirty-six acres near 25th and Arbutus undeveloped for many years, while the surrounding area was built up as a residential community. In 1967 Marathon announced plans to build a major regional shopping center. I lived a block away and was concerned about the impact on our community. The road system would have had to be enlarged and there would have been a lot of traffic in an area where there were many children. I became the spokesman for the community.

City Hall planners approved the plan and Marathon put on a slick public relations campaign of brochures and films that there would not be traffic problems. Finally, after two large stormy public hearings and a four-year fight, Marathon scrapped its plans and built a small shopping center to which we were not opposed. Marathon also offered to work with our group regarding the center's layout.

Volrich regards the episode as a turning point in Vancouver's planning and development, "the first example in our city of how a big developer could be influenced by the community."

Because CP is the largest landowner in Vancouver, this was only the first of the Volrich–Marathon battles. Another one centered around Marathon's on-again, off-again plans to redevelop two hundred acres in the city's False Creek area. Marathon's first proposal, made in 1971, was halted in 1977 in a dispute over the type of housing to be built. In 1979, Volrich, who was then mayor, announced that Marathon had offered to sell the city forty acres for $20 million. Marathon said the land could be used for a long-sought stadium for the city. It could have used the adjoining land it still owned for housing or commercial development. Volrich said he favored using the land for parkland and a community center. In any case, Volrich called the proposed deal "win-win for Marathon, lose-lose" for Vancouver, and rejected it.

Eventually, in 1980, Marathon agreed to a land swap with the provincial government of its False Creek property for several sites in downtown Vancouver. The province planned to use the land for the billion-dollar B.C. Place development, with a stadium as its focal point.

CP is also a major landholder on Vancouver's waterfront and leased a three-block-long pier from the National Harbors Board that the city wanted to use for a trade convention center. CP's lease still had ten years to run when in 1979 the city tried to get it to terminate the lease for one dollar as a goodwill gesture to the community. "But it did not turn out that way," Volrich says.

When I met Ian Sinclair, Premier Bennett had just stopped CP's takeover of MacMillan Bloedel and Mr. Sinclair was still resentful. When we met in my office, he said: "Mr. Mayor, why should we do any favors for the city when we've been treated so badly by your province?" I replied: "Your companies haven't done too badly in Vancouver. The lands acquired and developed have brought financial benefits to your companies."

Because of his strong resentment about MacMillan Bloedel, I didn't feel it was an appropriate time to ask what the price tag would be for canceling the lease. Mr. Sinclair doesn't like meeting reporters and when he was asked after our meeting what he would charge, he said "probably about $9 million." I said "No way." From then on, I urged Mr. Sinclair by phone and telegram to be more reasonable, and one day a Marathon executive said the company would accept $2.9 million. We were prepared to offer $2 million and negotiations over the $900,000 difference went on for four months.

One problem with the negotiations was CP's unwillingness to show us a financial statement confirming how much business the pier gave them. Also, they built into their financial calculations projections of increased profit from cruise ships docking at the pier in future years. But we argued that cruise operations are an uncertain business and that proposed American legislation restricting United States' vessels from taking on passengers at Vancouver also made their projections debatable.

The city finally won out. But a Marathon proposal for a $100 million redevelopment project adjacent to the convention center has been delayed because of what Marathon's 1981 annual report described as "concern of City Planning and Development Committee officials about the transportation of hazardous rail freight in the area." What the report omitted mentioning was that it is CP Rail that is carrying the hazardous materials.

Although Winnipeg is the home town of many CP executives, sentiment has not entered into the decades-long but still unsettled debate over whether the railway should move its extensive yards from the city's central core. The yards were the site of a spectacular explosion in December 1982 when a train of six runaway locomotives smashed into an empty propane tanker car. Fortunately, nobody was seriously hurt, but the accident prompted civic officials and action groups to renew their call for the yards to be moved outside the city, especially as the explosion occurred only two years after a similar collision in the yards.

In the city's early days, municipal officials pressured the

railway to pass through Winnipeg in order to attract settlers and commerce. As incentives, they offered a railway bridge already under construction, a $200,000 cash bonus, free land for a railway station, and exemption from all property taxes "forever" for land used for the railway. (Forever ended in 1965 when the railway started paying property taxes in the city.) But as E.T. Sale, executive director of the Social Planning Council of Winnipeg, has pointed out, "Winnipeg lost overall control of its environment in its willingness to accommodate the needs of the railway."

Proponents of relocation of the yards want the transfer, not only for safety reasons, but also because Winnipeg would then be able to improve the appearance of a large chunk of its downtown. Throughout the years, abortive attempts have been made to relocate the yards or to replace the existing narrow overpass bridges with new ones.

Despite the furor over the two explosions, no quick remedial action is expected because the matter is bogged down, repeatedly shunted between Winnipeg and the federal government, as well as being endlessly debated at the city council level. CP has counter-argued that moving rail yards does not necessarily solve the problem permanently. For example, when it built its new Agincourt yard in northeast Toronto in 1963, it was a rural area. Now, the yard is completely surrounded by suburbia.

In its dealings with Canadian cities, CP is not always the villain. Sometimes, the situation, instead of being a simple case of right and wrong, arises from both CP and its opponent lacking virtue. Such was the case in November 1982 when CP, at the crack of dawn, demolished a seventy-one-year-old railway station in west Toronto without permission from either municipal or federal authorities. The kamikaze attack touched off a howl of protest by historic preservation groups and city officials who had been toying with the idea of turning the station into a farmer's market. On the other hand, anyone who has waited for ages to clear government red tape could understand CP's impatience after months of stalling by Toronto's city officials in giving approval for tearing down the station, which CP said was dangerously close to its planned expansion of the commuter rail line nearby. The station was so rundown that the cost of turning it into a farmer's market would probably have been at least equal to building a market from scratch, but CP had offered to sell the station to preservation buffs for one dollar and contribute towards its moving costs.

The role of Toronto Mayor Art Eggleton in the incident was cloudy. CP officials charged that Eggleton knew they were going to demolish the station, but had asked them to wait until after the November municipal elections. Eggleton hotly denied this, then in a grandstand gesture cut off talks with CP over the redevelopment of its lands near Toronto's waterfront. Less than two months later, the talks were on again. The mayor and CP had reached the ultimate compromise. The mayor could say he won because CP agreed to partially fund a study of all the railway's "historic" properties in Toronto, ranging from stations to sheds. The dispute had also made the usually invisible Eggleton less of a phantom mayor in the eyes of the public. Conversely, CP could claim victory because it did not promise that it would not repeat tearing down its buildings without government approval.

Still, how many individuals could get away with breaking all the rules as CP did? If someone had got tired of waiting for government approval to build an addition to his home or for rezoning and decided to proceed regardless, it is a pretty sure bet he would have run into a lot of trouble. The stiffest punishment faced by CP was a maximum $5,000 fine, peanuts to a company like CP Rail which in 1982 made that amount in just seventeen seconds over an average forty-hour business week. On the same basis, it would take CP itself only three seconds to pay off the fine.

Besides erecting buildings on its vast land holdings, CP has also expanded its empire by tapping their rich mineral and oil and gas resources. The company likes to maintain that it stumbled into the mining business when it took over the construction of a line in 1897 from the financially troubled British Columbia Southern Railway Company and then bought that railway. The line was to run from Lethbridge, Alberta, to Nelson, British Columbia, via the Crow's Nest Pass in the Rockies. CP's claim that it acquired its mineral rights in British Columbia by accident, rather than by design, does not carry weight in view of its deliberate actions to acquire those rights.

In acquiring the B.C. Southern Railway, CP assumed both that railway's pledge to build the Crow's Nest Pass line and the ownership of the 3,755,733 acres B.C. Southern had received as a subsidy from the federal government. CP later sold the land at a $1.8 million profit and obtained a separate $11,000 a mile subsidy from the federal government to build the line, which it had previously considered doing without government assistance. The subsidy came to a total of $3,404,720. In turn, CP agreed without protest to charge only a half cent a ton per mile for grain—the perennially debated Crow's Nest Pass rate.*

At the same time, CP also made some astute purchases in British Columbia from an engineer named F. Augustus Heinze. These included a railway from Trail to Rossland, about twenty miles northwest, plus Heinze's smelter at Trail and the right to build a rail line as far west as Penticton. The smelter formed the nucleus of Cominco.

Why CP should want to say that it was an accident and not foresight that resulted in its getting the Trail smelter when it turned out to be such a lucrative purchase is puzzling. But that is what it did in a 1968 book on its history commissioned by CP and written by Queen's University School of Business Professor J. Lorne McDougall. McDougall said that CP only bought the smelter because Heinze refused to sell the railways alone. But McDougall then contradicted the thesis that CP backed into mining, writing that company executives believed they could use the smelter to encourage mining development. The mine cost $205,980 then. Today, Cominco has assets of $2 billion, and its millions of dollars in dividends to parent CP have helped finance diversification. CP got a double payback from its purchase of the smelter; it is a major producer of lead and zinc and is the carrier of that output.

Although the Crow's Nest agreement later became contentious, in 1897 many parliamentarians felt CP was getting the better part of the deal because it was being subsidized for

---

* See Chapter 8.

building a line for which it had been prepared to pay on its own. Thomas Sproule, Liberal-Conservative member for East Grey in Ontario, said during the June 10, 1897 parliamentary debate on the agreement:

We have given that company a great deal of money. The time ought to come when they should be satisfied and when they would not expect any more from us. . . . Have hon. gentlemen considered that this road would have been built without the country being committed to a dollar's expenditure? If we had not given them that money the Canadian Pacific Railway would have built that road anyway, because in their last report I find the following statement: "But even with these important facilities for handling the traffic of the mining districts, your company will continue to be at a disadvantage in competing with the American lines (which have already reached Nelson, Rossland and other important centres in these districts) until it shall have direct railway connections of its own. Until then the greater part of the mining traffic will be beyond its reach, and will continue to be, as at present, carried by the American lines southward. . . . The directors feel that they cannot too strongly urge the immediate construction of a line from Lethbridge to a connection with your Columbia and Kootenay Railway at Nelson, a distance of 325 miles, and anticipating your approval, they have already taken steps towards commencement of the work on the opening of the spring. . . ."

Therefore, I say we are justified in believing that Canadian Pacific Railway would have built that line whether they got a subsidy from the Government or not. But they have never been very dilatory about asking. They have succeeded admirably in the past, and they are always willing to ask.

CP executives in this century have been just as skilled as their predecessors in getting favorable terms for railway construction. Such was the case, for example, in the building of the Great Slave Lake Railway to Cominco's Pine Point lead-zinc mine, opened in 1965 in the Northwest Territories after explorations dating back to 1927. Although a 1959 Royal Commission recommended trucking the concentrates from the mine, Cominco said this mode of shipping would be uneconomical and that it would only develop the mine if a railway were built.

The federal government, which also viewed the railway as a way of opening up new areas for settlers, agreed and the government-owned Canadian National Railways built the line at a cost of $75 million. Pine Point was only charged $20 million. As Janet Macpherson wrote in a 1978 study of the mine for the Canadian Arctic Resources Committee, an environmental organization: "The government spent large amounts of capital to build a railway for the ultimate benefit of Canadian Pacific, Cominco's major shareholder."

The financial terms of the railway agreement were also favorable to Cominco. Although Pine Point began shipping in 1965, it did not have to pay taxes, royalties, or contribute to the capital cost of the railway until March 1968. In addition, between 1968 and 1978 the company benefited from not having to pay more than the flat rate charge on shipments exceeding the 215,000 tons to which it was committed annually. The government probably thought this was to its advantage since it did not expect Pine Point to surpass that amount. However, during that period Pine Point shipments were triple its actual commitment, which meant it was making windfall profits on the surplus. By the end of 1970, Pine Point's cumulative cash flow was $110.1 million, which meant the mine could have paid completely for the railway and still have had a healthy amount left over.

The question of land grants is not just applicable to CP's early days. Part of CP's vast land grants received when it built the railway are now owned by PanCanadian Petroleum. The significance of this is that while other oil companies either lease most or all of their land from the government or obtain licenses on specific parcels for a maximum of five years, PanCanadian owns 60 percent of its 15.4 million acres. By contrast, Imperial Oil's 1.7 million acres are mostly on Crown lands.

There are also tax advantages for owners of freehold land because they can deduct their exploration expenses from the royalties they must pay the government. These writeoffs reduce their royalties to an average of 22 percent, compared with the 30 percent paid by firms drilling on Crown lands. As a Canadian-owned company, PanCanadian also qualifies for the maximum grants offered under the National Energy Program.

Its large freehold ownership means PanCanadian does not

have to rush to drill on its land or hand it back, as is the case with companies that only have temporary access to the land. Consequently, PanCanadian, the largest owner of freehold oil land in Canada, has been able to take a more leisurely approach to exploration than its foreign-owned, multinational competitors.

One of the arguments used by the Liberal government in introducing its National Energy Program in 1981 was that the multinationals were not sufficiently reinvesting their oil and gas revenues in further exploration in Canada. But PanCanadian's record in reinvestment is not as good as that of major multinationals. Its reinvestment rate (capital expenditures as a percentage of cash flow) ranges between 70 percent and 100 percent, whereas the rate for both Shell Canada and Imperial Oil, two of the largest multinationals in Canada, far exceeds 100 percent. Indeed, in 1982, a year in which the oil companies were stung by the recession, Imperial Oil's reinvestment rate was 153 percent, double that of PanCanadian's 78 percent.

In addition, PanCanadian turns over a larger proportionate chunk of its dividends to its shareholders than Imperial and Shell do. In 1981, PanCanadian paid 55 percent of its earnings—or about $111 million—to its shareholders, compared with a 48.8 percent payout by Shell and 47.3 percent by Imperial.

But less of PanCanadian is publicly owned than Shell or Imperial. PanCanadian is 87 percent owned by Canadian Pacific Enterprises, Imperial is 70 percent owned by Exxon, and Shell 79 percent by Shell Investments Ltd. of the Netherlands and Britain. Thus, on a proportionate scale, CP retains more oil and gas funds for diversification within its empire than the big, bad multinationals of Shell and Imperial at which the NEP was directed.

CP's use of its muscle in cities and its use of taxpayer-financed land grants to build its huge empire probably would not arouse so much public hostility if the company displayed the qualities of a good corporate citizen in other ways. That it does not display such qualities is one of CP's biggest failings.

CP can make colossal blunders and be extremely obdurate, heartless, and foolishly shortsighted at times. Its arrogance in feeling it has a divine right to ignore governments and the public if they get in the way has made CP one of the most disliked companies in Canada. And even when it has no choice other than to do something beneficial for the public or its employees, it does it like a feudal lord dispensing ducats from his balcony.

The size of CP has tended to make many of its executives arrogant and autocratic in their dealings with consumers, customers, or elected government officials. The examples are many. There is the cavalier way rail passengers were treated before CP withdrew from the business five years ago. There is CP's stiff opposition to deregulation of freight rates, such as exists in the United States, and CP Air's dog-in-the-manger attitude about opening the transcontinental market to other companies besides itself and Air Canada, even though it acknowledges its own growth is due to the government giving it more routes. There is CP Rail's argument, after the derailment of a train carrying hazardous chemicals in 1979 at Mississauga, Ontario, that communities should know better than to have residences near railway tracks where accidents can happen. There is the company's insensitivity in planning to put a smokestack from a railway tunnel in the Rocky Mountains in full view of tourists at the summit of Rogers Pass. There is Great Lakes Forest Products' sudden interest in beautiful but marginally productive forest land that it had not used for two decades when wilderness park lovers wanted to turn it into a park.

And while other major corporations boast about their charitable donations in support of the arts, education, or medicine, CP is very low-key. Whether the low profile is due to not wanting a deluge of requests, modesty, or limited generosity is, therefore, difficult to judge. Other firms are not so reticent. ITT, for example, devotes two pages in its annual report to recounting its good deeds. Imasco sets aside a page in its annual report in order to list its community funding, and its tobacco division gets substantial publicity from its support of sports and the performing arts. Several Canadian companies and successful businessmen have also established philanthropic foundations to support community activities—the Carling O'Keefe Sports Foundation, the Paul G. Desmarais Foundation, the Eaton Foundation, the W. Garfield Weston Foundation.

CP does none of this. It does not sponsor performing arts groups on a continuing basis. There is no CP Foundation or one named after a CP executive. CP prefers to support different ventures each year, with its decision based on each proposal's benefits to a community. Using this criterion, CP has contributed towards such diverse projects as civic centers, concerts, transportation for the physically handicapped, and educational television programming. One subsidiary, Cominco, was one of three winners in 1982 of the *Financial Post* awards for business in the arts because of its underwriting the $150,000 tour expenses of the Vancouver Symphony Orchestra and contributing $50,000 towards a feasibility study for an arts center in Trail. CP Air provides short scenic plane flights, from which passengers' fees go to the Easter Seal campaign, and also flights as prizes in fund raising campaigns for other health causes.

On the political front, Ian Sinclair's appointment by the Liberal government as its mouthpiece in the business world for its "six and five" percent wage increase ceiling is due to the prominence of CP, rather than a favor in return for CP's donations to the Liberals. CP is an equal opportunity donor to the Liberals and Progressive Conservatives. In 1981, it gave $25,000 to each party, upped to $50,000 to each in 1982, according to the office of the federal chief electoral officer. (By contrast, Desmarais' Power Corporation gave $51,713.66 to the Liberals in 1981 and $29,388.72 to the Conservatives, reflecting Desmarais' leaning towards the Liberals. His son, André, is married to Energy Minister Jean Chrétien's daughter, France, and Transport Minister Jean-Luc Pépin is a former member of Power's board.)

But if it wants to be a good corporate citizen, charitable donations are not all that a company owes the public. CP is not alone in sometimes ignoring the public's welfare; the same could be said of automobile manufacturers who turn out lemons and coal-fired power stations whose emissions contribute to acid rain. However, that does not excuse CP. A company should not only feel responsible to its bottom line and its shareholders, but also to the public without whose purchases the company could not be in business. A company that is a good corporate citizen feels it owes something to the public. For its engineering skill, ranging from its railway to its two-year-old lead and zinc mine in the Arctic, the world's northernmost mine, CP deserves praise. But for its frequent lack of social conscience and disregard for the public, CP rates condemnation.

Despite CP's huge public relations machine churning out an awesome amount of material on the company's projects, CP has not been able to win the affection of Canadians for the company. Even a century after the company was formed, its reputation as a corporate citizen remains as hotly controversial as it was one hundred years ago, and unless CP undergoes a radical change in its dealings with the public, the controversy is likely to continue.

7

The Rank and File

In 1979, a former CP Rail employee, seeking revenge on the company because his toes got frozen on the job, left a track switch half open and derailed a freight train near Thunder Bay. The employee picked the wrong train—it was a CN freight train that went off the track.

Labor relations between CP and its 127,000 employees do not often sink to this level, but they have had their rough spots. Between 1950 and 1982, there have been more than forty strikes at CP companies, most of them over wages and fringe benefits, although some have also dealt with the loss of jobs caused by technological changes. The longest was a six-month walkout at CIP in 1982 as part of a near industry-wide strike by pulp and paper workers over wages. Subsequently, in the summer of 1983, CIP gave its employees a 24 percent wage hike over a two-year contract running retroactively from June 30, 1982 up to June 30,1984. That was a far cry from the 4 and 3 percent increases urged by Ian Sinclair as head of the federal government's business committee promoting wage restraints. Obviously, CIP was not listening to its master's voice.

Canadians as a whole have not suffered from work stoppages at CP companies for a decade, since there have been no nationwide railway strikes since 1973. However, there are rumblings of a national rail strike in 1984 due to the dissatisfaction of rail employees at CN as well as at CP over what they regard as unfairness arising from the federal government's 6 and 5 percent wage guidelines. Because Canadian National Railways is a Crown corporation, its employees are subject to the federal government's six and five ceiling on wage hikes for federal employees, and because they negotiate jointly with those at CN Rail, so are CP Rail employees.

The application of the guidelines gave CP a double benefit. Since CP Rail employs about one-fourth of CP's workforce, the wage restraints should prevent CP's payroll expenditures from growing as much as they would otherwise. At the same time, both CN and CP benefited from a six-month period of grace, during which their export freight rates were excluded from the government's restraint program. During this time, the two railways hiked their rates by about 12 percent, equal to the rate of inflation, but double the restraints' ceiling. This enabled them to make up for shortfalls in domestic freight rates that were subject to the restrictions from the start of the program.

In applying the wage restraints to CN and CP, however, the federal government, unwittingly or not, gave the rail unions an unexpected bargaining lever for when their contract comes up for renewal in 1984. According to Eddy Abbott, executive director of the Canadian Railway Labor Association, the railway unions' umbrella lobbying and research association, the railway workers could argue that "if they have to obey the wage restraints like the civil service, they should get the same benefits of cumulative sick leave for years of service, job security, and pensions indexed to inflation, none of which they get now."

As Canada's largest industrial employer, CP employs about sixty-thousand more people than CN, when both are at full employment. CP's staff is greater in number than the combined total of employees at General Motors of Canada, Imperial Oil, and the Hudson's Bay Company. CP's labor relations provide a portrait of major industrial issues affecting business today, ranging from the impact of technological changes to pensions and job safety.

CN and CP do not provide a public breakdown of how much they pay employees, but according to information submitted on request by both railways to the Canadian Railway Labor Association, in 1981 CN Rail and CP Rail combined laid out $2.2 billion in total compensation. That sum includes salary plus such benefits as life insurance, denticare, a drug plan, and pension payments. The dental plan, coincidentally, is operated at both

CN and CP by Great West Life Assurance, which is controlled by CP's largest shareholder, Paul Desmarais.

Pension payments account for 13 percent of gross payroll at CP Rail and 11 percent at CN Rail. The total compensation package amounts to one-half of the two railways' combined expenses. The average annual salary of a worker at CP Rail and CN Rail in 1981 was $21,821. By contrast, the average annual salary in 1981 for United States' rail employees was $26,698 (U.S.).

The ravages inflicted on employment by technological changes are most evident in the rail industry, where CP still has the largest proportion of its employees. Of the four major rail strikes in Canada—in 1950, 1957, 1958, and 1973—all but the 1950 strike, in which the major issue was wages, revolved around concern over job security in the wake of technological changes. "Automation has improved productivity at the railroads, but it has also wiped out thousands of jobs. It used to take hundreds of people to lay track; now a machine, with one operator sitting in the cab, does this," says Eddy Abbott of the Canadian Railway Labor Association.

At CP alone, rail employment has dropped from 84,000 in 1952 (equivalent to the total at Canada's eleven railways today) to 58,000 in 1962, 42,000 in 1972, and about 30,000 in 1983. That number is slated to drop still further. Years ago, five employees operated each train. They now have three-man crews and the railways want to reduce the crew still further to two engineers, getting rid of the caboose and its occupant. The main purpose of today's caboose is just to carry marker lights, which can be put on the freight cars, as is already done in France and England.

Over the last fifteen years, workers laid off as a result of technological changes have been paid 80 percent of their last five years' salary. This worked out to 12 percent more than they would have received under their regular pension plan, which is equal to about 68 percent of the best five salary years.

The workers have partly funded their own forced early retirement. "In 1962 when the industry recognized a fund would be necessary to help people face relocation problems, it was decided to set aside one cent an hour per employee out of their wages," says R.J. Cranch, national secretary-treasurer, Canadian division, Brotherhood of Railway, Airline and Steamship Clerks, Freight Handlers and Station Employees (BRAC). "The fund was not used until 1967–68 when CP's fund had grown to $6 million and CN's to $11 million, including interest."

At CN, since the 1970s, unionized workers have been able to retire early at age fifty-five, but at CP they must continue to age sixty, regardless of years of service. "Ian Sinclair used to say that a man is just becoming efficient at fifty-five and could work on, but must have independent means if he retires then and so does not need a pension," Cranch says. "We hope this attitude will loosen up under Frederick Burbidge and William Stinson."

Decline in railway employment due to technological changes first began in the 1930s when CN and CP started to build so-called "hump" rail yards. Under this system, cars are pushed up an incline or "hump" by locomotives and then descend by the force of gravity. Consequently, fewer engineers and yard crews were needed than when the operation was done on flat ground. But the axe did not really fall until after World War II when the railways, faced with increasing competition from trucks, planes, and cars, resorted to staff cuts as a way of keeping down costs. Labor was a natural place for them to look because their payroll and benefits accounted for 62 percent of their expenses, or 12 percent more than they do today. Unfortunately for the rail workers, their unions were unsuccessful in getting the retirement fund established until 1962, and by then more than thirty thousand employees at CP Rail alone had lost their jobs.

The biggest wipeout of jobs came in the aftermath of the diesel engine, which eliminated the need for firemen who had been essential on steam-operated railroads and enabled longer runs without having to change train crews. The ham-handed way CP went about implementing dieselization was guaranteed to provoke a strike, and that is exactly what happened. The firemen struck for nine days in January 1957 and again for two days in 1958, when the whole conflict might have been defused if CP had acted more tactfully.

The firemen did not challenge the necessity of the technological changes destroying their profession. What justifiably irked them was CP's neglecting to negotiate with them over a decision that would drastically affect their lives. There was no prior consultation regarding the impact on the firemen, nor were there any definite proposals to offset the adverse effects. CP's snub was bound to make the union intransigent in return. As W.E. Gamble, a spokesman for the Brotherhood of Locomotive Firemen and Enginemen, said:

If the company had seen fit to accompany its proposal on the diesel issue with a concrete blueprint, spelling out in detail what provisions it was willing to make for the 1,000-odd firemen who would be immediately cut off the payroll and the not inconsiderable number of other firemen who would ultimately lose their employment, the no-compromise position which the union maintained throughout might have been at least in some respects relaxed or modified.

The dispute over the firemen eventually went before a Royal Commission, a standard procedure with major contentious rail issues ranging from wages to freight rates. The 1958 commission, headed by Supreme Court Justice Roy Kellock, supported CP, saying that the functions of firemen in freight and yard service had "either totally disappeared. . . or are a mere duplication of what is discharged by others." Kellock also approved CP's proposal to his commission that it would not lay off firemen hired before April 1956. "The change from steam to diesel power which will cause the displacement of the firemen, has also resulted in effecting very substantial savings in the Company in transportation and locomotive repair expenses," he said. "The cost of protecting the firemen, in this case, can therefore be properly set off against these savings."

The firemen struck for two days in May 1958 over the Kellock Report but gave in when they found they lacked support from members of other railway unions, as well as labor as a whole. In those days when job redundancy was not a national issue and did not affect Canadians in every industry, public opinion was also against the firemen and in favor of companies' keeping pace with new technology.

Interestingly, one proponent of the view that the firemen were being unreasonable was Queen's University Professor J. Lorne McDougall, the author of a commissioned history for CP in 1968. In 1976, in a retrospective article for his hometown newspaper, the *Kingston Whig-Standard*, McDougall wrote: "If you believe that wages should be paid for valuable services only, but for no other reason, then it follows that the whole $355 million paid to CN and CP firemen in yard and freight service from 1950 to 1974 was a deplorable, even scandalous waste."

Providing job security to workers whose jobs have been wiped out in exchange for more modern methods can be a costly proposition, with the benefits of the technological advances not being realized for years, as CP learned. In 1956, it had estimated its carrying costs of the firemen would be $38 million and its annual savings $11 million, based on its calculations that its firemen would retire or be promoted to engineers within a decade. Its projections were wide off the mark. By 1970, CP had spent $110 million on the firemen and achieved only $2.5 million in savings. It took until near the end of the decade before the remaining firemen became engineers.

CP was not alone in summarily presenting major changes to rail workers as a *fait accompli*. CN was just as guilty. In 1964, without notice or consultation, CN decided to eliminate what it viewed as unnecessary train stops and crew changes, because dieselization allowed run-throughs. The first stops eliminated were two small communities, Nakina in Ontario and Wain-wright in Alberta. CN workers retaliated by booking sick in protest. A landmark ruling by an inquiry into CN's actions, headed by Justice Samuel Freedman, ensured that such high-handedness would not recur. Freedman said the workers should be given advance notice and that there should be negotiations between the unions and the railways to minimize the adverse effects on employees of technological change.

Most gains made by rail workers were the result of such federal inquiries, rather than corporate beneficence. Fairness in compensation was the result of government intervention, too. In January 1974, following a July 26 to September 10 strike over wages by CN and CP rail workers in 1973 (by far the longest of the four rail strikes since 1950), federally appointed Justice Emmett Hall drew up a three-part formula regarding compensa-tion that has been adhered to ever since. Justice Hall stated that the rail workers were entitled to three basics of fair play: 1. a raise that represents a catch-up to wages in comparable industries; 2. a share in the increased productivity of the economy; and 3. wage increases equal to the rise in the cost of living.

But Justice Hall's ruling had some unintended harmful side effects. In earlier days, when the railways looked for ways to improve their profit position, they could turn to automation as a way of making their industry less labor intensive and, thereby, reduce their payroll. However, by the 1970s, technological changes had gone about as far as they could go, and the railways had to hunt elsewhere for ways to improve profit. Two courses were open to them. They could squeeze more value out of their equipment by loading trains with only one item ("unit trains") and introducing differently shaped freight cars that stored greater quantities in less space. And, at the same time as they increased service to shippers, the railways could look at ways to economize in order to boost profit. Their choice was to continue cutting back on passenger service as well as freight service to areas where they felt there was insufficient traffic.

In these days of double digit inflation, the indexing of pensions to inflation has become a major issue, not just for rail workers but for Canadians in all industries. The idea is not new. The subject of indexed pensions for rail workers was investigated between 1974 and 1976 by Noel Hall, a University of British Columbia industrial relations specialist, at the request of the federal government. But even though the government authorized Hall to "particularly investigate and report with recommendations upon the cost of living indexing of pension benefits," he dodged the issue.

"Indexing may come about at some future time either on a partial or full basis, but if that is to happen, it will likely require a realignment of priorities at the bargaining table," Hall wrote. "In my judgment, railway pension plans properly belong within the scope of collective bargaining. . . . In my role as a Commission of Inquiry it would not be appropriate for me to make a recommendation which would have the effect of relieving the CNR, CPR, and Canadian Railway Labor Association from a responsibility that properly falls to them."

Hall did, however, single out CP for "glaring inequities" in its pension plan that, unlike CN, did not provide a supplement to soften the impact of inflation. In line with Hall's recommendation, CP introduced a 2 percent increase for each year of retirement up to December 31, 1976 for employees who had retired before January 1, 1973. This brought CP in line with CN, which had provided the extra money since 1970. CP also accepted Hall's suggestions for relaxing the criteria to qualify for survivor pensions. As a result, benefits were no longer cut off if a survivor remarried after one year, instead of after the previous five-year waiting period. In addition, the age requirements for eligibility were broadened from employees hired before the age of forty to those hired before the age of sixty.

Today, CN and CP have two of Canada's largest pension funds, ranking first and sixth in terms of assets according to the 1983 *Financial Post* five hundred top companies survey. In 1982, CN's fund was the leader with $3.2 billion in assets, and CP's fund had assets of $1.7 billion. The number of people involved at each company is equivalent to the size of a small city. CN's plan had about 71,000 active members and 28,000 retired ones; CP's had about 37,000 active members and 26,000 retired ones.

That progress on pensions and other matters has so often come from inquiries rather than collective bargaining illustrates a basic weakness in railway labor relations. No industry has as many different unions as the railways, which have fifteen covering the many trades ranging from engineers to yardmen, signalmen, clerks, and repair shop workers. With such a multiplicity of unions, contract negotiations could be non-stop throughout the year with first one union and then another and another holding talks. Nevertheless, this was the pattern of labor relations until a decade ago. The process was tiring for the railways and harmful to the unions because it diluted their bargaining strength.

The fragmentation was finally replaced by centralized bargaining in 1974 with the formation of the Associated Railway Unions as an umbrella organization for all the rail unions. The organization does not exist as a legal entity, and its purpose is only to allow joint bargaining by the individual unions. The unions can opt to bargain through the Associated Railway Unions on their own or in groups. However, because coalition bargaining deals with universal issues such as wages and benefits but, by its nature, does not cover individual union problems that may not affect other unions, the rail unions tend to prefer the group approach.

There is also a third party—the federal government—indirectly at the bargaining table. The government has the power to legislate striking rail workers back to work, and many of the arguments made by management are aimed at the government rather than the workers, who almost become bystanders in the proceedings. In the railways' view, they have had to maintain unremunerative lines and stations in areas where the amount of traffic, in their opinion, did not justify the service. Thus, they have viewed labor negotiations as a forum in which they could seek a *quid pro quo*: unless they were compensated more for providing what they regarded as uneconomic service, they would not enter any negotiations that could lead to their having to pay higher wages. The railways reasoned that if they willingly agreed to hike wages, even by a small amount, the government would interpret this to mean that the government regulations calling for "unprofitable service" were not hurting the companies.

As Stephen Peitchinis, a University of Calgary business administration professor, wrote in a 1975 study on collective bargaining in the railway industry, following the last major strike in 1973:

On many occasions it was quite evident that the "crises" in labor-management relations had nothing to do with labor-management relations. Rather, they were conflicts between the government and the railways regarding the nature and degree of controls imposed upon the operations of the industry. Therefore, from the standpoint of the application of continuous pressure on the government to review and relax the rigid regulations, it was to the industry's advantage to create a crisis situation out of every contract renewal, thereby forcing an examination by the Cabinet of the whole railway problem.

The strategy worked time after time, with the federal government providing more and more subsidies to the railways to make up for their claimed losses in providing service "in the national interest." The situation put Canadians in a no-win situation.

Maintaining such service hiked their taxes to keep the lines in operation. Canceling the service left many communities stranded.

Although the number of strikes at CP is nothing to be proud of, some of the strikes were part of industry-wide strikes by steel, rail, or pulp and paper unions. The three major strikes since 1974 at Algoma Steel, for example, have lasted fewer than twenty days, whereas Stelco had a 125-day strike in 1981.

Algoma also offers a case study of how local management and unions can jointly recognize a problem (with a little outside encouragement) and work out their differences. Workers and management were at loggerheads a few years ago over what the workers regarded as lax safety conditions at the main Algoma mill in Sault Ste. Marie. Their differences came to the boiling point in the fall of 1980 after four fatalities at the mill in the space of just six weeks. The deaths, the most ever suffered in such a brief span of time at Algoma, also concerned the community of Sault Ste. Marie. Algoma is its biggest employer, and families were worried that their husbands or sons might die, too. "Algoma's management did not recognize the right of a union committee to inspect the workplace or of the workers to refuse unsafe work, as called for under Ontario's Occupational Health and Safety Act, which had become law two years earlier in 1978," says Dennis Abernot, vice-president and chairman of the Compensation Committee of Local 2251 of the United Steelworkers of America, which represents Algoma workers in Sault Ste. Marie.

The four fatalities served as a catalyst for an overhaul of the working conditions at Algoma. The deaths prompted both Local 2251 and Algoma's management to send telegrams to Ontario's Department of Labor requesting an inquiry on safety practices at the mill. The resulting model safety program, of which both the company and the union boast today, has two morals to it. First, despite usual public doubt about government effectiveness, the government can be a positive force. Second, while Algoma failed to initiate the safer procedures on its own, it became a willing participant once it was pushed into bettering its safety record.

Ontario's Department of Labor began to tear down the barriers between the union and management by holding a three-day seminar in Sault Ste. Marie paid for by the company and attended by twenty-five union and twenty-five management people. "We hung out all the laundry and then began to build a structure," Abernot says. A three-tier committee structure was established, covering departments, divisions, and top union and management officials, backed up by a series of sub-committees on matters such as hygiene and overhead walkways. The responsibilities of the committees, frequency of meetings, duties of the chairmen, reporting procedure for injuries, discipline for violations of safety regulations, and safety precautions for employees were detailed in a three-hundred-page manual that is updated annually. As of 1982, the company agreed to bear the cost of printing copies for each of the twelve thousand workers.

In addition to revamping safety procedures, Algoma upgraded the general working conditions. The old, crowded change rooms, which Abernot says lacked adequate shower facilities and ventilation, have been replaced with brightly painted, air-conditioned units containing lots of showers and locker space for work and street clothes. The tables and benches in the lunch room have been replaced with full-scale kitchen facilities.

The upshot is both a much safer plant and a far better working relationship between management and the union. "Accident frequency is down from 29 percent to 18 percent annually and labor relations are 90 percent better," Abernot says. "We're being treated like human beings, rather than animals. Before, when a worker went to a supervisor and reported unsafe conditions, he was often ignored. Now, management listens."

Today's shaky economy has made job security a top priority of Canada's labor movement. About 10 percent of CP's workforce has lost their jobs or been laid off at various times throughout 1982 and 1983 in response to slumping demand for CP products. The opposite reactions of labor and management to the downturn are illustrated by the situation at Cominco, which in 1982 had its first operating loss since 1932. Labor's reaction was that, placed in perspective, the loss was not a catastrophe. In an October 1982 report on Cominco's financial outlook, the United Steelworkers of America, which represents Cominco's mining employees, pointed out that "since 1912, there have been only two years when operating deficits were incurred," and concluded: "Cominco's problems are short term. While the company may consider this period a 'crisis,' it will rebound as soon as the recession ends. It will curtail Cominco's investment pattern, but it will restart as soon as the North American economy rebounds."

Cominco's situation also provides a case study of two other issues in labor-management relations: whether the economy or modernization, or both, are to blame for layoffs; and if a seemingly over-generous contract settlement is as much a give-away as it seems.

Cominco blamed the layoff of 765 of its 3,600 employees at its Trail lead and zinc smelter on declining demand for these minerals. The United Steelworkers' Union blamed the layoffs on a $425 million five-year modernization program launched in 1977 at Cominco's facilities at Trail and nearby Kimberley, rather than on the recession.

Union leaders said that when they signed a two-year contract with Cominco in May 1981, the company told them that normal attrition should take care of any jobs made redundant by the modernization, which would make possible greater output with fewer workers. However, the contract did not include the indexing of pensions to inflation and, therefore, fewer people took retirement. That created a surplus of workers as the plant modernization program got underway.

On the other hand, the company could argue that the 1981 contract, covering two years, did give Cominco workers at Trail a generous average wage increase of 43.7 percent, including benefits. In actual dollars, though, the terms were not as great as they seem. While higher job classifications did gain substantially, lower levels did not: the salary of a technical supervisor rose $1,174 a month, or 43.5 percent, between May 1981 and May 1983, but a laborer's pay rose only 18 percent over the two-year period, or 9 percent annually, less than the rate of inflation.

When that contract expired, the company sought to regain what it had given away by refusing a wage increase in the first year of any new contract and trying to eliminate various fringe benefits, including a cost-of-living allowance, a crucial clause in recent contracts in all industries. A compromise agreement reached after a one-week strike awarded cost-of-living allowances in the second year of the two-year contract, but no wage increases unless depressed metal prices rose spectacularly.

The stance taken at Cominco, as well as the history of relations with the rail unions, shows that CP tends to be hard-nosed in its dealings with labor. The recession has kept worker-management conflict on the back burner, but as the economy improves and contracts come up for renewal, CP's traditional intransigence may lead to confrontations in all parts of the empire over the decade of the eighties.

· 8 ·

The CPR: No Longer the National Dream

Each day at 4:30 P.M., EDT, Canada's last remaining transcontinental passenger train, *The Canadian*, leaves Montreal's Central Station. Three days, four nights, and ninety-eight stops later, it arrives in Vancouver, having followed the route carved out one hundred years ago by the builders of the Canadian Pacific Railway. It passes through Ontario's granite Laurentian Shield and the vast plains of the prairie provinces, then climbs and twists up, around, and through the spectacular beauty of the Rocky Mountains.

It is a trip through CP's past, because since 1978 CP has not been involved in passenger train travel, and for years before, it gave this end of its business—the foundation of its empire—short shrift as it shifted to what it viewed as more profitable ventures.

CP likes to keep saying it has become much more than a railway, but the railway is still a leading contributor to CP's consolidated profit, providing about the same amount as the many CPE divisions do combined. In 1982, CP Rail accounted for 62.6 percent of consolidated CP profit. The future for diversification by CP, then, relies to a large extent on the former National Dream—a transcontinental railway that has become more profitable by operating, but not financing, passenger service.

The Canadian is now run by Via Rail, which took over passenger rail services from CP and Canadian National Railways in 1977 and 1978. Today's trip is a far cry from the luxury that passengers enjoyed on Canada's first transcontinental train, the *Pacific Express*. Its sleeping car contained sofas, a private state-

100

room, and a bath. As CP's archivist, Omer Lavallée, wrote in *Van Horne's Road*, published in 1974, it was nothing but the best back in the pioneer days of 1886 when the cross-country run began.

CP advertisements of the time said the dining cars "excel in elegance of design and furniture, and in the quality of food and attendance, anything hitherto offered to transcontinental passengers, local delicacies such as trout, prairie hens, antelope steaks, and Fraser River salmon succeed one another as the train moves westward." Dining cars had tooled leather benches, white linen tablecloths, and expensive silverware. Meals, Lavallée continued, were seventy-five cents, and a typical menu featured barley soup, broiled haddock, mutton, ham or turkey, filet of beef, potatoes, corn, peas, salad, cheese and biscuits, apple pie, tea and fruits. Champagne was two dollars a pint, and the fattest Havana cigars were twenty-five cents.

While the first CP transcontinental arrived only one minute late in Vancouver, *The Canadian* I took in 1982 was forty-five minutes late. Instead of the palatial stateroom of a century ago, I had a roomette so compact that I had to stand in the corridor to lift down the bed. The luggage rack was so small, a suitcase could not be opened. The dining car had plastic chairs and paper placemats, and the local delicacies of a century ago had been replaced by spaghetti and club sandwiches. Eggs and bacon, thanks to inflation, cost more than five dollars—equivalent to the cost of five superb dinners in 1886.

The cars on the train were more than twenty-five years old, the carpeting was faded and frayed, and the walls a depressing beige. The scenic dome viewing cars, introduced in 1955 by "Buck" Crump, afforded only a blurred vista because they were unwashed.

At an average speed of forty-eight miles per hour, *The Canadian* is considerably slower than going by car or bus. The ride is bumpier than a roller coaster due to the wear and tear caused by heavy freight trains using the same tracks, and the swaying and grinding makes sleeping nearly impossible. It is at times like these that one thinks envyingly and longingly of the smooth, quiet, more comfortable, close to two hundred miles per hour trains of France and Japan. It is also easy to understand why railways account for only 1 percent of travel in Canada.

The deteriorating quality of passenger train service in Canada has been the subject of debate for years. No one will accept the blame, although the parties involved are certainly quick to place the guilt elsewhere. Both CP and CN argued that there was no money to be made from passenger rail because travelers preferred going by plane. Train travel devotees said the railways were deliberately forcing the public to travel by other means because of the deplorable conditions on the trains, such as dirt and no air conditioning, and scheduling seemingly timed to just miss connecting trains. On top of these miseries, CP also charged rates that averaged 13 percent more than Via Rail's current charges. CN, by contrast, had introduced a number of discount fares in the 1970s, some of which were lower than Via's.

For the fact that the quality of service has not improved much since the takeover, Via Rail blames Ottawa, arguing that the government saddled it with the enormous financial burdens of high payments to the railways for inexplicit bills and old equipment that urgently needed costly overhauling. When Via Rail was established, it had no trains, tracks or stations—all these belonged to CN and CP. Via officials say the newest equipment they got had been built in 1953 and that the average age was twenty-nine years. Says Emery LeBlanc, public relations director at Via:

When Via was created, the railways were being reimbursed for 80 percent of their losses by the federal government and absorbing the other 20 percent, which was $56 million at that time. We argued we were taking away that $56 million and, therefore, should get the equipment for a token dollar. Instead, we had to pay book value for a total of $65 million, of which $52 million went to CN and $13 million to CP. If we had paid the then market value, some cars would have been appraised at a lower rate. The CP cars still had their 1953 carpet. We had to get the seats, carpet, and cushions replaced.

LeBlanc estimates the upgrading cost $500,000. Where did the money go? It went to CN and CP, which got paid to do the work in their shops that they had previously declined to do on their own initiative. But it was not only the rolling stock that needed modernization. CP only had a manual reservation system and CN was just edging into an electronic method. Via paid $15 million to Air Canada to develop a computer-based system. Moreover, CN and CP, despite substantial subsidies from the federal government dating back to 1968, have neglected to improve their tracks to make the ride less bumpy.

While Via's mandate is to provide passenger rail service, the actual operating of the trains is still done by CN crews on its former lines and CP crews on theirs. It is this arrangement that has led to the biggest financial argument. Via is billed by CN and CP for "long-run variable costs," which include expenses not directly arising from provision of services to Via. By contrast, Amtrak, the government-run passenger rail organization in the United States, pays only for services undertaken for it by the operating railways. As a result, Amtrak spends less than one-third of its budget on payments to the railways, whereas Via pays almost two-thirds of its budget to CN and CP. If the Amtrak system were adopted in Canada, according to the Canadian Transport Commission, Via would save between $25 million and $35 million.

In annual report after annual report, Via executives have pleaded for the variable contracts to be replaced with fixed price ones and for the railways to give more detailed, explicit information on their variable charges. Strange as it may seem, the federal government's Canadian Transport Commission, which oversees the railways, can demand detailed costing data, but Via is unable to do so because it is not protected by legislation. There is no Via Rail Canada Act that would give Via the legislative right to see the railways' costing data on which their charges are based. Moreover, it was not until 1980, three years after Via was established, that the CTC even began auditing CN's and CP's charges.

Those charges, which the railways maintain are lower than the actual costs, but which nobody has any way of verifying since the accounts are not made public, amount to millions of dollars. Based on Via's saying that two-thirds of its railway operating expenses are for CN's and CP's charges, CN and CP received close to $1 billion between 1978 and 1981. In 1982 alone, CN and CP together received $395 million.

This is not the only way CP and CN benefit. Under the old system, introduced in 1968, in which the government covered 80 percent of their losses, they would have received $800 million and had to absorb the $200 million difference. Under the new system, CN and CP have not only managed to get out of a business in which they no longer wanted to be, but they have also saved that $200 million.

Certainly, the payments have done wonders for both companies' balance sheets. In 1978 at CP, when Via began taking over CP's passenger routes, CP's "passenger revenue" was $61.8 million—or almost three times 1977's $21.5 million. Although CP operates some commuter trains in the Montreal area, CP executives say most of the passenger revenue comes from Via. Between 1978 and 1981, CP's passenger revenue was $265.6 million, or four times the combined total between 1975 and 1977.

Combined with increases in freight revenues, the spurt in passenger revenue has helped to more than double profits at CP Rail from $54.8 million in 1977 to $127.2 million in 1981. Moreover, while freight revenue still far surpasses passenger revenue, the Via payments have upped the performance of passenger versus freight revenue. In 1977, CP's passenger revenue was 1.9 percent that of freight; by 1981, its passenger revenue had climbed to 4.3 percent that of freight.

Via's takeover of passenger services has certainly been a good deal for the railways, if not for Via or the Canadian taxpayer whose taxes go to support a shrinking system. While Via has tried hard with innovative marketing ideas and the introduction in 1982 of LRC (light, rapid, comfortable) cars, and while its volume of passengers has risen in response, it still has a long way to go. A major blow occurred in the fall of 1981 when Transport Minister Jean-Luc Pépin axed 20 percent of Via's network without parliamentary consultation or consent.

With a stroke of a pen, Pépin chopped the number of daily trains from 163 to 150, the number of passengers by 15 percent, and the number of passenger route miles by 19 percent. The direct run to the Maritimes was killed, and the second daily transcontinental train, which ran through Jasper and attracted hordes of big-spending overseas visitors, was ended. The reduction also set back Via's initial goal of reaching a 60 to 70 percent load factor (the ratio between the number of passengers and number of seats in a train) by an unspecified date. In 1981, the load factor had climbed to 53 percent from 30 percent in 1976.

Pépin claimed the cutback would save $100 million, which could be used to buy new equipment for Via. The $100 million is equivalent to one-fourth the amount of money the government paid Via in 1982 for providing rail passenger service and equal to the cost of Via's ten new LRC trains used between Quebec City and Windsor. It could be argued that the cutbacks in service in the rest of Canada were used to provide new service for the south-central part of the country.

Despite the cutbacks, government subsidies still represent 70 percent of the money Via spends, according to the 1982 annual report of the federal auditor-general, which blamed the situation on a lack of adequate government control over Via's finances. According to the report, none of the payments by the federal government to Via have been fully audited since its inauguration, and Via has not provided the government with market projections that support its forecasts of future passenger growth. "The general lack of information has compromised the Department of Transport's ability to provide ministers with reliable information for decisions on significant matters such as route structures, service levels, and Via's capital and operating requirements," the report said.

Pinning the blame for Via's problems is as difficult as catching an elusive butterfly. Via says CN and CP are at fault, because of their high charges based on costing data which Via is barred from seeing. The auditor-general says it is Via that has not been adequately audited. These are items that cry for the creation of a Via Rail Act that would set down specific rules. But, the bottom line remains that without federal handouts, Via would be awash in red ink. That leaves the future of passenger rail in Canada in grave trouble, because a cost-conscious federal government might be inclined to shrink Via's route network even further.

The obvious loser in the toss-the-ball situation regarding rail travel in Canada is the public. Via now has about 925 passenger cars covering 14,100 miles, or an average of one car per fifteen track miles. Amtrak has 2,000 passenger cars on its 24,000 mile system (one car per twelve miles); France, 17,000 cars over 20,000 miles (a ratio of nearly 1:1); Germany, 17,000 cars over 17,000 miles (a 1:1 ratio) and Japan, 26,000 cars over 13,000 miles (a 2:1 ratio).

Improving the car situation in Canada does not seem promising. LeBlanc of Via maintains that getting the railways to provide more equipment is a struggle. "For example, we were supposed to get four new trains in April 1981, but did not get them until June of that year. Via has no clout." By contrast to Via, which contracts with outside firms for its equipment, Amtrak has taken an equity position in a new company that will develop high speed trains. The formation of the new company also has an added attraction for Amtrak's former president, Alan Boyd, since he is chairman of the new firm.

Although CN and CP receive money for operating passenger rail for Via, their main source of revenue is freight. About 40 percent of all freight transported in Canada goes by rail, and in 1981, freight accounted for $1.7 billion of CP Rail's revenue while passenger service accounted for only $7.3 million. Although the railways are facing increased competition from trucking, especially on the busy route between Montreal and Toronto, CP's trucking operations, the largest in Canada, help the company make up in road transport what it loses in rail.

It's not only CP executives who prefer moving goods rather than people. Railway engineers say they earn more money hauling freight than passengers. Passenger train employees are scheduled for a certain period each month and paid for that amount, but freight assignments are paid by the mile; as a result, workers can amass all their mileage in three weeks and have the rest of the month off.

The hub of CP's traffic flow system for rail freight operations is Room 100 in Montreal's Windsor Station. The classroom-size room is dominated on one side by a thirty-six-foot-wide wall-to-wall green board with color-coded symbols indicating what is happening with CP's 1,300 locomotives and 800 cabooses. A handful of shirt-sleeved men sit peering into computer terminals or having terse telephone conversations with the regional offices over special dedicated lines between the various locales.

Occasionally, the quiet is pierced by a squawk from various operators over the intercoms. On a particular day in February 1982, as Earl Baynton, systems operations center director, turned up the volume for me: "Give him the equivalent of two units [referring to locomotives] and that will make him good for 5,600 tons." "Holy Jesus," came the reply. Baynton, a thirty-eight-year employee of CP, and very proud of the center, flushed and quickly turned off the intercom.

The center, opened on April 1, 1973 ("We're fools once in a while, but not too often," Baynton says), has two big pluses for both CP's present and forward planning. In contrast to the previous system of receiving reports a day later by telegraph, this method provides constant status reports on traffic and a quick indication of weather or other problems that necessitate adjustments. The information is updated twice per eight-hour shift. At the same time, it makes it possible to measure productivity on an ongoing basis. This yardstick is then used to determine how many locomotives the company should be ordering for delivery several years later. With locomotives costing $1.5 million, all railway companies want to limit purchases as much as possible through increasing usage of existing equipment. "We have a productivity standard, but are always testing it," Baynton says.

Better equipment utilization is a top priority with all railway companies because of the industry's low return on net rail investment (book value of property, minus debt). CP's return— 7.6 percent in 1981 and 1980—is higher than the 4 percent average in the United States, but still considerably lower than the 16.5 percent that the Interstate Commerce Commission in the United States has calculated is desirable for the industry.

One of the industry's major problems is that much of its equipment is idle, sitting in rail yards or at shippers' docks, waiting for loading or unloading. According to industry statistics, equipment is sitting still an average of 90 percent of the time. It is Baynton's job to improve that record, and his major tool is the colorful thirty-six-foot board. He quickly rattles off its components:

The locomotives are tab coded in different colors, according to the yard shop that maintains them. Blue is for Montreal, red for Toronto, brown for the Prairies, and black for Calgary. Yellow tabs indicate cabooses. Each locomotive has a four number code indicating its model. For example, the 3,000 series are 2,000 horsepower locomotives made by General Motors and the 5,500 series, GM's 3,300 horsepower model.

Turquoise tags indicate time-sensitive, transcontinental traffic and the numbers on them represent the type of commodity and date that shipment started. White tags show that trains will be run west from Calgary. The yellow horizontal line across the board is the main cross-country track; the black lines are subsidiary routes, and the brown lines are branch lines.

At the top of the board an overhead map illustrates the grades the trains must climb and descend. There are clocks for each time zone and sunshine, storm, and snow symbols for the weather. Different colored tacks designate the schedule and type of maintenance for equipment. Baynton predicts that eventually this information will become computerized.

Red arrows indicate traffic disruptions due to derailments or severe weather problems such as avalanches. In instances where CN tracks are nearby, CP detours its traffic around the trouble spot via CN lines; however, if the CN track is lighter than CP's at that spot, CP is unable to use its heavier cars. "Obstructions on the Dryden–Kenora route in northwestern Ontario cause the toughest rerouting problems, because the only available detour is out of the way via Fort Frances or Sioux Lookout," Baynton says.

Guided by past experience, the operations center sets weekly volume targets, which are fine-tuned on a daily basis. Each morning at 9:30, Baynton briefs CP Rail's boss, Executive Vice-President Russell Allison, and Robert Gilmore, the vice-president of marketing and sales. An hour later, the traffic dispatchers in Ontario and Manitoba discuss the daily outlook by conference telephone, while at 12:15, the western dispatchers do the same.

To improve the utilization of equipment, in 1979 CP introduced the concept of high-priority empty freight trains. The system, first called XT and now using the number 300 on the cars, is the first of its kind in Canada, according to CP. It averages ninety cars in length and leaves five times weekly from Vancouver for Toronto.

Every Thursday, CP Rail's five distribution centers in Montreal, Toronto, Winnipeg, Calgary, and Vancouver develop a processing plan for the following week in order to make certain there are no surpluses or shortages. Their decisions are based on a 155-page computer printout on the last location of the cars, destination, departure and arrival dates, contents, how much CP is paying or charging for the car, and the car's physical characteristics, including capacity and door size. If the car is not CP's, the computer printout enables the company to determine where the car is to be returned so as to reduce its per diem payments.

Also helping to speed up the turnaround time on trains, and thereby improving the bottom line on CP's balance sheet, are the automated classification yards common to the rail industry. These yards have a computer-based sorting system that sets switches automatically for routing cars to the correct track for becoming part of the right train. CP's biggest automated yard is its Alyth Yard in southeast Calgary, which was the most advanced of its type in North America when it was opened in 1970 at a cost of $14.5 million. Alyth is 170 acres in size, has 73 miles of track, and can handle 3,000 cars daily. Large as it is, Alyth is only one-tenth the size of the largest American freight classification depot—Union Pacific's $40.5 million complex in Nebraska, which is 1,700 acres with 200 miles of track in two yards and can handle 6,000 cars daily.

The railways' major focus these days is on their multimillion-dollar track expansion and improvement programs. During the 1980s, CP plans to spend $7.6 billion (in 1982 dollars). One $660 million project alone, a restructuring of a twenty-one-mile passage through the Rogers Pass in the Rocky Mountains, costs nearly as much as the company's entire $800 million capital spending program over 1976–1980. One measure of the impact of inflation is that in 1980 it was predicted the Rogers Pass work would cost $420 million out of a total budget of $5.4 billion. The currently forecasted $7.6 billion outlay is six times the amount spent by the fourteen major American railroads in 1981 on roadway improvement.

Although the Rogers Pass is only one-fourteenth of CP's spending budget, it is a crucial element. For train travelers, the Rogers Pass—located 150 miles west of Calgary between Golden and Revelstoke, British Columbia—is a spectacularly beautiful journey. The train inches for several hours along a ribbon of track four thousand feet high in the midst of mountains eleven thousand feet high with perpendicular, snow-covered cliffs, spotted with fir trees and waterfalls on one side, and a stomach-turning sheer drop on the other. The ride is everything a scenic-hungry tourist could crave.

But for CP, the climb that is so exciting for travelers—and which CN avoided by building its line farther north—is not what it wants a century after carving out the route. With expectations of a huge jump in westbound traffic of bulk commodities such as coal, potash, and grain, CP wants to reduce the climb and add track so that more traffic can go through with lower fuel consumption. Total westbound rail traffic via CP is now about thirty-four million metric tonnes and CP expects this to climb to fifty-six million by 1990. The export value of westbound coal, grain, sulphur, and potash has been forecast at $12 billion in 1990 (at 1980 prices), compared to $4.5 billion in 1980.

Westbound traffic has always exceeded eastbound and this trend will continue throughout this decade. By 1986, projected eastbound traffic will equal only 7 percent of westbound, compared to 15 percent of westbound in 1974. Reflecting this, three-quarters of CP's massive spending program will be in the West.

To put the enormity of the $7.6 billion into perspective, it is three times CP Rail's 1982 asset value of $2.6 billion. The Rogers Pass work alone exceeds the original cost of the whole transcontinental line. The main thrust of the Rogers Pass construction is to reduce the grade from 2.6 percent (2.6 feet for every 100 feet of track) to the 1 percent maximum throughout the rest of the system. The construction will also include a nine-mile tunnel, which will pass under an existing five-mile one. The new tunnel will be the longest in the western hemisphere and two-thirds the combined total of CP's eighty-five other tunnels. The tunnel will feature a "doorway" ventilation system: after a train passes the halfway point, a "door" will shut, allowing the first part of the tunnel to be cleared of exhaust. The system will enable two trains an hour to go through the tunnel rather than one.

In planning the construction, CP engineers had to figure out where to run the new tunnel, how to avoid the eighty known avalanche slide paths in the area, and determine how the track could traverse thirteen rivers, creeks, and streams. With the obvious technical expertise all this demands, it was surprising to many, including Parks Canada, that CP initially planned to locate its tall ventilation shaft, with its smoke emissions, smack dab in the line of view from the summit of the Rogers Pass.

Even CP acknowledged the shaft would be an eyesore in an April 4, 1982 brief on the project to the federal government. "The vent shaft for the tunnel, depending on its location, may pose a permanent visual impairment at the Summit monument of Rogers Pass. It is also possible that at some periods, smoke will be visible at and near the vent shaft. The new second main line will be visible from the Trans-Canada Highway in several locations and will further reduce the wilderness experience of the (Glacier) National Park." Fortunately, Parks Canada got CP to shift the shaft to a less noticeable location, and the company, on its own, planned a tree planting program to hide the tracks.

Reducing the grade of the Rogers Pass is critical if CP is to cash in on what it feels will be a boom in westbound traffic in the late 1980s and onward, even though railway car loadings in 1982 were at their lowest in fifty years. Bulk freight trains now require six extra locomotives to enable them to climb the Rogers Pass. It takes twenty minutes to add the extra locomotives and up to ninety minutes to push up the mountains. Leveling out the grade will eliminate the need for the extra locomotives and, thus, lower fuel consumption—and since no time will be lost in adding more locomotives, more trains will be able to make the trip, with the ultimate goal being twenty-four compared to the present fifteen.

In the predicted boom in Canada's exports to the Pacific Rim countries, most of the railways' hopes are pinned on coal. CP Rail predicts that it will be carrying 30.7 million tonnes of the total 55 million tonnes of coal expected to be shipped by 1986. In 1982, CP carried 15.3 million of the total 28 million tonnes of coal headed west. (Total CP westbound traffic of all goods by 1986 is forecast at 48.7 million tonnes.) For CP, an increased demand for coal would be good news not only for CP Rail, but also for Fording Coal, among Canada's top five producers, and

PanCanadian Petroleum, which owns substantial coal reserves.

There is general agreement that demand for coal will indeed more than double by the year 2000. World coal reserves that can be economically mined with today's technology represent more than five times the energy in the proven oil reserves of the Middle East. In 1980, according to a survey for a world conference on energy, Canada had 3.4 percent of the world's 13.6 trillion tonnes of coal resources, including substantial reserves of thermal coal, which is expected to be in growing demand for the production of electric power.

How well Canada and other coal exporting nations fare depends on how buoyant the economy is in its major customers, Japan, Korea, and Taiwan, which use imported metallurgical coal in the production of steel. Japan is the major buyer, and when its demand for steel slides, as it did in the 1982 recession, it erodes coal exports from Canada and elsewhere. Consequently, the Canadians have been trying to edge into other markets. Fording, for example, has made sales to Brazil.

The Canadian railways are not alone in preparing for more coal traffic. Railroads in the United States are also gearing up to cash in on the expected boom and to help their country sprint well ahead of the Canadians. However, capital expenditures by the American railroads have not been nearly as heavy as for CP and CN. One major American railroad, Union Pacific, spent $86.9 million in 1981 on roadway improvements, less than one-sixth the cost of CP's Rogers Pass work alone. Moreover, the American railroads are already hauling far more coal than their Canadian counterparts. In 1981, Union Pacific, one of the forty so-called Class I railroads (revenue over $1 million) in the United States and the third largest in terms of rail revenue, carried 31.3 million tonnes of coal, compared with 13 million tonnes taken by CP.

The big question, though, is whether the demand for coal will be as high as CP was predicting before the 1982 recession hit. In addition, although Canada ranks fourth in the world in coal sales, it faces stiff competition from the United States, Australia, and South Africa, which all produce substantially more coal than Canada and have their coal mines located nearer ports, making their transportation costs lower. CN's "shareholders," the Canadian taxpayers, and CP's could each justifiably wonder whether there will be enough freight business to warrant their huge spending programs, especially as their parallel rail lines mean each will only get a portion of the traffic.

The planned combined capital spending by CP and CN in the 1980s brought to a head the decades-long debate over the Crow's Nest Pass rate, which had allowed farmers to ship grain at a half cent a ton per mile since 1897. The railways maintained that if the rate was not abolished they would not be able to afford their $18 billion capital spending program, and this in turn would harm the outlook for Canadian exports. CP, for example, said that while grain represented 20 percent of its volume, it only provided 8 percent of its revenue and half of that came from government subsidies for maintaining branch lines for grain shipments.

The Crow's Nest rate was one-fourth to one-fifth the average rates for coal, sulphur, and potash. It cost twice as much to send a letter, at thirty-two cents, than the fifteen cents per bushel for shipping grain. At first, the low rate presented no problem, but as grain exports began to soar, the railways found that the more grain they shipped, the more money they lost. With grain shipments expected to increase from twenty-six million tonnes in 1981–82 to thirty million by 1985–86, the railways argued that the increased volume would be a further financial drain on them. They were supported by Transport Minister Jean-Luc Pépin, who said the railways could lose $2.4 billion between 1981 and 1985 if the Crow rate was not changed.

The ramifications of what came to be known as the Holy Crow were not realized in 1897. At the time, it was only an incentive scheme designed to encourage construction of a railway line from Lethbridge in southern Alberta to Nelson in southeastern British Columbia. The main purpose of the line was to hold back the influence of the United States, whose railroads were already running near the border. In return, CP was paid a subsidy of $11,000 a mile. At the same time, the government, pressured by prairie farmers who felt CP was overcharging them, agreed to keep grain rates at 0.5 cents a mile.

The rates both helped and hurt western Canada. On the plus side, they enabled Canada to compete in world grain markets by wiping out the economic disadvantage of having its nearest coastal port one thousand miles away. On the negative side, the rates were so cheap that bread and cake manufacturers did not have to build plants in the West, but were able to carry on their production at existing facilities in eastern Canada. That has helped crimp industrial development in the western provinces.

Determining just how much the railways have lost on grain shipping depends on whose estimates are being used. In 1980, CN and CP estimated their combined revenue shortfall totaled $552 million; shipping groups said it was $392.3 million; Clay Gilson, a University of Manitoba professor commissioned in 1982 by the federal government to study the matter, placed the amount at $469.5 million. A study commissioned by the federal government in the 1970s and conducted by Carl Snavely, a Washington economist, said 1980 losses would be $670.7 million. And still another study, conducted around the same time as Gilson's by the Alberta, Saskatchewan, and Manitoba wheat pools, said the losses were $467.9 million—close to Gilson's figure.

While even most farmers' groups agree that the Crow rate was outdated and depressed the railways' revenues, the impact has been softened by extremely generous government subsidies. Moreover, grain, as a percentage of total volume of business, is projected to level out in comparison to increased traffic in coal, sulphur, and potash. According to CP figures, it shipped 4.4 million tonnes of grain west in 1981. By 1986, it expects such shipments to increase only slightly to 5.9 million tonnes.

On the subsidy side, the railways did extremely well. Since 1972, the government has been supplying the railways, rent free, with hopper cars (funnel-shaped cars in which grain is discharged through the bottom). The government stepped in because CN and CP said they would not buy any more railway cars for grain while the Crow rate was in effect. At the same time, CP rejected an offer by the federal government to share the repair costs for one thousand boxcars used in shipping grain. CN accepted the offer. Nevertheless, both railways were rapidly withdrawing boxcars, traditionally used to haul grain, from grain service at the rate of about 1,800 annually. This cut farmers off from valuable export sales. For example, in 1977, according to the Canadian Wheat Board, prairie farmers lost two million tonnes in sales and another one million in 1978, making a total loss in revenue of $460 million.

Between 1972 and 1982, with both CN and CP refusing to expand their grain car fleet, the federal government purchased 11,285 cars at a total cost of $427 million and leased 2,000 at a cost of $300 million to the railways at no charge. In addition, it contributed half the repair cost—$22.8 million—for another 7,215 boxcars. And on top of that, Ottawa laid out another $1.1 billion in subsidies over the past eleven years for the continued operation of prairie branch lines. The governments of Alberta and Saskatchewan also each purchased 1,000 cars, totaling another $125 million in free equipment. The significance of these payments is highlighted by the railway's 1982 results. According to CP, the railway's net income without these subsidies would have been $56 million; with them, CP made $117.9 million. In return, CN and CP are committed to maintain nearly 16,000 miles of branch lines until the end of this century.

But that is just part of the generous deal the railways have got on grain transportation. In 1977, Ottawa authorized $700 million for the upgrading and rehabilitation of branch lines. Adding it all together, the railways in just one decade received close to $2.5 billion in compensation for carting grain.

In February 1983, after three years of promising and then dithering over changing the Crow's Nest rate, the federal government announced what Pépin grandiosely called "the greatest exercise in compromise since God created Adam and Eve." The Trudeau government's solution called for the removal of the unrealistically low Crow rate, along with the retention of the format of subsidies for the railways that had resulted from the original rate and the matching of these subsidies with similar funding for grain farmers.

Each year until 1986, when the revised system will be reviewed, Ottawa will dole out $651.4 million of taxpayers' money to CP and CN. Originally, the government planned to split the money between the farmers and the railways. But it changed this proposal following opposition from western grain pools, which were afraid farmers would not ship their grain by rail and, therefore, would not need the pools' storage elevators. In addition, the railways will get $72.5 million annually for the purchase of grain cars and another $167.5 million for track improvements. In return, grain farmers will be paying twice as much to ship grain by 1986, and the railways must abide by performance guarantees or lose their subsidies.

The only winners in this modification of the Crow rate are the railways. They will get paid more by the farmers and still receive subsidies. But the grain farmers at least did not lose. They remain the only Canadian farmers to get government subsidies, and should also benefit from the improved service pledged by the railways in return for the restructuring of the Crow rate. Grain remains Canada's most heavily subsidized export industry.

The higher rates come at a difficult time for grain farmers, however, since they are being squeezed by a severe drop in grain prices, as well as high financing costs on loans made at peak 1982 rates. In addition, Argentina, Australia, and the United States, Canada's major competitors in the world grain markets, are increasing their subsidies to their grain farmers. Whether the revisions also contribute to the axis of power shifting more to western Canada remains to be seen. But under the restructured rate, the West, which already has dominance in oil, could become more of an industrial center through the $75 million Ottawa will provide for the development of agricultural processing industries there. The higher rail fees for grain could also encourage some grain farmers to switch to hog and beef production. This could seriously affect livestock farmers in Ontario and Quebec because they will have to pay higher livestock feed prices, as a result of the changed grain freight rate, whereas western farmers can feed their livestock with grain grown in the area. In 1982, Ontario had a record number of farm bankruptcies, of which half were livestock producers.

For the railways, which were making a profit even before the Crow revision, the changes sparked an immediate hike in their spending plans for track improvements, primarily in western Canada. CP Rail upped its 1983 spending by $135 million, of which about 70 percent was taken care of by the subsidies in the new federal compensation program.

Changing the Crow's Nest rate does not mean that rates on other goods will fall, but neither will they be under as much pressure to rise anymore to compensate for the low grain rates. As the railways view the situation, instead of just four-fifths of their business providing what they regard as necessary revenue growth, all five-fifths will.

Throughout the years it has been argued—by those favoring nationalization of CP to the most ardent free enterprisers such as CP executives—that CP and CN should be unified, since they cover the same territory and often run parallel only a few miles apart. CN was created in 1919 and went into official operation in 1923. In between, in 1921, Thomas Shaughnessy, CP's president, proposed that the four lines then operated by the federal government (Canadian Northern, Intercolonial, National Transcontinental, and Grand Trunk Pacific) be combined with CP. He said operations would run singly, but ownership of the lines would remain separate.

Shaughnessy's proposal was rejected for three reasons. First, the government would have been obliged to guarantee dividends on CP's stock. Second, it was felt it would create a virtual monopoly in most of Canada. Third, the apparently improving financial performance of the government-owned railways at that time gave rise to a false impression of their potential earning power.

In 1925, two years after CN's debut, a special Senate committee on the railways resurrected Shaughnessy's proposal. Any surplus produced by joint management would go towards a stipulated dividend to CP, with any remaining money to be divided between CN and CP in proportion to their valuations. This proposal, which seemed to the public to be written by the railways for the railways, also died.

But its death was temporary. A decade later, Shaughnessy's successor at CP, Edward Beatty, revived Shaughnessy's idea, but in a slightly different manner. He called for outright unification, which would eliminate duplication between the two systems and thus lead to an annual savings in railway operating costs of up to $75 million. Naturally, CP was to do the managing. Beatty's idea also disappeared in the face of fears about a monopoly, abandonment of service to smaller communities, and job losses by railway workers.

Still, the concept keeps cropping up, even though its fruition is highly unlikely. One leading current proponent is Carleton University's Julius Lukasiewicz, an engineering professor and a longtime student of Canada's railway operations: "It makes no sense to duplicate railway operations."

Although CN and CP are not unified, the lack of competition between them over freight rates makes them seem like identical twins to Canada's close to seventy thousand rail shippers. This situation is due to thirty-seven words in Section 279 of the 1967 National Transportation Act, which allows the railways the right to meet behind closed doors and set common rates: "Railway companies shall exchange such information with respect to costs as may be required under this Act and may agree upon and charge common rates under and in accordance with regulations or orders made by the [Canadian Transport] Commission."

Adding to this freedom is a CTC policy not to require railways to quote joint rates that take advantage of the most direct route between origin and destination over the rail lines of both carriers. As long as one railway has a "reasonable" route over its own lines, it is free to oblige captive shippers to take that route, whatever the cost and delivery time implications.

Section 23 of the National Transportation Act allows shippers to appeal rates on the grounds that the public interest is not being served, but most shippers have been discouraged from acting since the burden of proof is on them and the hearing process is costly and time consuming, running from three to seven years. Little wonder that since 1967 only fourteen appeals have been made under Section 23. Of these, nine were discontinued prior to a hearing.

"It's in the interest of the railroads to drag out cases as long as possible in that the shipper pays the higher rate throughout the entire length of the case and no retroactive refunds have to be made," says Donald Wallace, transportation director at Consolidated-Bathurst Inc. For example, in the five years (1976–1981) that their Section 23 case against CP and CN was before the Canadian Transport Commission, fifteen western Canada pulp shippers paid $15 million in extra freight charges.

CP Rail, with the backing of CP Chairman Frederick Burbidge, has proposed an arbitration process that would call for a decision within six weeks. CN, however, is opposed and the government has placed the idea on the back burner. Shippers place more priority on revising Section 279.

By contrast, since 1980, when the U.S. government deregulated the railways as part of an overall transportation deregulation policy aimed at increasing competition, shippers and railways have operated successfully without collective rate making. This was made possible by the 1980 Staggers Rail Act: "In regulating the railroad industry, it is the policy of the United States Government to allow, to the maximum extent possible, competition and the demand for services to establish reasonable rates for transportation by rail."

This step was taken to help the railways as much as the shippers, because it made it possible to raise rates within certain government parameters without getting government approval. The government decided on this course since railroad earnings were the lowest within the transportation industry. Without being allowed to increase earnings, government calculations indicated that there would be a capital shortfall among the railroads of between $16 billion and $20 billion by 1985.

Deregulation appears to be helping both the shippers and the railroads, although a subsequent spurt in mergers has raised concern among smaller lines that these "megarailroads" could woo former shipping customers. Shippers are now being offered prices that reflect demand and supply, as well as low "backhaul" rates (on return trips of previously empty freight cars), rebates and contract rates in which the railroads provide rate guarantees in return for volume guarantees. One of the most innovative is a twenty-year contract between Illinois Central Gulf and Hoosier Energy. Hoosier advanced $9 million to ICG so that the rail line could be upgraded. In return, Hoosier got a lower freight rate than it would have otherwise. The lines also have been willing to gear their rates to individual customers more than in the past. For example, during a 1981 glut of grain-carrying cars, some lines offered 10 to 15 percent reductions or two free carloads for every ten carloads.

The innovations paid off for the railroads as well as for the shippers. In the first full year of the Staggers Act, the railroads reported a 4.13 percent rate of return on net investment, the highest in more than three decades. Profit margins have also risen and are ahead of those in Canada. For example, the profit margin at csx, the leading railroad in the United States, rose to 9.8 percent in 1981, compared with 7.1 percent in 1978. By comparison, cp Rail's 1981 profit margin was 6.1 percent, versus 4.4 percent in 1978. "This newly competitive environment encourages and rewards timely, creative service and pricing initiative," csx said in its 1982 annual report.

The federal government has been wrestling with what to do about Section 279 for more than a year. So far, Transport Canada has commissioned an outside report by a University of British Columbia transportation professor, held a conference of shippers, their associations, and the railways, and invited position papers from the conference's participants. In September 1983, Transport Canada will decide whether to write a policy paper simply reviewing everyone's arguments or to go further and prepare a discussion paper, with recommendations for legislative change, that would then go to the federal Cabinet.

The issue is made thornier by the impact of the increased government subsidies to the railways in the revised Crow rate. Some shippers feel that the higher subsidies will increase the railways' rate of return and, therefore, Section 279 should be eliminated as a counter-balance. Others maintain the removal of Section 279 would result in a still greater rate of return. East coast shippers are concerned that if Section 279 is dumped, they will face a double whammy of rising rates, because such action would come on top of plans to reduce the subsidies they receive when they ship westward in order to compete with central Canada's merchandise.

What will likely push the Canadian government into taking action is not so much pressure from within Canada, but the impact of U.S. deregulation on trans-border shipments by Canadian firms. Before deregulation, the Canadian railways would route trans-border shipments for as long a distance as possible across Canada. Now, to lower their shipping costs, shippers are sending their goods to the nearest border crossing and transferring them to American railroads that offer rebates, a practice not allowed in Canada. The Americans also have the advantage of knowing what the Canadian lines would charge, since unlike the Americans, they publish their rates.

Outside of their dislike of Sections 23 and 279, the rail shippers' major grievance against the railways is that in 1981, with only twenty-four hours' telephone notice, CN and CP imposed a 2.3 percent fuel surcharge, increasing the annual freight bill for major shippers by several hundred thousand dollars. The railways had imposed a 1.7 percent fuel surcharge in 1979, but that did not anger the shippers as much as the 1981 action.

The railways maintained the surcharge was necessary because they had budgeted for only a 38 percent increase in 1981 over 1980, and instead, their fuel costs had risen by 50 percent. On behalf of the shippers, who were dubious about the railways' mathematics, the Canadian Manufacturers' Association sought a meeting with both railways. CP turned out to be somewhat more obliging than CN, according to shippers who attended. CN refused to submit cost justifications and CP's had mathematical errors. The shippers were suspicious that with railway revenue dropping due to less traffic caused by poor economic conditions, the only way the railways could increase revenue was through a fuel surcharge. Shippers also wondered if both railways needed as much as 2.3 percent, which they were unable to verify with the skimpy data available.

The meeting left the CMA unhappy, and it subsequently wrote to federal Deputy Transport Minister Arthur Kroeger. The September 28, 1981 letter, written by CMA's then manager of transportation, Rod Taylor, did not mince words:

The railway assertions with respect to the 1981 fuel price increases are not consistent with the experience of our members who purchase diesel fuel, nor with available fuel price indices. Further, based on the early figures supplied by the carriers, we have a disquieting suspicion that revenue obtained through the surcharge may exceed any unanticipated cost increases by year end. Additional discomfort results from the belief that at least part of the surcharge borne by manufacturers is serving to offset fuel costs incurred in movement of grain at statutory rates.

Although the CMA did not ask the government to roll back the increase, Kroeger did reply on November 2, 1981, that any such charges should be temporary.

Shippers say that although CP is privately owned and CN is a Crown corporation, each is equally tough in negotiations, although CP appears softer on the surface. "CP is more American in style—friendly, but hard," says William Sheffield, traffic manager at Stelco. "CP tries very hard to understand your problems and get them to fit into their optimization approach, but their situation comes first. CN, before its profit center days, used to have some people who were not of high caliber. But now they are emulating CP's style."

Adds Rod Taylor: "The people in charge at CN now come from the marketing side and they take a very hard-nosed, practical approach that if something is not profitable, they should get out of it. CP is less hard-nosed on the surface, but whether it means anything is hard to determine. Some shippers prefer CN, because they know exactly where they stand."

CP Rail is no longer the embodiment of the national dream. Long ago it provided a transcontinental link between settlements in the new confederation of Canada. Today, it is part of a new dream of railway executives and shippers that Canada will expand its international trade. The emphasis is now on freight, and passenger service has been abandoned. The question for the company is whether the demand of overseas customers for Canadian goods will be as great as CP is hoping.

· 9 ·

The Mississauga
Nightmare

CP Rail is proud of its record in pioneering new technology and methodology in Canada. Its accomplishments include developing the first electronically operated unmanned "robot" locomotives used for extra power through the Rockies, the first "unit trains" (trains hauling only one product), computerized tracing of car locations, which bypassed the previous telephone system, experiments with solar energy generators, computerized system of waybills for repeat shipments, and computerized records of car movements in rail yards.

It is also proud of its safety record. In 1978, CP Rail won the International Golden Spike of the U.S. National Safety Council for the twenty-fifth year in a row for "outstanding public and employee safety activities." One year later, in November 1979, CP earned a not so welcome niche in railway history when one of its trains, loaded with chemicals, derailed in Mississauga, Ontario.

The derailment involved twenty-four cars on a 106-car train traveling from London to Toronto. Of the twenty-four cars, nineteen were carrying such dangerous chemicals as toluene, propane, and chlorine. Fire spread through most of the cars, some exploded, and the chlorine-loaded tank car suffered a large hole. Because of fear over the consequences of the escape of deadly chlorine gas, close to 250,000 people were evacuated from Mississauga and surrounding areas for up to five days.

The cause of the accident was found to be a "hot box" in its right rear journal box. As a subsequent hearing explained, almost all railway cars have eight wheels upon four axles. The axles at their extremities are called journals. The journals bear the weight of the car and are housed in journal boxes. Inside the journal boxes are bearings resting upon the revolving journals. Modern bearings are roller bearings, but the majority of journal bearings, including the ones in the toluene car, are friction or plain bearings.

With plain bearings, a wedge rests on the bearing, which in turn rests upon the journal with an oil-soaked pad supplying lubrication between the bearing and journal. If the pad stops working, the bearing and journal will be in direct contact and the journal will overheat. If not detected, as was the case in this derailment, the journal will burn off and the tank car will collapse. Some railroad lines have installed so-called hot box detectors, developed in the 1950s and usually stationed twenty to thirty miles apart. CN started installing such devices in 1967, but CP installed only a few, arguing that if the detectors were in place, the crew might become too relaxed in their inspections.

By 1980, about 70 percent of the railroad cars in the United States had roller bearings, compared to 39.7 percent of CN's fleet and 38.8 percent of CP's, according to the Canadian Transport Commission. Although the pace of installing hot box detectors in Canada was only half that of the United States, their advantages had been detailed in 1970, nine years before the Mississauga derailment, in a federal safety inquiry. The CTC had never ordered their mandatory use.

The Mississauga derailment was not only a nightmare for the thousands of residents evacuated because of the accident. It could turn into a $3 billion nightmare for CP. The incident led to the largest damage suit in Canadian history in terms of numbers of people suing. There are 389 lawsuits, representing more than one thousand people. Individual claims range from $200 to $200,000. The city of Mississauga, which had a parks building damaged, keeps revising its claim upward to reflect the impact of inflation. It now stands at around $1 million. The company could have to pay more than $100 million in damage claims if it loses the hundreds of lawsuits. But the financial impact on CP would be more than the actual dollar amount of the claims it would have to pay, because CP has calculated that for every dollar it pays out in general claims, it has to generate $30 in revenue.

The cases probably will not be heard at least until 1984 in the Ontario Supreme Court. The issue is expected eventually to wind up in the Supreme Court of Canada. The case could establish a legal precedent, not just in the number of people involved, but over the point of law at stake. With the exception of a handful of cases, the suits are over economic loss, and Canadian law is not clear as to whether such losses are compensable.

In addition to all the lawsuits, the derailment has given birth to something of a growth industry. The Ontario attorney general's office wrote an "instant" book on the event. There were two federal reports—a one-man Royal Commission study for Transport Canada by Ontario Supreme Court Justice Samuel Grange, which became a bestseller, and a follow-up report by the Canadian Transport Commission. Mississauga's feisty mayor, Hazel McCallion, also plans a book on the subject. Any hard feelings she may have against CP have not prevented her from keeping a white CP hard hat on her credenza. "I collect all sorts of hard hats," she snaps. "I got this one when I dedicated the GO Transit line, operated by CP, in this area, along with Ian Sinclair."

Ontario Attorney General Roy McMurtry, who coordinated public authorities during the crisis in his then position as Ontario solicitor general, received a huge photograph of the disaster from his staff, with an inscription to the "Real Mississauga Miracle." McMurtry has stuck the picture in an anteroom off his office. "I'm too embarrassed to hang it publicly," he says.

But what should have been the most important aftermath of the derailment—dramatic improvements in railway safety along the lines of the Grange Report—has not materialized. During the CTC hearing, three similar derailments occurred in Canada, and in 1981 there were 127 derailments across the country of trains carrying dangerous commodities. It was not until 1982 that CP started setting up specialized rapid-deployment teams to respond immediately to derailments involving chemical products. All twelve teams were not in place until the summer of 1983, nearly four years after Mississauga.

Nor did the accident give any immediate impetus to the federal government's efforts, started in 1975, to develop a universal dangerous goods code for rail, truck, marine, and air transportation. The code, not expected to be ready until late 1983, will mean that the different transportation industries will no longer have inconsistent regulations and standards, some of which date back to the early 1900s. Transport Canada officials say the Mississauga derailment's impact upon the code has been for the new regulations to require more information to be given in shipping documents on dangerous goods shipments.

CTC regulations, issued in 1981, either watered down or ignored Justice Grange's recommendations. Here is a comparison of what Justice Grange suggested and the lighter measures the CTC, following a report stressing the draconian cost of greater safety measures, actually imposed:

Grange	CTC
• All train cars should immediately have roller bearings installed.	• 75 percent of the fleet should have roller bearings by the end of 1987.
• Immediate installation of bottom fitting protection on tank cars.	• Schedule of installation to be proposed by June 1982.
• If a dangerous goods train does not have roller bearings, it should not exceed 4,000 feet.	• No limit on length.
• No point within built-up areas (500 or more people) should be more than 20 miles from hot box detector protection.	• Hot boxes should be phased in between 1981 and 1987 in communities with a minimum population of 10,000.
• Maximum speed of 25 miles per hour through built-up areas.	• 35 miles per hour speed limit.

Much of the CTC's report dealt with whether roller bearings were better than plain bearings, as Justice Grange concluded, or close to being of equal utility as the CTC believed, due to improvements in engineering of plain bearings.

The CTC calculated that the cost to all of Canada's eleven railways of converting their trains to roller bearings would be between $27 million and $42 million annually—for a maximum total of $252 million—or less than 20 percent of implementing Justice Grange's recommendation. The annual combined minimum cost is just slightly more than the $22 million spent on preliminary work on CP's Rogers Pass construction project. The total maximum combined amount for both railways is less than half the cost of the $660 million bill for the Rogers Pass work. Moreover, as the CTC noted in its report: "There are significant operational cost savings of roller bearings relative to plain bearings."

The CTC, which seems at times to have written its report with a calculator, opposed shorter trains, saying they would be costly and could increase the number of level crossings and thus level crossing accidents. "Reducing the length of trains will have a very substantial impact on the economic operation of the railways, requiring additional crews, additional motive power, and additional rolling stock."

As for Grange's proposed twenty-five mile per hour speed limit, the CTC maintained this particular speed would cause the train to rock, whereas the higher thirty-five miles per hour would not. Besides, added the cost-conscious report: "From an economic point of view, the cost of such a speed limitation under these conditions is substantially below the cost incurred by the twenty-five miles per hour Grange recommendations." The train involved in the Mississauga derailment was estimated to be traveling between forty miles per hour and fifty miles per hour when the accident occurred.

Pointing out that it cost $100,000 to install hot box detectors and $8,000 each year to maintain each unit, the CTC said nobody at its hearing supported Grange's five-hundred population benchmark for installation. "Considering the capital cost, the economic burden of such a massive hot box detector program is not warranted at this time, if at any time."

The CTC calculated that a total of only two hundred hot boxes would have to be installed by 1987, at a total installation cost, for CN and CP together, of $20 million and a yearly combined maintenance bill of $1.6 million. In May 1981, the CTC ordered

CP to install 154 hot boxes by the end of 1983, two years ahead of CP's original schedule. That would cost CP about $15 million. If CP had installed the boxes in 1978, when prices were lower, the cost per hot box detector would have been $25,000 less.

According to the CTC, CN ranks first in safety and CP second in North America in the number of accidents per train mile. In view of this record and CP's considerable achievements in new technology, it is astounding how sloppy its procedures were on its freight trains, as outlined by the Grange Report.

Grange found that CP crews were ordered not to use their rear view mirrors because CP was concerned about the crews relying on the mirrors instead of looking out the window. Wrote Grange: "I have a feeling reasonably close to conviction that if rear view mirrors had been used on the ill-fated Mississauga train, this Report would never have had to be written."

Grange also discovered that: 1. record keeping was inadequate; 2. there was no consistency regarding where inspections during travel on curves should take place or in the language for communications during and after such inspections; 3. no event recorders were installed (such as the "black boxes" on airplanes); and 4. there were no speedometers, windshield wipers, or window defrosters on cabooses.

In retrospect, Ontario Attorney General Roy McMurtry says he was not impressed with either the CTC's or CP's posture during the Mississauga crisis. "CP's preoccupation appeared simply to be to get the line reopened," he says. "The CTC was not as involved as it should have been at the beginning of the emergency. For the first few days, they did not have any senior personnel on the scene."

In 1984, five years after the derailment, the lawsuits will likely finally go to court. At the time of the accident, CP reimbursed people quite generously for out-of-pocket expenses. One resident recalls "receiving $450 when I was staying at relatives' and all I bought was a shirt." The court cases revolve around those people who did not accept compensation.

Although CP is the main target in the lawsuits, some people are also suing the Chesapeake and Ohio Railroad, from which the cars that eventually derailed were transferred, and Dow Chemical Canada Ltd., producer of the chemicals, as well as Mississauga city officials and McMurtry regarding the evacuation. The gargantuan caseload has led the Ontario Supreme Court to take an unprecedented step in appointing two separate judges— one for the pre-trial work and the other for the trial.

The case is taking so long to reach the courts for several reasons. First, the law enabled people to take two years after the derailment to sue CP and the other companies. Second, the lawyers had to iron out a sensible pre-trial routine. The usual proceeding in court cases is for each side's lawyer to conduct "examinations of discovery"—pre-trial questioning under oath. Considering that most of the plaintiffs in this case had similar stories, as well as the number of defendants involved, examinations of discovery could have taken forever. The logistics had to be worked out as to which cases could be used as samples. A class action lawsuit, covering all the claimants, was not possible because not everybody suffered identically, a criterion for class action cases. Instead, it was decided that everyone who wanted to sue would do so as a group in the category that their claim fit.

The nub of the legal argument is over the nature of the damages being sought. "Most of the losses are economic losses unassociated with physical or personal injury, and there is uncertainty regarding whether such costs are legally recoverable," says Joan Lax, one of four lawyers at the Toronto law firm of Weir and Foulds representing the city of Mississauga. "Traditionally, such losses have not been recoverable. Public policy has been that each person should bear his own economic loss."

The city of Mississauga is one of the few plaintiffs that suffered actual property damage. One of the derailed tank cars landed against a parks and recreation building, severely damaging it.

Mrs. Lax says the plaintiffs will argue that the accident "was so clearly foreseeable and avoidable, that they should recover damages. They will argue that when a train full of hazardous commodities goes at a great rate of speed through a municipality and is not protected with hot boxes, the railway runs the risk of this type of catastrophe."

CP is expected to say at the hearings that it was not solely at fault and to throw the blame largely on the Chesapeake and

Ohio, which was the last to service the journal box that failed. It may also repeat some of the rather far-fetched arguments it used at the hearings to cast blame elsewhere. These included attacking the firemen for hosing the chlorine car and saying that municipalities allowing residences near railways should know in advance that such accidents can happen.

In addition, the cases will deal with who should bear the liability for the evacuation. CP argues that the evacuation was unnecessary and that, therefore, the cost should be borne by the various government authorities. Those authorities, in turn, maintain that, based on advice from Dow Chemical and government environmental experts about wind changes, the evacuation was essential.

Fixing the blame is not the only matter of debate. Who pays the legal fees is also a hot topic. In normal lawsuits, the loser pays one-half to two-thirds of the winners' costs. In this case, the plaintiffs maintained that CP should foot the entire bill, primarily on the grounds that since a few clients were representing all the plaintiffs, CP was spared the cost and nuisance of defending itself over and over. However, CP said it would not agree to consolidating the lawsuits if it had to pay all the legal fees, and the Ontario Supreme Court ruled in CP's favor.

Thomson Rogers, a Toronto law firm, is handling most of the individual cases. Four lawyers have been assigned to the caseload. "We got involved through a client whose business is in Mississauga," supervising lawyer Laurence Mandel says. "He had 650 employees and many of them asked us to represent them, too; it mushroomed from there. When we decided to take on the case, we said we would not just represent big claims. Some of our clients are only claiming $200."

Because the cases are strictly concerned with claimed damages, no safety recommendations will be made. Nevertheless, Mandel says the cases have critical implications for CP and other railroad companies. "If damages are awarded, the plaintiff is not just compensated; it is also a warning to the defendant to clean up its act. For instance, following malpractice suits over surgeons leaving sponges in bodies, doctors now do sponge counts. Certainly, CP has to be concerned about its future operations."

CP, however, seems to favor moving more deliberately, as CP

Rail Executive Vice-President Russell Allison said in a September 1981 interview in *Canadian Transportation and Distribution Management* magazine:

We think an improvement in the marshalling of dangerous goods is essential and we support that. However, we do not subscribe to the idea that lowering the speed in which dangerous commodities are moved improves safety. Likewise, the rail system is such that it's not practical or economically possible to route dangerous commodities around cities.

I think that through the years we've done a very good job of improving the handling of dangerous commodities. There has been the occasional derailment, such as in Mississauga, but it must be remembered that at Mississauga, while it was a very spectacular derailment, there were no personal injuries. And we're anxious to ensure that there will never be any personal injuries. The other point I meant to make earlier concerned roller bearings. We fully support equipping cars that haul dangerous goods with roller bearings. But it will be a major undertaking—it cannot be done overnight. Maybe the cars that are handling the *most dangerous* commodities should be equipped first.

That there were no injuries as a result of the Mississauga accident was due to good luck, and even four years later CP has had to be forced into taking safety precautions. The most recent instance occurred in the summer of 1983 when CP replaced track in midtown Toronto only after complaints by nearby residents that it was unsafe gained public attention and they had sought the assistance of a local organization that had lobbied for safer rail transport following the Mississauga derailment. The organization, the Metro Toronto Residents Action Committee, said the worrisome track could result in a repeat of the Mississauga derailment. One day later, CP, which had ignored the residents for three months, replaced it.

Only a few months earlier in March, a Via Rail train operated and serviced by a CP crew crashed into several train cars loaded with sulphur near Calgary while traveling at an estimated sixty-five miles per hour. That was nearly twice as fast as the speed limit laid down by the Canadian Transport Commission after the

Mississauga incident. Moreover, it was found that the crash in which five people were killed might not have been as bad if CP had fixed an automatic emergency brake that one of its own machinists had found to be defective and "not fit for the road in this condition."

Apparently the lesson of Mississauga is still not fully appreciated by CP.

·10·

Weak Sisters

In its early days, Canadian Pacific depended mostly on people for its revenue. They rode CP's trains, cruised on its ships, later flew in its planes, sent parcels by horse and wagon and then by truck express, and stayed at its hotels built alongside CP train and plane routes.

Today, CP no longer has passenger trains or ships and its only direct contact with most Canadians is through its planes, hotels, and the recently formed parcel delivery express service, called Canpar. These are among the least profitable of CP ventures, the weak sisters in the empire. In some cases the poor showing is due to uncontrollable economic circumstances, as in the case of CP Air. But in other instances it is due to either disinterest or a lack of competitive instinct.

Although CP's hotels were built as luxury hotels, they have slipped behind newer places that offer bigger, more modern rooms. While CP Hotels is a small contributor to corporate revenue, it still ranks second in terms of sales in Canada's lodging industry—ranking behind Scott's Hospitality, which owns Commonwealth Holiday Inns. By contrast, according to the annual survey of *Foodservice and Hospitality* magazine, Canadian National Hotels ranks ninth in sales.

CP Hotels is growing at a slower rate than its competitors, however. Between 1977 and 1981, CP Hotels' revenue doubled, compared with a 213 percent increase at Delta Hotels, a 162 percent increase at Commonwealth Holiday Inns, and an 118 percent rise at Four Seasons Hotels. CP did do better than CN Hotels, which registered only a 37 percent increase in revenue.

While other Canadian hotel chains are aggressively expanding at home and American controlled outfits are also growing in Canada, CP Hotels has been at a near standstill. CP has opened a handful of new hotels in the United States, Germany, and Israel, but although it has hotels across most of Canada, even in smaller cities like Brandon and Thunder Bay, it still is not in either Vancouver or Ottawa.

At one time, CP drew up plans for a hotel to be connected to its Granville Square offices in Vancouver. World-famous architect Arthur Erickson of Vancouver designed a building, but the city of Vancouver refused to approve a building permit and CP subsequently dropped its plans. CP also once considered the Ottawa market at the suggestion of Duff Roblin, the Manitoba premier who was president of Canadian Pacific Enterprises between 1968 and 1974. That idea died, too, and the site on the Rideau Canal is now being used by Westin Hotels for its first hotel in the nation's capital.

Of course, few corporations are willing to build new hotels, with construction costs per room now averaging $110,000. The old rule of thumb used to be that room prices would be one-tenth of 1 percent of the construction cost, but that is no longer possible as the spread widens between the building costs and what most people are able to pay. Instead, what hoteliers are now seeking are management contracts.

CP Hotels is gradually moving into this type of business, but it is far outpaced by Delta Hotels, Canada's fastest growing hotel chain, with sales climbing to close to $100 million in just twenty years in business. Going the management route allowed Delta to grow a lot faster and to save money. Delta also differs from CP Hotels in its choice of locations. CP's hotels originally grew up along its railway, and several are in resort areas. All seek conventions. Delta, on the other hand, has avoided the resort and convention market, eliminating the need for costly large lobbies, ballrooms, and convention facilities.

Despite its size in the hotel industry, CP Hotels makes very slim profits, with most of the money due to increased room rates and food prices, rather than increased business. Occupancy at the Royal York, CP's largest hotel with sixteen hundred rooms, averages around 71 percent, below the industry average of 75 percent. By contrast, the occupancy rate at Delta's one-thousand-room Chelsea Inn in Toronto is around 96 percent.

Although CP Hotels' bottom line is not as profitable as it might be, it is unlikely CP would ever sell the chain. "It's an advertising exercise and a window on the world," says a former financial executive with the chain. "Besides, the hotels are sitting on very valuable real estate." In addition, Ian Sinclair is said to have a soft spot for the hotel business dating back to 1961 when he managed the Royal York Hotel during a nearly year-long strike.

Many of the chain's hotels have become part of Canadian folklore. Château Montebello, a 105-square-mile fifty-three-year-old hunting, fishing, golf, and tennis resort that bills its hotel as the world's largest log cabin, was the site of the 1981 economic summit of the western industrial nations. Famous guests in years gone by included Harry Truman, Bing Crosby, and Perry Como.

The Royal York, the largest hotel in the Commonwealth, was opened in 1929 at the start of the Depression. Many regard it as having Toronto's most comfortable hotel lobby. The hotel has passed into Canadian legend as the center of merriment during the Grey Cup football festivities. In 1948, a horse was ridden into the lobby at the time of the game; another year, a guest jumped from the mezzanine to the lobby, without breaking any bones or furnishings. Guests in the six-hundred-dollar-a-day Royal Suite on the sixteenth floor—which has a dining table that can seat twenty-two people, a living room with fireplace, and two bathrooms—have included Queen Elizabeth and Prince Philip.

The pecking order in the Royal York's dining room, the Imperial Room, is revealed by who sits at table number thirty, the best table, which is at the front left corner. The worst table for watching shows is at the back left corner behind a pillar. That table, however, is popular at lunch for businessmen wanting quiet, discreet meetings.

Until recent years, entertainment at the Royal York always featured top nightclub performers. For Tony Bennett, always a sellout, the hotel would get Steinway pianos from the same store in Toronto, Paul Hahn Ltd. But with the hotel now attracting tourist groups as corporate and luxury travelers head to newer hotels in the city, the Imperial Room introduced burlesque-type entertainment during the summer season, starting with a night-club act in July 1982. This show obtained a deservedly cutting review from *Toronto Star* critic Rob Salem: "Tacky . . . playing to an imagined, lowest common denominator . . . a turkey." A similar "Las Vegas" show was also started at CP's Château Champlain in Montreal.

It is not only the entertainment that indicates standards at most of CP's hotels are sliding. Behind the scenes is not always a pleasant sight. For example, side stairwells at the Royal York have paper-littered steps and walls gray with age and grime. The kitchen floor is covered with flour and scraps of food.

CP has spent millions of dollars renovating its hotels—such as the Royal York, Banff Springs, Château Lake Louise, Château Frontenac, Château Montebello, the Empress in Victoria, and the Algonquin in St. Andrew's-By-The-Sea in New Brunswick. But because these famous hotels are fifty to seventy-five years old, the money has gone towards things guests do not see, such as air conditioning, stainless-steel kitchen equipment, interior fire escapes, smoke detectors, and wiring, rather than on paint. "Most hotel companies try to set aside 1.5 percent of their revenue for improvements, but CP had fallen behind in this and had to spend nearly all of its budget on wiring and so on," says former CP Hotels Chairman and President Donald Curtis. Now, the chain is spending $17 million on renovating some of its oldest hotels.

In addition, although CP has been in the hotel business since 1886, one year after completing its railway, it did not modernize its accounting system until the 1970s. Until then, accounts were ad hoc and outdated, former hotel employees say. "When I arrived in 1972, it seemed that the hotels' controller kept the books in an envelope in his pocket and that he kept losing the envelope," Curtis says. Two former accountants, who asked not to be quoted by name, say that until a decade ago, the hotels only did manual bookkeeping and that they were never up to date regarding cash control and accounts receivable, two crucial areas in a business so dependent on daily receipt of money.

"We introduced specific reporting requirements covering cash management and receivables, such as requiring bi-weekly and weekly reports on anticipated inflow and outflow," says one of the ex-accountants, now a senior executive in Canada's entertainment industry. "In the past, there had been no financial projection reporting. We compared the figures with the industry norm in order to budget more accurately and make better management decisions."

With hotels located around the world and reporting until the 1970s done mostly by letter, accounts were never up to date. That system was finally replaced by each hotel putting its data on a computer disc, making possible speedier accounting by the head office in Toronto. One of Curtis' proudest accomplishments was the introduction of what in its time was the largest computer system in the Canadian hotel industry. It recorded guest registration and billing, night audits, payables and receivables, and payroll. Curtis is also proud of expanding Château Flight Kitchens, CP Hotels' airline catering business. "Originally, CP Air was our biggest customer, but eventually it became our smallest one as we signed up more airlines," he says. More kitchens were also added in Canada and in Mexico City to the original two in Montreal and Toronto.

Before joining CP Hotels, Curtis had been in the hotel business in Europe and South Africa for more than twenty years. At one time he was senior vice-president of Club Mediterránée, of which the principal shareholder was Baron Edmond de Rothschild. The baron later figured in CP's move into the Israeli market through managing two of Rothschild's hotels there.

Since leaving CP Hotels, Curtis has become a hotel consultant for Canadian, American, and Italian clients. "When I joined CP Hotels, there were eleven hotels in the system, grossing about $60 million," Curtis recalls. "It grew to thirty-one hotels with two under construction and revenue in excess of $200 million."

Curtis' first task was to buy back the hotels from Canadian Pacific Railway and private owners. "It was part of the profit center re-organization in which every company was to stand on its own two feet and in which it would be easier to monitor the results of each company," he says. Just because the hotels and railway were in the same family did not mean the hotels got favored treatment in the buyback. "We had to negotiate each purchase as if it were from an outsider," Curtis recalls. "The hotel and railway companies each made different evaluations and the matter finally went to arbitration."

Being part of the CP empire did not necessarily mean ready access to banks, Curtis recalls. "At the time I joined, CP's management contract for the Skylon Tower Restaurant in Niagara Falls was expiring. They were not going to renew and I was afraid it would be blamed on me. We decided to buy it, but our loan requests were rejected by two major banks." A bank finally came through, and since then the Skylon has been a steady moneymaker.

Since 1978, CP Hotels has been run by Gordon Cardy, a leading member of the "establishment." At one time his family owned the Brock Hotel in Niagara Falls and Toronto's King Edward Hotel in the days when it was the watering hole for the city's corporate elite. Cardy is married to a member of the Dunlop-Cochrane hardware business family. Despite his wealth, Cardy does not seek special treatment at the various hotels he runs. "Donald Curtis, who preceded Cardy, used to demand that he have a special suite and be picked up by limousine, whereas Cardy insists on not having this treatment," says a former CP Hotels executive.

Cardy was general manager of the Royal York for ten years and vice-president of CP Hotels' central region before becoming president after the abrupt departure of Curtis and most of his managers. Curtis' expansionary outlook had clashed with the consolidation sentiment of his superiors, especially when the multimillion-dollar structural renovation program and aggressive expansion began to create losses for the chain. "Curtis seemed to be taking CP into almost any old country," says a former employee. "In Israel, we did very, very well. But Germany has teething problems. Curaçao was fair to middling, and we pulled out of Mexico and the Bahamas."

While CP Hotels needed more money in order to be competitive, its wobbly financial performance prevented it from getting an outside infusion of money from investors.

Over the years, senior CP executives have predicted that CP Hotels would become a publicly traded stock, as are several other CP companies. Curtis says his objective was to whip the hotels into shape for going public, but that the chain still lacks a consistent success record.

Like the hotel chain, CP's parcel shipping service is one of CP's oldest businesses outside of its railway. It was started in 1882, four years before CP's first hotel was built and just one year after construction began on the railway. Besides age, the parcel shipping and hotel divisions share another characteristic—poor financial results. CP folds in its express division results with those of its trucking operations, which showed losses of more than $2 million in 1979 and 1980 and only slim profits of $4.9 million in 1981 and $1.3 million in 1982.

Although it is a leader in diversification, CP, like many companies, sometimes looks elsewhere for inspiration in how to run its business. Such was the case with its Canpar small parcel delivery system started in 1976. Canpar is largely a carbon copy of the organizational methods, even down to the number of columns in waybills, used by United Parcel Service, the giant U.S. firm with which CP first considered a joint venture and then fought unsuccessfully to keep out of Canada. CP attributed the similarity to wanting compatibility with UPS, with which it briefly had an interline arrangement between Canada and the United States. Other companies have not found this necessary.

The origin of Canpar dates back to the 1950s when CP bought Smithsons Holdings, which owned a number of major eastern Canadian trucking companies. As John Sanderson, director of marketing for CP Express, told the Ontario Highway Transport Board during 1978 hearings on parcel delivery, Smithsons was bought because more people were moving into the country at a time when passenger rail service was being reduced. Consequently, CP had to find another way to send small parcels, and Smithsons' trucking routes paralleled the dropped rail routes. Still, CP Express continued losing customers because people living outside a town had to come into it to send or pick up parcels. In 1975, the company did an in-depth study on courier services and concluded there was a large market for small shipments. According to Sanderson's testimony, outside of Canada Post, which had a 51 percent market share in Ontario, no courier had more than a 10 percent market share, providing a golden opportunity for CP.

Glenn Smith, president of United Parcel Service Canada Ltd., says that also in 1975, UPS approached CP and three other major trucking carriers, including Kingsway Transport, then owned by Paul Desmarais, about a possible joint venture in Canada. CP eventually broke off the talks and in 1976 set up Canpar, the same year that UPS got a license to operate in Toronto.

Subsequently, CP led a group of couriers in opposition to UPS in its application before the Ontario Highway Transport Board to expand its coverage beyond the city. In a peculiar move, the board's chairman, E.J. Shoniker, asked Canpar's attorney, Richard Zimmerman, to write the board's judgment denying UPS' application. UPS appealed the ruling to the Ontario Cabinet, saying Shoniker's action was improper. UPS was granted a new hearing in 1980 under a new chairman, who gave it a license. Smith says the hearing process cost UPS $3.5 million.

The 1978 hearing revealed that Canpar's only major difference from UPS was its name. All its structure and systems were lifted from UPS, as the following exchange between Sanderson and the board shows:

Q. Delivery time in Canpar?
A. Same as UPS. The policy is to deliver five-day a week service to all of the areas served, and by served I mean where Canpar pick-up services are provided.
Q. Automatic daily pick-up stop for customers signed up to the Canpar service, like signed up to the UPS service. What is your situation?
A. Same as UPS, except the charge is $5.00 per week rather than $4.00 per week.
Q. One shipping document for all packages. What is your position opposite UPS?
A. It's identical to UPS. . . .
Q. UPS uses a metering system; does Canpar use a metering system as well?
A. Yes it does. . . .

Q. Alright. Proof of delivery. How do you stack up opposite UPS in this regard?

A. The same procedures as UPS.

Q. Three delivery attempts?

A. The same as UPS.

Q. Refused or undelivered packages returned? Without charge and without instructions from the shipper?

A. Same as UPS.

Q. Simplified C.O.D. procedure. You follow exactly the same format?

A. Yes we do.

Q. Address correction. Have you the same feature? You do exactly the same thing as you charge for it?

A. Yes, and we charge the same amount.

Q. .85¢?

A. Yes.

There are some areas, however, in which Canpar does not manage to parallel UPS. Whereas UPS does not charge for tracing parcels, Canpar charges five dollars. UPS' Smith says tracing actually costs one or two dollars but that "if a customer entrusts a package to you, why should you charge him for information?" And, although its record may have since improved, testimony before the 1978 Ontario Highway Transport Board hearings stated that in a sample one-month survey, 12 percent of Canpar's parcels were delivered one day late, compared with 1 percent by UPS. No public surveys have been conducted since then.

Canpar has not been a happy experience for CP, and under increasing competitive pressure it may become even less so. While Canpar is nationwide, UPS is still confined to Ontario, although Smith says expansion, possibly first into Quebec, is planned. In addition, in a move that will help it compete with the airline courier operations and firms like Purolator and Emery, which have their own planes, Smith plans to tie UPS Canada into the parent company's fleet. "For example, a plane flying between Boston and Louisville could stop en route in Montreal and Toronto," he says.

With Canpar, both the future and the past are troubled. Former Canpar employees have harsh recollections of the company and its working conditions. "Canpar went through supervisors like water," says a former supervisor who worked there from 1977 until 1980. Now a Toronto Transit Commission driver, he asked not to be identified.

Most transportation companies, including cp Express, operate with day and evening fulltime supervisors. But Canpar felt that two fulltime shifts were too expensive, so it hired university and highschool students on a casual basis.

The only way to make a profit from small parcel delivery is through high volume and drivers were pushed hard. If they made 100 stops, the company wanted 110. They were chastised for requesting overtime, if they made more stops or were held up by snowstorms. There were also problems with the loading system at Canpar's main terminal on Queen's Quay in Toronto. The trucks had a two-foot-high step and a six-foot-high door and were loaded from a five-foot platform. It was elevated to make cleaning easier, but workers often fell between it and the vans.

Truck maintenance was also poor. Often, light bulbs were not replaced and alternators and batteries were not checked regularly. A Canpar executive once scolded me for buying a $60 filing cabinet.

cp Hotels and Canpar show that even the most powerful corporations have their weak spots that are hard to fix.

Airsick

One of the few things Canadians will admit to liking about Canadian Pacific is CP Air. They praise its food—served on china, unlike the plastic dishes of Air Canada—and its service as being superior to that of the government-run airline. For CP's balance sheet, however, there is little to praise.

CP Air's profit in the last five years has never come close to that of CP Rail, or even to that of the Soo Line Railroad, a short, 4,400-mile system (one-fourth the length of CP Rail) in the midwestern United States, owned 55.7 percent by CP. In 1981, when CP Air lost $22.8 million, the Soo Line contributed $23 million. In 1982, CP Air had a record loss of $39.2 million and the Soo Line, despite a decline in profits, still contributed $13.6 million.

In fact, CP Air has been borderline financially or in the red since it was started in 1942, except for the two excellent years of 1978 and 1979. Obviously, CP Air is lucky to have such a wealthy parent. How many other businesses would be able to stay alive for forty years in such poor condition?

The past few years have been tough for the airline industry around the world, and of all CP's troubled divisions, CP Air has been the most in the public eye. The airline, whose finances have never kept pace with its ambitions for growth, is in its worst slump since 1976. Back then, when it was only $5 million in the red, it was saved from bankruptcy by Big Daddy in Montreal taking care of the payroll. Now, after rolling up total losses of $62 million over 1981 and 1982, the airline has to fight hard to survive.

One of CP Air's problems in this fight is that it risks damaging itself in the process. Frenzied cost cutting on the airline's package tours, for example, contributed to the recent losses and at the same time created ill-will at travel companies. They said CP Air's cut-rate fares threw the industry into an unwanted price war at a time when Canadians were deciding to save their money, rather than go on package tours.

In 1976, CP Air was reeling when it had only one major problem. In the early eighties it faced a whole onslaught of difficulties. A $1 billion fleet expansion program, encouraged by the long-awaited opening by the federal government of more transcontinental routes in Canada to the airline, collided with rising fuel and interest rates, the recession, declining passenger travel, a fierce fare price war against Air Canada, and new competition for traffic to the Far East and Australia.

In March 1983, the United States threatened to disrupt a discount fare program, mostly offered by Air Canada, which serves far more U.S. points than CP Air, for thousands of Canadians flying to the United States. The dispute was not over the discount fares; they simply served as leverage in a three-year row between Canada and the United States over Canada's refusal to allow Continental Airlines, a U.S. airline, indirect access to Canadian passengers flying between Canada and Australia. Previously, this business went to CP Air or Qantas, the Australian airline. Faced with the anger of thousands of Canadians who had booked the cheap flights, the Canadian government caved in and said Continental could offer Vancouver-based travelers the same rates as CP Air to fly to Australia. The Vancouver customers would board Continental in Los Angeles.

Within weeks of this bad news, CP Air was also faced with another danger to its Far East business when Cathay Pacific Airways of Hong Kong started flights between Vancouver and Hong Kong. As a result, CP Air reduced its weekly flights to Hong Kong from three to two, with the potential of losing more business to Cathay if the large number of Hong Kong immigrants in Canada who decide to visit their birthplace opt for their hometown airline.

CP Air was by no means alone in its financial suffering. Government-owned Air Canada, Canada's number one airline with revenue about two and a half times that of CP Air, had a $32.6 million loss in 1982—the largest in its forty-six-year history—in contrast to 1981, when it had a $40 million profit. The industry worldwide suffered a $1.87 billion (U.S.) loss in 1982 on top of a $2 billion drop in 1981. The recession has cut sharply into air traffic growth. The maximum annual growth this decade is expected to be only 1 or 2 percent, compared to close to 9 percent in most of the 1970s.

In the midst of this, CP Air has shown some signs of a forward looking, fighting spirit. It has linked forces with Eastern Provincial Airways, a former foe, and with Sir Freddie Laker, who has been in the dog house in the British travel industry since his charter airline went messily bankrupt in 1982.

CP Air and EPA agreed in late 1982 to integrate both their flight schedules into Toronto from the west and east coasts, and their ticket, reservation, and promotional operations on passenger and cargo traffic. For the much smaller EPA, whose revenue is just over one-tenth that of CP Air, the agreement gave it the last laugh in a long-running feud with CP Air over routes to the Maritimes.

The deal with Sir Freddie, signed in December 1982, calls for CP Air to fly customers of his new holiday company from the U.K. to Canada and the United States. This could provide a form of insurance to CP Air in that it can count on a steady volume of business from Sir Freddie's clients at a time of surplus capacity at most airlines. On the other hand, Sir Freddie's re-entry into the travel business came when the number of Britons flying to Canada and the United States was down drastically.

In 1979, the then president, Ian Gray, predicted that by 1985 CP Air would have an annual growth of 13 percent, seventeen more planes, two hundred more pilots, and as much as 45 percent of the domestic market. But instead of 1982 and 1983 turning out to be a period of buoyant expansion, the company instituted a vigorous program to become trimmer. It sold several planes, shelved its fleet purchases, laid off more than a thousand employees, froze wages, reduced departmental budgets by 10 percent, shrank the number of its domestic runs, lengthened the working day, postponed expansion of its main facility in Vancouver, and began to raise fares in a struggle to stay afloat.

It even cut down on its post-signing celebration after finalizing contracts with its main union, the International Association of Machinists and Aerospace Workers (IAM). In the past, the company used to serve cognac and champagne. In 1981, the IAM was sent half the bill for rental of the room used for the signing ceremony and the coffee (no liquor) that was served.

Fuel prices account for about 30 percent of airlines' expenses, and the tripling of oil prices between 1979 and 1981 was particularly bad news for CP Air because of its heavy reliance on long international routes, which account for close to 40 percent of its revenue and include flights to Tokyo, Hong Kong, Lima, Santiago, Buenos Aires, Lisbon, Rome, Milan, and Amsterdam. In 1982, according to the company's annual report, each one cent per gallon rise in the price of fuel resulted in a $1.8 million increase in the airline's fuel bill. Pushing up CP Air's fuel bill, as well as those of other domestic airlines, was the rise in oil prices following the 1981 Ottawa–Alberta oil pact committing the federal government to allowing Canadian oil prices to rise to world levels.

CP Air's use of orange paint on its planes not only adds to its maintenance bills, but also increases fuel consumption by 0.5 percent. This may seem small, but it amounts to about 750,000 gallons costing $1 million at 1981 prices. Eastern Airlines, for example, shaved its annual fuel and maintenance bills by $2.5 million as a result of stripping the paint off its planes and polishing the silver metal instead. CP Air has not changed its planes' color from orange to silver, but its cost cutting program has affected the on-board flight style in other ways.

CP Air has largely built customer loyalty through food superior to Air Canada's. Now the challenge of the airline's food service manager, Bruno Marti, is to maintain that reputation while decreasing costs. He says CP Air annually serves about five million meals worth an average of about eight dollars each. Vancouver, one of the airline's busiest points, buys about $4 million worth of food yearly.

Five years ago, we dictated to caterers what we wanted; now, we're asking caterers what they can give us that will save money. For example, at Buenos Aires, the caterer also does the catering for the

Argentina airline, which bought five-ounce beef tenderloin portions, compared with our six-ounce. By taking the same size as the Argentina airline, we got a break in price. We also fly to Fiji, which imports most of its meat, but has pork, chicken, and fish, so we use their foods instead of imports to cut down our bills.

To reduce wastage of food, due to about 10 percent of travelers not eating on flights, CP Air has also switched from regular cooking of meals to pouch-packed foods that stay fresh if not opened.

Liquor bills have also come under close scrutiny. "In the past, we carried four types of Scotch and three of Rye; now, we find that one brand of premium Scotch is enough," Marti says. In addition, the miniature self-serve bottles have been replaced by large bottles poured by flight attendants. Marti says that the cost of the free wine drunk by full-fare passengers is slightly defrayed by discount Skybus travelers who must pay for their drinks, but that the plane must still be equipped with enough dishes and glasses for a full load, because they may be used on the next flight.

Not even the dishes and cutlery are immune from Marti's cost-cutting campaign. Except for first-class passengers, stainless steel rather than silverware is now being used, which eliminates a lot of time spent polishing. Dishes are now being made for the airline with thicker rims that do not chip as easily as the fine china that had to be replaced frequently. Following the 1978 acquisition by CP of Syracuse China, CP Air started to switch to Syracuse-made dinnerware from its former Japanese-made china.

In view of CP Air's troubles, it is worthwhile to compare its strategy with that of more successful and more troubled airlines. Although CP Air is badly off, it is not the sickest North American airline. In the United States, Braniff Airways went bankrupt in 1982, a victim of its ill-timed, overly ambitious, heavily debt-financed expansion. It had added service to sixteen more American cities and seven more countries since 1978.

Pan American World Airways had to sell its New York headquarters and hotel chain to stay in business. Unsure of the best strategy, Pan Am first reduced its flights to only money-making routes or "jewels" and then later increased its number of flights "to fly our way" into profitability. At United Airlines, which suffered the largest losses among the major American airlines during much of 1982, flight turnaround times were quickened and more emphasis was placed on longer, more profitable flights. By contrast, Air Canada, one of North America's most profitable airlines in 1981—a rotten year for most—is considering emphasizing shorter haul flights.

Obviously, airline executives do not know the magic formula for success in tough economic times. But two that seem to have a fairly firm grasp are full-service Delta Airlines and the discount People Express. Delta was the world's most profitable line until 1982, when it suffered its first losses since 1953 due to increased competition resulting from deregulation of the air industry in the United States. Unlike CP Air, which withheld its fleet expansion until after it got more routes in 1979 and then was unable to buy because of money problems, Delta has a fifteen-year advance planning system for flight equipment. It sticks to this plan, even if faced with unexpected crises, such as fuel shortages or the 1981 air controllers' strike. It never backs down from a fleet improvement program because of financial limitations.

At the other end of the scale is People Express, one of the most successful deep-discount airlines that have sprung up in the United States since deregulation in 1978. People Express gives no free meals. Snacks and beverages must be purchased, in contrast to free non-alcoholic beverages given CP Air's discount Skybus passengers. Because there are no food galleys, more seats—and paying passengers—can be added. It costs three dollars per bag to check luggage, and most passengers are encouraged to carry on their suitcases. People Express also flies out of an old terminal in Newark, New Jersey, which is cheaper to rent than space at glossy new terminals. People has no vice-presidents, or even secretaries, which is unusual in the airline industry. CP Air, for example, has eight vice-presidents and Air Canada had thirty until 1983 when seven lost their jobs as part of an overall reduction of 500 people from the previous 3,600 in management.

But one of the main reasons the two airlines can keep operating costs down is their lack of unionization. People Express has no unionized employees; at Delta, only the pilots are unionized. People's pilots are paid half the $100,000 that is the rate for members of the Airline Pilots Association. With a surplus of pilots in the United States, People's is able to get away with the lower salaries.

The big advantage of being union-free, however, is that workers can do more than one job. At People's, for example, pilots load baggage. Consequently, the airline needs fewer employees and can improve productivity, currently a favorite corporate buzzword. People's has a profit-sharing program as an incentive to employees to work on their multiplicity of tasks.

During its recent downturn, CP Air asked the IAM for concessions along the lines of what is done at Delta and People's. Under management's plan, workers in one trade would cross over to another in their down time. Thus, an aircraft mechanic might spend his off-duty time as a baggage attendant. In turn, baggage handlers would help with the formerly exclusive IAM responsibility of pushing planes out from the gates. CP also wanted to replace the usual three shifts with schedules tied to the busiest flight times and to remove plane overhaul checks from union to management supervision.

Management maintained that this "worker flexibility" would result in tremendous efficiencies. But the IAM was firmly opposed. "CP is a long-established company and plans to continue forever," says Ralph Steeves, IAM's general chairman in Vancouver. "They're not in business just to make money in a particular year." Besides, the IAM is already extremely concerned about technological changes threatening mechanics' jobs. Steeves says:

As of now, pilots write up maintenance requests in a log which they hand to the chief mechanic who writes up a work order and gives it to a supervisor. But computer programming is now being installed in the cockpit that allows flight personnel to enter snags. That sets in motion an order repair scheme and re-ordering of inventory, all done by computer. CP is already installing 1,500 terminals at its operations center here in Vancouver. In addition, new electronic equipment, which is almost self-repairing because it tells you what has gone wrong, is being developed. As a result, fewer people will be needed, but those who do stay or are hired will be paid extra since more skills will be required.

Outside of their disagreement over workers taking on more than one job, management and labor get on fairly well at CP Air. The last strike was in 1973. Steeves says CP Air paid one-half to one cent more per hour than Air Canada before the government's wage restraint program, gives longer vacations, and has a more generous pension plan. In 1980, the company hired a fulltime counselor to help employees with drug or alcohol problems, and has also encouraged employees to participate in community activities. Over the years, workers have built a forerunner of today's kidney dialysis machine and donated it to a Vancouver hospital and have overhauled dental chairs and equipment for shipment to Third World countries.

Steeves gives much of the credit for the generally amiable labor relations at CP Air to Ian Gray, who became president in 1976 after spending his entire career at the company. "He's tough, but very fair," Steeves says.

Gray retired in the spring of 1983 after forty years with the airline. The company's imported new president and chief operating officer, Daniel Colussy, formerly president of Pan American, the world's second largest airline, succeeded Gray as chief executive officer.

In the airline industry these days, many executives have a background in finance or marketing. People Express Chairman Donald Burr has a business administration background, Pan Am Chairman Edward Acker started out in investment counseling, and both Delta President David Garrett Jr. and Air Canada President Claude Taylor started as passenger agents. Taylor, an accountant, was a vice-president of strategic development, government and industry affairs, and public affairs before becoming president.

Gray, however, was an engineer who used to chip in and help mechanics change plane tires. His engineering background made him well equipped to know which planes would be the most fuel efficient, a prime requirement as fuel prices soared. Colussy, who left Pan Am in 1981, is credited with that airline's recovery in the late 1970s from heavy financial losses earlier in the decade. His marketing background will be useful as CP tries to get rid of its red ink.

Compared with CP Air's flamboyant founder, Grant McConachie, who had a stock of inflatable globes to help demonstrate his view that CP Air should be a global airline, Gray seemed colorless. He spoke in a rapid, quiet monotone, drove a small car, and refused to be picked up by staff at airports. His windowless office was located in CP's hangars in Vancouver, to which he moved executives from luxury downtown quarters during the airline's 1976 crisis. He made it a point to have early morning coffee in the cafeteria with other employees.

Gray was a strong believer in good communications with employees, especially during hard times when workers were anxious about their jobs. He held coffee klatches with management from across the system several times a year, as well as with union leaders. During the 1976 crunch, Gray cut back on the number of company newsletters, but in 1982, with layoffs frightening workers, he instituted a bi-monthly newsletter to provide speedy, blunt answers during the setback. The newsletters gave summaries of layoffs, the outlook for future reductions, and what was happening to the industry as a whole. At the time, it must have been grim reading.

While CP Air shares all the economic problems common to most of the world's airlines, it also has an additional problem that beleaguered airlines in the United States do not face. While there is no major government-owned airline in the United States, in Canada nearly all the regularly scheduled, competitive major airlines—both national and regional—are government supported. Federally owned Air Canada controls Nordair. Pacific Western Airlines, Canada's third largest airline, is owned by the Alberta government. Eastern Provincial Airways has received considerable financial help from the provinces of Nova Scotia and Newfoundland, and Quebecair has had generous support from the Quebec government.

Air Canada was founded in 1937, just five years before CP Air. Air Canada's creator, Finance Minister C.D. Howe, originally intended Canadian National Railways and Canadian Pacific

Railway to own the airline jointly, and throughout the years, with the two airlines' prices, plane sizes, and schedules being similar, the question has been raised as to why Canada needs two transcontinental airlines. Opponents say airports, which are federally funded, would be smaller if there were only the one carrier. Those in favor of two lines say that CP Air has often been the leader in price fare wars and that a regulated monopoly (such as Bell Canada, for example) would not benefit consumers. Indeed, when the Trudeau government called for wage and price restraints in 1982, both Air Canada and Bell were unwilling to accept the government's 6 percent limit and asked for a 25 percent hike in prices.

Over the years, government policy has favored Air Canada, holding CP Air back from lucrative routes in eastern Canada. This policy was originally set forth in 1943 by Prime Minister Mackenzie King:

The government sees no good reason for changing its policy that TCA [Trans Canada Airlines—the original name of Air Canada] is the sole Canadian agency which may operate international services. Within Canada TCA will continue to operate all transcontinental systems, and such other service as may from time to time be designated by the government. Competition between air services over the same route will not be permitted.

It was not until 1959 that CP Air was allowed by the federal government to start a transcontinental flight from Vancouver to Montreal, and it took another eight years before it got permission to start a second flight. Subsequently, in 1970 CP Air was allowed to expand its flights to obtain 25 percent of total transcontinental capacity. In 1978, the ceiling was raised to 35 percent; in 1979, it was raised first to 45 percent and finally, in March of that year, all restrictions on CP Air's transcontinental market shares were removed. Following the decision, Air Canada employees were urged in their staff magazine, *Horizons*, to prepare for battle:

Fasten your seat belts and get ready for WAR, because we're into the most important fight of our lives and winning the battle will require the participation of everyone on the Air Canada team. It could be called the Battle of the Transcon and the enemy is the increased competition facing us on our cross-Canada routes.

The change, however, has had little impact on Air Canada's dominance. One out of every two dollars spent by Canadians on domestic air travel still goes to Air Canada.

Air Canada's hub and spoke system, in which its routes fan out from a core, provide it with cost efficiencies that CP Air's more linear system lacks. According to Brian Campbell, an American airline manager and consultant who has advised both the Consumers' Association of Canada and the federal government's bureau of competition policy, Air Canada is the most hub and spoke oriented airline in North America. "About 35 percent of its departures are from Toronto and Montreal, compared with 33 percent of American Airlines' flights leaving from Chicago and Dallas, and 28 percent of Delta Airline's flights going from Atlanta and Dallas."

Adds John Blakeney, a lawyer specializing in aviation with the Consumers' Association of Canada, "CP Air is effectively shut out of the major hub and spoke centers of eastern Canada. Air Canada's positioning at Toronto International and Montreal's Dorval airports puts it in a perfect place to control traffic in eastern Canada. Taking the lid off CP Air's transcontinental market share was a good step, but without giving it the additional opportunity to develop a feeder network, it can't have the same efficiencies as Air Canada." In recognition of this weakness, Daniel Colussy is reshaping the airline's operations into a hub and spoke structure radiating from Toronto and Vancouver, which he claims will cut $25 million from its annual costs, the equivalent of 64 percent of CP Air's 1982 losses.

Air Canada executives would also like to shut CP Air out of the international market. They have frequently suggested that Canada have just one international airline, operated by Air Canada, of course.

Also contributing to Air Canada's continued dominance is its better borrowing position. Air Canada gets money from the government at very low cost, an advantage made possible by the taxpayer footing the differences between the rate given to the airline and what it costs the government to borrow at the higher rates of the marketplace. Borrowing costs CP Air much more, even if it borrows from parent CP at interest rates slightly lower than those the banks would charge.

One of the most curious government rulings in the gradual evolution of CP Air's becoming a truly national airline occurred in 1980 when the airline applied to the Canadian Transport Commission for permission to start a twice-daily non-stop Toronto–Halifax run. As Air Canada was already flying non-stop to Halifax from Toronto, CP's competitor for the new route was Eastern Provincial Airways (EPA), the Maritimes' regional airline.

EPA supporters at the Canadian Transport Commission's January 1980 hearings said that the profitable Halifax–Toronto run would help EPA make up losses from money-losing local flights. CP Air was supported by the Halifax Board of Trade, the Nova Scotia Tourist Industry Association, and local exporters and importers who felt CP Air's national and international service would help business. The Board of Trade's brief said:

Canada does not end at Montreal. . . . It has been shown elsewhere in Canada that competition on the same route between two carriers results in a marked improvement in scheduling and in cabin service. This, too, would be most welcome in this region.

The CTC's reaction was to favor CP Air, pointing out that EPA could be worse off if, as expected, the Toronto–Halifax run were to lose money in its initial years. "I wasn't surprised by the decision," says EPA President Harry Steele. "I didn't expect a courageous decision by the CTC because the people appointed to its Air Transport Committee do not give regional airlines much support."

Following the ruling, EPA, with the support of the Maritime premiers who sent telegrams to Prime Minister Trudeau, lobbied hard to get it reversed. Their lobbying worked. On June 27, 1980, ten days prior to CP Air's inaugural flight, the federal Cabinet reversed the CTC's decision and gave the non-stop Toronto–Halifax route to EPA, at the same time canceling its non-stop Montreal–Halifax service. Subsequently, CP Air decided to launch a Montreal–Halifax route, which began in March 1981, eight months after it would have begun the Toronto–Halifax run. It gave up that route in 1982 as part of the terms of its operational agreement with EPA.

Halifax Board of Trade officials say the Cabinet's ruling temporarily hurt tourism in Nova Scotia. "When CP Air was first authorized to come to Halifax, it implemented a special advertising program in western Canada which resulted in a substantial number of people making plans to come to the Maritimes that summer," says Gordon Lumis, general manager of the board. "When the federal Cabinet overturned the decision, we received a number of calls from motel and hotel owners who were complaining that it had resulted in cancellation of bookings they had received for hotel rooms."

While the United States has deregulated its air industry, Canada's airlines are still treated as if they were a utility, like hydro electric and telephone companies, entitled, according to the government, to regulated rates. The airlines believe they are similar to utilities, too, because they serve many markets and customers.

Canada's airline industry is divided on a geographical basis between carriers. Under a 1981 fine tuning of the status quo, the regional airlines of PWA, EPA, and Quebecair may only fly non-stop between distances of under eight hundred miles, although the size plane to which they are restricted is able to fly longer distances. Local carriers are not permitted to become regional carriers, and Wardair lost its bid to move from running one-way domestic charters to become Canada's third regularly scheduled transcontinental airline. With the regionals competing against one another as well as the nationals, industry observers believe a shakeout leading to mergers is inevitable.

One of the ironies of the divvying up of markets is CP Air's ambivalent position. Its growth, as Ian Gray has said time after time, was due to its pressuring the government for more routes. But that is as far as CP favors widening competition. CP Air executives argue that CP had to wait years for more markets, so why should other airlines not have to wait?

"It is indeed ironic that it took CP Air twenty years to gain the opportunity to compete on an equal footing with Air Canada,"

Gray has often said. "But since CP Air has obtained this right, there has been considerable further deregulation of the industry. Changes in charter regulations now make it possible for charter services to be operated anywhere in Canada on a 'scheduled' basis, with very few limitations. Further, in spite of a clear regional air policy which defined the geographic areas of the country in which the regional carriers could operate, every regional carrier is now serving Toronto."

When Gray made the standard pitch to a 1982 parliamentary transportation committee hearing on air policy, the committee members could not pin him down as to whether he was for or against greater competition. Perhaps the best summary of Gray's views came from committee member Pierre Deniger, who favors greater competition: "You are 100 percent behind the status quo for others. You want other airlines restricted, but all the doors left open for you."

Despite the CTC's loosening of its regulations, Air Canada's dominance is unlikely to diminish. President Claude Taylor has periodically floated the idea of the airline becoming privately owned like CP Air, and this proposal has been endorsed by the Consumers' Association of Canada, which is concerned about the lack of competition in Canada's airline industry. Says Blakeney:

Before the end of the 1980s, there are likely to be fewer inter-city air carriers than there are today and these remaining few will be either government-owned or effectively controlled by government.

Air Canada's dominance would then become an immutable fact of Canadian economic life. Such an outcome would have little appeal, if any, to Canadian consumers. A decrease in the level of industry competitiveness, coupled with the substitution of political accountability through the marketplace, will mean less choice and unnecessarily higher fares as a result of a lack of pressure to innovate and improve efficiency.

Canada's regulated competition duplicates American airline transportation policy before deregulation began there in 1978, with the two major differences of none of the American airlines being owned by the regulator and no airline having the dominance Air Canada has. The largest pre-deregulation market share held by one airline in the United States was 20 percent, whereas Air Canada has a 64 percent market share.

At the outset, deregulation in the United States led to fierce price wars, as well as to some imaginative give-away programs. Air Florida, for example, offered free stamps for use in buying groceries, Republic Airlines gave children free seats in exchange for cereal box tops, provided the youngsters traveled with an adult in off-peak seasons, Western Airlines offered a $100 round-trip fare between any two points in the continental United States and Alaska, and several airlines had a $99 New York to San Francisco fare. By contrast, the bus fare between the two cities during that period was $133.

Although getting financing proved an insurmountable obstacle to many airline hopefuls, sixty-eight more carriers emerged in the United States, many of them serving local communities. Despite this, the market share of the ten transcontinental carriers decreased only slightly from 73 percent to 70.2 percent, according to Civil Aeronautics Board (CAB) statistics.

At the same time, the financial results for the airlines have been disastrous, with record losses in 1981 and 1982 of $400 million and $550 million (U.S.), respectively. Detractors of deregulation say the red ink has been caused by deregulation, but supporters say the real problems are the recession, high interest rates, increased fuel prices, and the 1981 air traffic controllers' strike. Because there were fewer controllers, the U.S. government restricted the number of flight slots at twenty-two major cities in order not to pile too much work on control tower personnel and, thus, increase the potential for accidents. Airlines have been reluctant to give up money-losing slots for fear that when business recovers they will be out in the cold.

Even though 1981 and 1982 were terrible years overall, most U.S. airline presidents still support deregulation. Moreover, some airlines did well in the United States. Compared with 1980, the national or so-called "trunk" carriers suffered an 8 percent drop in traffic in 1981, the first year of deregulation, and had a loss of $600 million, but the smaller regional carriers had total profits of $270 million and a 20 percent increase in traffic.

The American airlines are optimistic that 1983 will be kind to their balance sheets, especially as fuel prices are expected to decline by about 12 cents a gallon, or below what they were in 1980. Fierce discounting at below the actual cost of providing seats, however, could result in a shakeout among the weaker companies. Canadian airline executives maintain that without deregulation they offer bargain fares that equal or excel those in the United States, a claim that travelers might contradict.

Canadian airlines have never really determined whether the discount-seeking customer or the business and first-class traveler is their target. Instead, they have tried to cater to both markets. For the luxury traveler, there were two choices of meals and lots of free liquor. For the bargain traveler, there were no meals and low fares. CP Air has led the way with both marketing strategies, as well as the return to higher fares in order to stanch financial losses.

There is nothing like competition at a time of decreased air travel to force airlines to provide giveaways and make bargain hunters happy. Both Nordair and CP Air have offered free car rentals and a "baker's dozen" deal, whereby everyone buying twelve one-way tickets between Toronto and Montreal could get a thirteenth ticket free. Pacific Western Airlines has provided a lucky numbers game, with winners receiving vacations, hotel weekends, and cash prizes. Eastern Provincial Airways has run a similar contest in which the winners could get a year's free use of an $80,000 Ferrari, among other prizes. Most airlines also give away free liquor or champagne. Both CP Air and Air Canada acknowledge that the unlimited free liquor on CP's "Empress" class and Air Canada's "Connoisseur" service has led to much more drinking than among passengers who had to pay for their drinks. CP Air attendants are instructed to avoid the problem of "pigs in space," as they call drunks, by serving only single drinks, and only two rounds of wine; they are to stop serving "when excessive consumption is evident."

In an effort to get more business travelers, CP Air also offered throughout 1982 two free plane tickets, for use anywhere in Canada, plus $500 to executive secretaries who filled out CP Air questionnaires on the travel habits at their company. In addition, the secretaries were asked to plug CP Air's more expensive first class and Empress class (full fare economy) to executives.

The lone exception to the giveaway binge has been Air Canada, which did not feel compelled to give any goodies. However, Air Canada's better financial position enables it to start fierce price wars, which it can withstand better than the financially wobbly CP Air. It was Air Canada, for example, that launched a brief period of cut-rate weekend fares in early 1983. But the short-lived price wars, free drinks, and prizes do not compare with the freebies that airlines in the United States now offer, which relate specifically to the price of tickets. They allow frequent fliers to "earn" free travel when they fly consistently with one line, plus "mileage credits" (added up from their plane trips) towards fare deductions, free upgrading from economy to first class, and discounted hotel rooms. The airlines have found the promotions build customer loyalty and increase traffic.

Although Canadian airline executives say that average economy fares between equidistant points are about the same or identical in Canada and the United States, the Consumers' Association of Canada says this is an over-simplification. "There are many more seats at lower fares in the United States," CAC's Blakency says. "Moreover, these are offered over shorter distances than in Canada. There are no discounts in Canada between places less than four hundred miles apart, unlike in the United States."

Nineteen eighty-four will be a crucial year for CP Air, with Daniel Colussy on the hot seat over whether his strategy works. How he does will not only determine CP Air's future, but will also be watched with interest by the many other troubled North American airlines desperate for rosier financial results.

But whether CP Air survives really depends on how much its parent company wants it to keep flying. Many of its planes are purchased by CP, then leased to CP Air, which bears the debt charges. These charges account for the bulk of the airline's long-term debt. In 1981, CP Air's lease obligations to CP Ltd. were $340 million at interest rates ranging from 6 to 11 percent. The 1981 obligations were up $100 million over those for 1980, and in 1982 these rose by $150 million to $492 million. In January 1983, the leases were sold to CP Air by CP in exchange for common shares and the airline's assuming any related outstanding debt. As a result, CP Air's high debt to equity ratio was reduced and its interest obligations were lowered, both of which should brighten the airline's financial picture.

The fate of CP Air is important not only to the airline's employees and CP, but also to the airline's home province of British Columbia. CP Air is one of British Columbia's top ten employers. Outside of the forest industry and provincial government, it is the province's major employer. In 1980, according to company data, CP Air paid close to $170 million to 5,482 employees located in the province, purchased $221 million worth of goods there, and paid $4.6 million in taxes.

Ian Gray has said the airline has been given until 1984 by CP to pull itself together, a year that is expected to be one of recovery for the airline industry generally. But in 1982, various CP Air officials appeared to be holding advance funeral services for the airline. "We're struggling to survive," the airline's public relations director, Jim McKeachie, said in March 1982. "I'm losing 25 percent of my staff. We don't want to say for posterity how bad things are."

Around the same time, Gray was giving a similar story to the parliamentary transport committee on the air industry. Some committee members said CP Air could always dip into the CP money pot for help. Not so, according to Gray. "They invested a lot of money in us and expect a return. The board meetings can be pretty hot and heavy."

In May 1982, during a Canadian–American conference on regulatory changes in the airline industry, a similarly nervous remark was made by Glenn Hunnings, CP Air's assistant vice-president for public affairs, who specializes in government and regulatory matters. Max Ward, founder and president of Wardair, had just summed up his view of the competitive outlook for the Canadian airline industry. "Only CP could afford to run nose on nose with Air Canada if they're prepared to do it," Ward said. "We wonder how long they will, too," Hunnings murmured.

But the company would much rather hold on to the airline, even though, as CP Air executives keep saying, it is only a small cog in CP's empire.

· 12 ·

Poor Henry

Little Cornwallis Island in the Northwest Territories is the sort of bleak, desolate country that only a visionary explorer would seek out. Snow so hard it could be sliced with a knife stretches out in every direction on this tiny, thirty-square-mile island, six hundred miles north of the Arctic Circle and three thousand miles north of Montreal. In the winter, there is no daylight. In the summer, there is no darkness. Winds of up to eighty-seven miles per hour whip the island. The temperature occasionally rises to forty degrees Fahrenheit; more often it drops to forty-five below. The windchill factor can reach seventy degrees below zero. The water surrounding the island is a sheet of ice, except for six weeks in the summer when the ice breaks into huge floes.

There are no trees or insects. Flowers peek up at ground level for just a few weeks in the summer. But there is a profusion of wildlife—fifteen-hundred-pound polar bears unafraid of man, flares or rifles; hares; walruses; seals; and foxes that change color from red in summer to a protective white in the winter.

Since the fall of 1981, two hundred people have been living on this tiny remote outpost in stylish comfort as they mine the island's rich treasure of lead and zinc. The $162 million project, built by Cominco, is the world's northernmost mine and has reserves for at least twenty-five years of mining. Called Polaris after the star in the Little Dipper that points navigators north, it will make Cominco, already the world's number one lead producer, the largest in zinc output as well. The mine itself is the world's eleventh largest lead-zinc mine. It will help make Canada the world's top lead-zinc producer and consolidate the country's position as number three in dollar value of mineral production after the United States and the Soviet Union.

Among Cominco's lead-zinc mines in Canada, the United States and Greenland, Polaris will be the second largest zinc producer, at about one hundred and eighty-seven thousand tons a year and, thus, a hefty financial asset to Cominco, which already is a hefty asset to CP. Until 1982, when it had its largest loss in fifty years, Cominco had been a significant contributor to its parent. It accounted for 8.6 percent of CPE's net income in 1981 and for 17.5 percent in 1980. Cominco's combined dividends of more than $200 million paid to CP over the years have also helped fuel CP's expansion and diversification.

The Polaris project has also provided an invaluable education for another lead-zinc project that Cominco is investigating in northwest Alaska. Called Red Dog, the site is one of the world's largest zinc deposits with a richness of ore content exceeding even the very high-grade Polaris ore. At current depressed metal market prices, the lead, zinc, and silver in the ore would be worth up to a blockbusting $16 billion.

If the Red Dog project gets underway, it will not be until 1984 because it must first get approval from a long list of federal and state agencies over road access to the remote site. The proposed route is being fought by environmentalists, since it would cut across either national park lands or land that is ecologically fragile. But the Polaris project has helped Cominco develop mining processes for a remote, ecologically fragile environment where wildlife must be protected, and because Polaris is substantially staffed by Inuit, Cominco has become familiar with native habits and is willing to make concessions in order to get the project underway. As at Polaris, the schedule for native peoples working at Red Dog would be geared so they would have plenty of time to continue their traditional hunting and fishing. Unlike Polaris, the Red Dog project gives the Inuit living in the Red Dog area a significant financial stake, calculated to work out to a minimum of $1 million annually over about a fifty-year period.

The Polaris mine is only a speck in the vast, resources-rich Northwest Territories, which cover 37 percent of Canada. The Northwest Territories are two million square miles, or more than seven times the size of Texas. But only twenty thousand of Canada's twenty-four million population live there.

Although lead and zinc are found in southern Canada, including at a Cominco mine in southeastern British Columbia, the company has gone so far north because of the richness of the ore on Little Cornwallis. For every ton mined, 25 to 40 percent of what is milled is actual ore and the rest scrap, compared with 3 percent to 6 percent ore richness at Cominco's other Canadian mines.

Mining in the Canadian North is not new to Cominco, which has been active there for almost fifty years. Even before Polaris, the company derived 60 percent of its zinc from north of the sixtieth parallel. But from a technological standpoint, the Polaris mine is as much a milestone as the building of the railroad was a century ago for Canadian Pacific. Both required engineering ingenuity and opened up new frontiers for Canadian industry. Whether the impact on the environment and culture of the North will be as positive as the economic potential remains a question.

Although the mine is the focal point of Polaris, very few of the two hundred employees actually work there. Today's high degree of mechanization in mining means only eight people work per shift in the mine.

The main challenge in operating the mine is not to melt the sparkling white permafrost covering the rocks, which would make mining impossible. To keep the tunnels frozen, the temperature is maintained at twenty degrees, but the dryness makes it feel warmer. Another big challenge is maintaining the engines of jeeps and mining equipment. Because of the cold, engines are kept running, even when vehicles are not being used, and overhauls are done weekly.

Since the ore can be shipped only in the summer, a huge storage shed was built with capacity for a year's production. It can be spotted from miles away because of the huge Canadian Maple Leaves painted on it.

Because of the site's remoteness, it was decided to build the mill on a barge in Quebec and then tow it the three thousand miles north. It was the first time such a technique had been used in Canada and one of the few times it has been done in the world.

Insurance for the two-week trip was one million dollars. Cominco calculates that the barge advanced production time at Polaris by nine months. If the mill had been erected on site, it would have taken until July 1982 to hook it up and the site's remoteness would have pushed up the price tag by the cost of flying in labor and supplies. The mill was actually built in Trois Rivières, where construction workers, suffering from a depressed market, were willing to sign a no-strike clause.

The barge hull is used for oil storage, while the topside houses concentrating equipment, machine shops, diesel generators, shower room, supply room, and offices. To conserve energy, Polaris uses the surplus from the diesel generators at the mill to heat its living quarters. The exhaust from the generators drives the concentrating equipment. Cominco executives estimate this reduces the mine's annual heating by "several million dollars."

The materials for the housing and much of the food and mining equipment were taken in by sealift in the summer of 1981. Fresh food supplies are flown in every week. Polaris charters twin-engine planes at an annual cost of five hundred thousand dollars to transport people and cargo from Resolute sixty miles away. The winds are often so strong, however, that flights to Resolute from Montreal (three times weekly) and Edmonton (twice weekly) are postponed. The springtime flight I took from Montreal was delayed from a Monday until Friday because of high winds. In between, we twice got as far as Frobisher Bay, about halfway, but were forced by the winds to return to Montreal.

At Polaris, every effort is made to make the workers, most of whom are in their twenties or thirties, feel comfortable. Each miner has his own brightly painted room and bathroom, and on each of the three fifteen-room floors there is a lounge with free fruit and beverages provided. The workers also have access to a swimming pool (used as a reservoir in case of fire), basketball court, exercise room, pool table, movies, and television. A tuck shop sells candy, magazines, Inuit art, and T-shirts inscribed "I escaped from Little Cornwallis Island." A hydroponic garden, with each worker having his own space, was started to provide some greenery in the treeless environment.

The dining room is arranged in a non-institutionalized way

with small tables instead of long rows of tables and benches. The annual food bill is $1.4 million and covers such fine fare as roast beef every Sunday, T-bone steaks each Wednesday, lobster, choice of omelettes, pancakes and French toast for breakfast, as well as fresh pastries each day. At Christmas in 1981, dinner included stuffed Arctic char, turkey, ham, scampis, baked Alaska, and chocolate mousse, and each worker received a $1,000 bonus, pen and pencil set, and a book on Inuit life. In 1982, though, with Cominco on an austerity program and workers' wages frozen at Polaris, time off at Christmas was given instead.

Although visitors are wide-eyed about the excitement of being in Canada's far north, employees do not regard it as an exciting adventure. They cannot go for long walks because of the dangers of frostbite and polar bears, and can never open a window. In the winter, the combination of the dark interior of the mine and the twenty-four-hour darkness outside is depressing. The feeling of loneliness and isolation is intensified because workers cannot bring their families, although couples are allowed if they both have jobs at the site. Telephone calls bounced off a satellite, at Ottawa rather than Northwest Territories area rates, are frequent.

Money is the only reason Polaris has attracted workers. They earn seventy-seven hours of pay for a sixty-six hour week, which works out to about forty thousand dollars annually. Polaris, however, does not pay the highest wages in the Canadian Arctic. Some mines pay about three dollars an hour more. Where the workers make their money is in overtime. The mine operates six days a week in two shifts, running from seven o'clock in the morning and seven in the evening. Under Canadian legislation, miners are supposed to work only eight hours a day; Polaris employees, however, work eleven hours. The company says part of that extra time is spent on meals and getting to and from the mine, only a few minutes' drive. The miners are not allowed to walk the few hundred yards from their accommodation to the mine because polar bears have been spotted nearby.

Besides setting a precedent in its location, Polaris also has several significant economic and cultural features. It was planned when there was a buoyant minerals market, but it opened when the outlook for Canadian metals was the most depressed in decades. Thousands of workers, including those at other Cominco mines, were being laid off. While Polaris had purchase commitments for its first year's output, the future is not as bright.

On the economic side, there is also the question of why Polaris is exporting its lead and zinc concentrate for smelting in European refineries, instead of doing its own processing and thereby creating more jobs for Canadians. In the early 1970s, the federal Department of Indian Affairs and Northern Development calculated that if Polaris, as planned, produced at least one hundred and fifty thousand tons of lead-zinc concentrates annually, the revenue gained by insisting on domestic processing would be $80 to $150 million over ten years.

Although Polaris could have been opened in the early 1970s, since its pre-development stretched back to the late 1950s, the company put the project on hold because the federal government, then under the Liberals, refused to grant an export license unless Cominco built an east coast smelter. Cominco countered that there was already excess smelter capacity in the world and that the cost of modernization of its major smelter at Trail exceeded $500 million alone. Moreover, in mining, financial returns from smelting are lower than from other parts of the process. In the 1979 federal approval of Polaris under the short-lived Conservative government, Ottawa simply called for a smelter feasibility study to be completed by the fifth year of the mine.

On the cultural side, the Polaris mine has been both an opportunity for the Inuit population to participate in the North's development and a challenge to their environment and traditions. It has also provided a taste of what will happen in the future because there are thirteen other known lead-zinc deposits in the vicinity. Polaris could be the logical staging area for future activity, since it has its own air strip, port facilities, and mill.

Of the two hundred employees at Polaris, about sixty are Inuit, recruited by a former Royal Canadian Mounted Police officer who speaks Inuktitut, the native language, hired by Cominco for that purpose. The company also worked in conjunction with the Inuit Development Council, the industrial strategy wing of the Inuit. Native foods such as Arctic char and caribou are served at the mine, and the Inuits' shifts are geared to their hunting schedules. They work six weeks, then have four off, whereas employees from southern Canada work ten weeks and get two off.

The consultative and hiring practices at Polaris show the lessons companies have learned over the past fifteen years in starting projects in the North. Before Cominco opened its other Northwest Territories mine at Pine Point near Great Slave Lake in 1965, it did not inform the community of Fort Resolution, forty-two miles away, of its plans. Under an agreement Cominco signed in 1969 with the Department of Indian Affairs and Northern Development, the company agreed to employ only six Inuit trainees out of a total work force of four hundred. Even though Cominco did make an effort to hire more native people from Fort Resolution, which has a population of Indians and Métis, the lack of a road was an obstacle. Even the completion of the road in 1974 was not entirely beneficial—alcohol and drugs became readily available at Pine Point, and Fort Resolution residents complained that outsiders were noisy and insulting, according to a 1978 study of the project for the Canadian Arctic Resources Committee, an environmental organization.

Not all of the blame for the lack of Inuit at Pine Point can be ascribed to Cominco, according to the report's author, Janet Macpherson. "One notable failure occurred when Cominco arranged a line cutting with the Indian Band Council of Fort Resolution. Only seven out of the thirty miles of line were cut and cleared when the first pay day occurred. When the Fort Resolution people failed to return to complete the job following the pay day, Cominco crews were dispatched to cut and clear the remaining twenty-three miles and clean up the campsite."

Northern mining projects like Polaris also bring into play the tug of war between protecting the unique environment of the area and developing its vast potential of oil and minerals, thereby enriching Canada's economy and exports. Such conflicting needs, both of which are important but frequently not compatible, often result in various divisions of a government department being aligned against one another. For example, the Department of Indian Affairs and Northern Development has to look out for the often-conflicting areas of native interests, the environment, and development in Canada's North. The result often satisfies neither the pro-development nor the pro-environment sides.

One such case pitting the mining industry, in which Cominco was the most vociferous spokesman, against the environmentalists concerns the Polar Bear Pass on Bathurst Island northwest of Little Cornwallis Island. The Pass is one of the one hundred and forty sites in northern Canada identified during the 1964–1974 United Nations International Biological Program (IBP). The program's purpose was to pinpoint areas of special biological importance and set them aside as ecological reserves. The one hundred and forty sites cover about 7 percent of Canada's North.

Polar Bear Pass, which runs across the middle of Bathurst Island, is one of six sites designated by the federal government for this purpose and the only one on which public hearings have been held. It was selected because it has one of the largest concentrations of birds and animals in the High Arctic—fifty-three species of birds, wolves, polar bears, caribou, foxes, and walruses—and a wide variety of vegetation, including one hundred and twelve types of moss. This variety has prompted many environmentalists to call it the most significant IBP site in the Northwest Territories. It is also regarded as a traditional and essential hunting area by the Inuit.

As one Inuit hunter told hearings on the Pass, held in January 1981 in Resolute Bay:

If they are going to continue exploring on Bathurst Island, we are really going to be in trouble, including my children. We would like to have a little protection for our generation, to receive the hunting ground for the future and not just for today. I'm not just talking about today, but for my children's children. What are they going to say to us after we are gone, what are they going to ask us? They are going to say why did you let this happen? That is the protection I would like to see for our own generation.

Just how much mining potential the Polar Bear Pass has is a matter of contention. But Cominco holds twenty-three mining claims in the Pass, and its explorations determined that a vast, high value, lead-zinc deposit lay beneath nearly all of the proposed site. Contradicting its descriptions of the potential wealth in the area, however, Cominco established only one claim, on the 1.8 square mile "Tutko property" in the eleven hundred and fifty square mile Pass, and then allowed this claim to lapse in 1981. The federal government banned exploration and mining on the proposed site in 1978, but Cominco had not planned to do any work on the site until 1981 anyway.

The federal government's 1980 assessments of the area's mineral potential were lukewarm. The Department of Indian Affairs and Northern Development said there was "low potential" for minerals and "possible potential for oil and gas." The Geological Survey of Canada, which is usually more optimistic, felt there was only "moderate potential" for minerals and for oil and gas.

Canada's mining industry predicts that world consumption of most minerals will double over the next twenty years and that the Northwest Territories, as Cominco Executive Vice-President Harold Fargey has described it, is a "happy hunting ground." Of Canada's two hundred and eighty mines, only ten are in a North rich in unmined copper, gold, lead, radium, silver, tungsten, nickel, and zinc.

Cominco was not the only CP-related company opposed to making the Polar Bear Pass an International Biological Program site. Panarctic Oils, of which Cominco and PanCanadian Oil own 16.75 percent, wanted to drill on the site and build an oil pipeline across it. In the September 1980 hearing on the Pass, Fargey expressed the industry viewpoint:

Cominco is not opposed to the creation of game sanctuaries, wilderness parks or International Biological Program sites. It is, however, very much concerned that vast areas of our country may be set aside for such purposes without due and appropriate consideration of other values, including mineral values.

Taking into consideration existing parks, wildlife and bird sanctuaries, caribou ranges, international biological sites and new proposals of various groups for specific land use consideration, it is not difficult to visualize off-limits signs for economic development applying to from 50 to 60 percent of Canada north of 60 degrees.

Fargey also argued that mineral exploration provided jobs for the Inuit and that existing exploration "seldom, if ever, is in conflict with biological values. Cominco finds it difficult to accept in logic that Inuit hunting is compatible with the intent of the proposed ecological site while mineral and petroleum exploration is not."

Later in his testimony, Fargey got involved in a rancorous exchange with Murray Coulican, executive director of the Canadian Arctic Resources Committee. In that exchange, Fargey revealed what might be described at best as facetiousness and at worst as a lack of commitment to his earlier statement that Cominco was "not opposed" to IBP sites.

Coulican: What you are saying is that there should be no lands set aside that did not allow mineral exploration or development anywhere?

Fargey: The tip of Sicily is okay.

Coulican: I was wondering if Cominco had done any work or had positive recommendations of areas which it considers could be valuable to be set aside for some kind of conservation where there is no interest on the part of the mineral industry?

Fargey: Mr. Chairman, we do not have any specific sites or designations.

Coulican: Would it be fair to summarize the position of Cominco is only the leftovers that are left after industrial interests have been able to cover the area, only what is left over should be available for any kind of long-term conservation?

Fargey: That would be a gross misinterpretation of my remarks.

Coulican: I do not understand. First, you are saying mineral exploration should be allowed everywhere, but then you have no positive proposals to put forward as to where conservation could take place, and yet you say it is not what is left over that is available to conservation. I don't understand how you fit those together, and perhaps you could clarify this and we would not have a disagreement.

Fargey: I don't really think I have any comment on that. I obviously cannot speak for your thought processes and how they work. I think our position is fairly clear.

Fargey made Cominco's position on IBPs even clearer in an eight-page November 1981 "Dear Neil" letter to G.N. Faulkner, assistant deputy minister of the Department of Indian Affairs and Northern Development (DIAND):

Expansion of mining activity in the North will depend in large measure on the ability of the industry to contain high costs now associated with northern operations. The industry is looking to governments, both federal and territorial, for help in this regard; not for help in the form of subsidies, but in the form of relief from regulation which in many cases substantially burdens costs. It is looking to governments to lower rather than to raise road blocks.

In particular, the mining industry is looking for clear signals that government is genuinely interested in raising the priority of northern economic issues. In our view, a decision to alienate or seriously restrict mineral development from an additional 150,000 square miles of the North would be a clear negative signal, one which could be expected to weaken investor confidence in northern mineral development.

The fate of the Polar Bear Pass site is still undecided, but one indication of the way the federal government is leaning was DIAND's September 1981 preliminary report. It said that development of pipelines, oil drilling and mining would not disrupt the ecological value of the site. Understandably, the report infuriated environmentalists. The Canadian Arctic Resources Committee called it "the worst one we have ever seen in the field of environmental assessment and management." Not so understandably, Cominco executives were also irate. In his November letter to Faulkner, Fargey described the report as "biased and lacking in balance."

Fargey was particularly angered by the report's statement that resource development would only be permitted in areas of existing claims, because many of the proposed IBP sites do not have permits or claims on them. It has sometimes been said that if a decision angers both sides, it must be a fairly good compromise, but in this case the decision seems to reflect a determination not to take a stand.

Cominco has a history of being involved in environmental disputes like that revolving around the Polar Bear Pass. In the

1930s, a disagreement over pollution from Cominco's Trail operations allegedly harming the environment across the border in the State of Washington went all the way to the World Court at The Hague. More recently, Cominco has been involved in another legal battle over allegedly dumping several tons of mercury into the Columbia River that flows past Cominco's Trail facilities. The case shows how the real issue of messing up the environment can be lost in a tangle of arguments over legal technicalities and precedents made possible by sloppy government preparation of pollution control orders. In this incident, adherence to the technicalities and precedents outweighed protecting the environment.

In 1980, Cominco was charged by British Columbia's pollution control board not with polluting the river, but for not reporting its dumping or taking samples to the board. There was no evidence that Cominco's dumping of mercury into the river, a process that had been going on since the plant opened way back in 1898, had caused any environmental harm to the Columbia, one of Canada's biggest rivers. Still, the dumping of mercury became a worrisome issue to those concerned about the environment, especially after findings in other parts of Canada of how mercury has contaminated fish.

Cominco maintained that the government's control orders were invalid because they were signed by an assistant director, whereas the province's Pollution Control Act specified that the director must sign such orders. Later, the legislation was changed to allow the assistant director's signature, but it did not come into effect until August 1980 and the Cominco incident occurred in March 1980. In addition, the order was stamped "pollution control branch" instead of "board." In the strict letter of the law, there was no such thing as a pollution control branch.

Cominco fought the case through five different courts in British Columbia. Since the maximum fine it would have had to pay was only $30,000, obviously Cominco was more concerned about other matters. "Their legal fees would have been way more than $30,000, so it is the bad publicity that must have concerned them," says Donald Skogstad, the Crown counsel on the case.

Because CP is involved in so many industries, mining is only one area in which it must wrestle with the conflicting goals of economic development and preserving the environment. These twin concerns also affect CP's transcontinental forestry operations. Forestry is the only business in which CP has more than one company. It has four—Pacific Forest Products in the West, Great Lakes Forest Products in Ontario, Commandant Properties in Quebec (a small operation localized near Montebello), and CIP Inc., in Quebec and the Maritimes.

They make CP a major player in the crucial race in Canada to save the country's rapidly disappearing forests and thereby preserve Canada's position as the world's top newsprint producer and second largest pulp and paper maker. With world demand for forest products expected to increase by at least 50 percent by the year 2000, Canada, and the CP forestry companies, stand to do exceedingly well provided that forest regeneration in the country improves. As of now, Canada's forestry companies spend only half the $500 million annually that the Canadian Pulp and Paper Association says is necessary. The federal government has set a goal of spending by government and industry of $650 million by 1987 to make possible a 40 percent increase in replanting of cutover forests by the year 2000. However, the structuring of the plan puts most of the burden on the provinces and forestry companies.

But the industry is strapped for funds because it committed itself to billions of dollars in expenditures on expansion and modernization just before it fell into what turned out to be its worst slump in thirty-five years. There is little money left for investing in the future. At CP, the four forestry companies are among the lowest contributors to net income. In fact, in 1982, they contributed the biggest losses—$97 million—of any segment.

The crunch is serious for Canada because it has already lost ground in its share of world trade in manufactured forest goods, its proportion dropping over the past twenty years from 31 to 19 percent. Although Canada has 10 percent of the world's productive forest, two-thirds of the merchantable wood is lost annually to fire, insects, and disease. The government's goal of a 40 percent rise in Canada's harvest by the year 2000 equals an average annual rise of only 1.8 percent, behind the 2.1 percent rate of increase expected in world consumption.

Not only Canada's prestige as a leading forestry products producer is at stake. So are thousands of jobs and the country's balance of trade. One out of every ten jobs is directly or indirectly related to the forestry industry, and more than three hundred communities are totally forestry-dependent. Industry exports account for 17 percent of total exports and, at $12 billion, equal the combined export earnings of Canada's farms, mines, oil and gas wells, fisheries, steel mills, and chemical and fertilizer operations. Forestry also accounts for 20 percent of new investment in manufacturing equipment.

Because 37 percent of Canada's land area is forest, the general impression is that the resource is endless, and Canadians have not realized until recently how much has disappeared. For example, Great Lakes Forest Products annually cuts the equivalent of two hundred square miles, which is equal to the size of Thunder Bay, where its main mill is located. For the average-size daily newspaper, about two hundred and fifty trees must be felled each day.

Canadian companies just keep cutting up to two hundred miles away from their mills, while Scandinavian countries and the southeastern United States do much of their cutting on reforested land. Consequently, Scandinavia is able to harvest almost as much as Canada from a forest area only one-third as big. Canada's unthinking, wide-ranging forestry push means more roads have had to be built, at a cost of up to $100,000 a mile, which also pushes fuel bills higher.

Part of the problem in Canada is the late awakening of governments to the necessity of better forest management. Their recognition of the acuteness of the problem was essential because they are the main landowners. The provinces own 87 percent of Canada's forests and the federal government owns another 5 percent. Nevertheless, the federal government's Canadian Forestry Service did not start collecting inventory data on Canada's forests until 1979. In that year, Ontario became the first province to establish "forest management agreements" (FMAS) with pulp and paper companies. The FMAS, which run twenty years and provide free seedlings to forestry companies, replaced the

province's five-year licenses and meshed responsibility for logging and silviculture, which were formerly kept separate.

Although the FMAS are an improvement, environmentalists are
critical because they are negotiated in private between the company and the government with no input from native peoples,
tourist camps, and wilderness associations. In addition, they are
aimed at increasing production, which wilderness groups fear
will cut into recreational use. Before the FMAS, the government
could arbitrarily withdraw an unlimited amount of land for
other uses. Now, there is a 5 percent ceiling. By 1985, forty-five
million acres will be covered by FMAS in Ontario out of a total of
82.2 million acres of productive forest. By contrast, only 10.4
million acres have been set aside for parks and wilderness areas.
Also worrying environmentalists is the chronic lack of foresters
to monitor the agreements. In Canada, there is only one profes-
sional forester for every 50,000 hectares of managed forest,
compared to one per 19,000 hectares in Sweden and one per
11,000 in Norway. (One hectare equals 2.5 acres).

CP has been in the vanguard of both the forest regeneration so
essential to Canada's future and the battle between wilderness
lovers and forest companies over who should have the use of
Canada's forests. Pacific Forest is regarded as the leader among
Canada's forest products firms in regeneration, while Great
Lakes Forest Products has been a leader in corporate advocacy
against more wilderness parks.

Bruce Devitt, chief forester at Pacific Forest and formerly a
sixteen-year veteran of the British Columbia Forest Service, has a
favorite story he likes to tell about reforestation:

I took a group of environmentalists for a drive, first through the forest
where they were talking away and then into a clear cut where they
became quiet. I took them closer and showed them that about 400 tiny
seedlings per acre had been planted. They were somewhat impressed,
but felt there were not enough trees. So I drove them to an area that had
been replanted with 400 trees per acre in 1948 and the trees were so
thick that the sunlight could not be seen at some spots.

Devitt spends much of his time outdoors at Pacific Forest's
sixty-five acre research station, greenhouses, and nursery lo-

cated near Victoria. Pacific Forest has operated the site since 1964 (Great Lakes Forest Products did not start planning a nursery until 1982). Devitt knows the history of each tree, including one planted in 1977 by Ian Sinclair. It is the only live one in a cluster of four. "Thank goodness it didn't die," Devitt laughs.

When CP built its railway, it also ran agricultural research stations to help immigrant farmers, and Devitt believes Pacific Forest reflects this tradition. "For every cubic meter of wood that is cut, eighty-two dollars comes into the Canadian economy," he says. "Canada has a gold mine in its own backyard with its forests and should take care of them. The forestry industry should be spending three dollars per cubic meter to grow a new crop, but on a Canada-wide basis only one dollar is spent. By contrast, we spend about $2.60."

Over the past seven years Pacific Forest has developed a computer model system on which it "grows" forests and can determine the consequences and costs of various programs and revise them accordingly. Of particular interest to the company is the development of improved seeds that will result in trees with wider diameters. Much of the experimental nursery is devoted to cross pollination and grafting to produce supertrees. That would mean that fewer trees would have to be planted, requiring less labor in a province given to frequent strikes by forestry workers, and more end uses in manufactured goods would be possible because of the bigger diameter.

Although Pacific Forest is regarded as a leader in reforestation, it was not happy when it was asked to compromise over its logging operations near the Whistler Mountain resort area in British Columbia. Pacific Forest's timber license there dated back to the turn of this century, but as the Whistler resort area expanded, the logging operations became visible from the ski slopes and highways. Finally, a plan was drawn up to slow down the rate of Pacific Forest's logging and restrict it to less visible spots. District forestry officials say that while Pacific Forest wanted to continue logging, it was "cooperative" in drawing up revisions.

The same cooperation, however, was lacking in the battle

between Great Lakes Forest Products and environmentalists over a proposed wilderness park on marginally good forest land owned by Great Lakes but not yet cut by it. The fifteen-hundred-square-mile area involved is one hundred and seventy miles north of Great Lakes' headquarters in Thunder Bay, near Armstrong and Lake Nipigon. It is known both as Whitewater Lake for the large lake there and as Ogoki–Albany for the two major rivers in the region.

A wilderness park differs from other parks in that it is left wild and entry is possible only by canoe or foot. No motorized travel, including motorboats, is allowed. About 10 percent of Ontario's parkland has been set aside for wilderness parks. The Ogoki–Albany area is regarded as a "living zoo" by wilderness lovers because of its boreal (coniferous) forest of black spruce, jack-pine, and balsam fir, as well as poplar and birch. North of the area there are no trees and south, there is a mixture of evergreen and deciduous. Besides spectacular beauty, the region contains such rare features as bald eagles and fish hawks as well as other wildlife such as moose and timber wolves. There are also ancient Indian rock paintings and grave sites, and wild rice, which has been traditionally harvested by local natives. The area is not devoid of motorized travel, however. There are several fly-in wilderness camps that would have had to be reached by other means if the area was designated a wilderness park.

The forestry industry is northwestern Ontario was concerned that the proposed wilderness park acreage, two-thirds of which would be in the northwest part of the province, would result in a severe shortage of lumber supplies. But according to environmentalists and also topographical maps of the provincial government, the Ogoki–Albany area holds mostly poor timber and thin, rocky soils that make the economics of cutting the area dubious. Great Lakes had the southern half of the proposed wilderness park under license since 1957, however, and based recent mill expansions on the premise that all the wood in the licensed area would be available for cutting. Just how much of their license was at stake is a matter of contention. The Ontario government says only 6.3 percent, the company says 13 percent.

Great Lakes' license was originally for twenty-one years and expired in 1978. The company obtained a four-year extension that expired March 1, 1982. Thus, technically, the company had no legal claim on the land, which like most forests in Canada is owned by the Crown.

Although it did not log the land during the original license, Great Lakes maintained that it needed the black spruce, which supplies strong fiber for pulp, for its future production. Chairman and President Charles Carter said the company would not run out of fiber "if there is no erosion of cutting limits through wilderness capacity." But environmentalists said Great Lakes was not dependent on this particular tract of land.

"Of the 24,000 square miles that Great Lakes has, this area has some of its poorest land," said Ron Reid, executive director, at the time, of the Federation of Ontario Naturalists (FON). "The shallow soil, rock, and northerly climate makes regeneration difficult." In addition, the amount of land lost by Great Lakes to the park would be made up by the company at other places. Great Lakes has rights to the largest licensed area in the northwest region—24,000 square miles, as well as a first claim on another 19,000 square miles formerly owned by Reed Inc. near Dryden in northwest Ontario. Great Lakes bought Reed's Dryden assets in 1979 primarily, industry analysts believed, for the land, since Reed's miserable pollution record necessitated a costly cleanup.

FON's Reid also said Great Lakes would not have to fear running short of wood if, like other forestry companies, it did not waste its existing resources. "Great Lakes specializes in black spruce and cuts around poplar and birch, whereas in northeast Ontario, forestry companies use these trees to make waferboard." Because Great Lakes is restricting its choice of woods, it is having to cut farther and farther away and truck its felled trees up to two hundred miles to its mills.

Usually, a conflict between environmentalists and corporations sees the corporation on the defensive as the environmentalists hold press conferences and issue press releases expressing their viewpoint. But the proposed Ogoki–Albany park was one of the few times a company had gone on the offensive, with

Great Lakes, despite being part of an industry-wide slump, spending thousands of dollars on a media blitz of advertising and promotional material.

Before continuing with this saga, it is necessary to point out that Great Lakes is not a dark ages company totally opposed to pollution control or protection of the environment. Its record has been quite good. Ontario Ministry of the Environment officials say there has been a "complete turnaround" at Reed's former Dryden operations, where Great Lakes' $340 million modernization program has included installing a bank of equipment to reduce air and water pollution. Great Lakes has also been a pioneer in the use of the "closed cycle" of recycling processed wastes within a plant so that only clean water is discharged into adjacent waterways, a process installed at its Thunder Bay kraft pulp mill. It used the method to partially decrease the pollutants it was dumping into the river near the plant, which were killing fish. This process was used after an attempt to discharge the material in lagoons resulted in wind-blown foam wafting towards nearby houses. While the discharge was halved, the solution was far from perfect.

Great Lakes' public relations campaign to promote its view of the proposed Ogoki–Albany park was by no means the first corporate advocacy program revolving around the restricted use of public lands. Such tactics had been used for several years, especially by oil companies in the United States. Great Lakes' effort was the first of its type in Ontario, however. The thrust of the campaign was that there should be multiple use of the forests, instead of the closing of some areas to wilderness devotees. The tone of the advertisements adroitly played on the dislike of northerners for southerners who come for a week or so to the north for a wilderness vacation, but make their living several hundred miles away while three-quarters of the northwest Ontario economy is forestry-related.

Great Lakes developed a prototypal northerner called Henry whose main leisure activity of going fishing in a motorboat was being threatened, as the following example of Great Lakes' advertisements describes:

HENRY, A SECOND CLASS CITIZEN?

Henry is a hard-working citizen who pays his taxes and wants to enjoy a few simple pleasures. He has a motorboat and likes to go fishing. So, what's wrong with that? The problem is the motorboat. Because he prefers to travel by motorboat he is banned from huge areas such as Quetico and there are those who would like to ban him from other huge tracts of forest land. It seems they want such areas reserved for canoeists and backpack campers.

We are in favor of canoeists and others who enjoy the solitude of the forest and agree that some lakes and rivers should be reserved for this sport which many of us enjoy too.

However, it is getting a little far out when some of our canoe enthusiasts want to take over such huge areas as the Whitewater Lake Candidate Wilderness Area for single purpose use.

This area also encompasses valuable timber land which we have held under licence and paid taxes on since 1957. The major expansion of our mill in recent years was based on the availability of this wood. There is no alternative area that is economically feasible for us to harvest.

We fully appreciate the needs of recreationalists and support their quest for greater enjoyment in our forest lands. But we must also remember that people like Henry and most others in Northwestern Ontario owe their livelihood directly or indirectly to the forest.

The campaign earned grudging high marks from environmentalists. "They were slick and effective in their style and presentation," says Arlin Hackman, executive director of the Algonquin Wildlands League at the time of the controversy and now with the Federation of Ontario Naturalists. "They were targeted at the working population of northern Ontario, with the language in them effectively used to divide their employees from southern elitists."

Just how much good the advertisements did Great Lakes is

debatable. They stirred up local sentiment favoring the company, but conversely, they brought public attention to the opposed environmentalists. "It did us untold amounts of good," says Bruce Hyer, a Thunder Bay wilderness outfitter and leading proponent of the proposed park. "I had been trying for five years to create interest in the park and I was finally getting publicity."

The advertisements were later followed by a company-made half-hour film, echoing the same themes and shown on Thunder Bay television in prime time bought by Great Lakes. Although at the beginning of the program a statement said it had been paid for by Great Lakes, viewers who did not pay close attention could have been confused. The commentator in the program was also the television station's commentator, and his questions to Great Lakes' executives were slanted towards the company's viewpoint.

Off and on throughout their war of words, the environmentalists and Great Lakes' executives met to express their opposing views. Hyer and Hackman said they found the extroverted, jovial Carter more open-minded than his junior executives. Still, no compromise was ever reached.

Finding a compromise was left up to the Ontario government, which in June 1983 designated only one-third of the area sought by the environmentalists as a park and gave the rest to Great Lakes to log. Moreover, the power of commerce won out even further over the attraction of tranquillity since the new park (called Wabakimi Waterway Park after another major lake in the region) has been left open by the government to mining and commercial tourism, although not to logging. Motorboats are also allowed, so poor Henry has not been deprived at all.

· 13 ·

Rivals and Buddies

On Friday, February 26, 1982, Canadian Pacific and Canadian National called a press conference at the second-floor Governor-General's suite in the Hotel Westin in Toronto. There, over coffee, tea, and muffins, the rival companies announced a new joint venture, called Telecommunications Terminal Systems, to sell telephone equipment and systems to business and government, with the goal of reaching $50 million in sales by 1987.

The establishment of Telecommunications Terminal Systems was the latest hand-in-hand move by CN and CP, which over the years have established a relationship that oscillates between rivalry and friendship, if a cosy business arrangement is in their interests. Previous joint ventures include CNCP Telecommunications, which evolved from a jointly built transmission network and integrated sales force in the 1960s to a formal partnership in 1981.

But telecommunications is not the only area where their interests coincide. In the 1960s, they proposed replacing their railway tracks in downtown Toronto with a $1 billion redevelopment project called Metro Centre. That project died, following stiff opposition from civic action groups, but a son of Metro Centre, somewhat bigger in scale, was proposed in 1982 by the two companies and is under consideration by municipal officials.

The close relationship between CN, Canada's second largest federal Crown corporation in terms of assets (after Petro Canada), and CP, the country's largest private enterprise, is founded on similarities of outlook and approach. Both advanced similar arguments calling for the lifting of the Crow's Nest Pass rate. Both enthusiastically dropped rail passenger service. Shippers find them equally hard-nosed. CN also paid CP the compliment of basing its divisional profit center organizational structure on CP's model.

The harmony between the companies only goes so far, however. Before Frederick Burbidge became president of CP and Robert Bandeen of CN, they met for lunch once or twice a month at Montreal's St. James's Club, an exclusive men's club. "We used to discuss the potential benefits of standardizing CN and CP rail equipment, which differ slightly in length and width, but our respective mechanical departments were against it because they did not want to do what the opposition was doing," Bandeen says.

The two rival companies continue to bicker and compete over other areas of business. In the 1970s, CN and CP briefly flirted with jointly owning a time and management computer services company, but Bandeen says the venture was a "disaster."

Until 1980, CN and CP jointly owned the 925-mile Northern Alberta Railways Company. That year, CP sold its 50 percent interest to CN for an undisclosed sum. According to CP's 1979 annual report, its investment, at cost, in Northern Alberta Railways was $23.3 million. "We could never agree on how to operate it," Bandeen says. According to him, joint ownership resulted in unnecessary expenses that single ownership would have eliminated through consolidation of the operations into that firm's existing large rail network. "The annual administrative costs were $3 million because it had its own management, office building, and repair shops. When two firms own something jointly, each looks for its own selfish advantage and this does not produce the best results."

But while the Northern Alberta Railways partnership dissolved, CN and CP are still jointly involved in two other rail ventures. They jointly own the Toronto Terminals Railway Company, which operates Toronto's Union Station, as well as the Detroit River Tunnel, purchased in 1982 for about $25 million, along with 274 miles of track in southern Ontario, from Consolidated Rail Corporation (Conrail) of Philadelphia. The tunnel gives them a major gateway to the midwestern United

States, linking CP to its midwest railroad, the Soo Line, and CN to its midwest line, the Grand Trunk Corporation.

When it will help their profitability, both companies are ready to cooperate. But if the bottom line will be hurt, they are just as ready to fight. One such instance occurred in November 1980 when CN told CP that it intended to cancel a fifty-year-old arrangement allowing special interswitching rates on CN's tracks in Montreal East. Oddly, although the legal department at CN and CP are among the largest in Canada, neither company could find a written basis for the agreement in their files; nor were there any legal documents or letters at the Canadian Transport Commission or in the public records.

Interswitching arrangements enable one railway company, without tracks in an area, to use the tracks of another railway as if they were its own and thereby charge similar rates. Such arrangements are usually limited to just four miles, but the long-standing agreement between CN and CP stretched out much farther to include the Montreal East refineries of such major oil companies as Imperial Oil, Gulf Canada, Shell Canada, and Texaco Canada, as well as major chemical producers like Union Carbide. This meant CP was able to do business in and out of this lucrative area as if it had been a point on its own line.

Even though CN did more business in Montreal East, it fretted that the arrangement was giving potential CN business to CP on a silver platter and announced the cancellation. What CN did not take into account was the furor canceling the agreement would cause at the shipping departments of the oil companies. With Montreal East no longer being a competitive rail point, they feared they would either become captives of CN or have to pay rates perhaps four times as high to continue shipping with CP. If, as an alternative, CP picked up the extra charge in order not to lose its shippers, it would have had to pay $6 million annually to CN.

CP, backed up by the irate shippers, applied to the Railway Transport Committee, a division of the Canadian Transport Commission, to get CN to rescind its cancellation. In a January 2, 1981 ruling, the committee said it would not hold a hearing on the matter because "at most, the shippers will lose a previously and existing competitive choice between carriers." However, the committee said it would re-examine the situation "if this loss of choice should mean some financial or service prejudice to a shipper in the future." Although the committee decided not to interfere, the continued protests of the shippers forced CN to restore the original agreement.

The main area of cooperation between CN and CP is the telecommunications industry, self-described as "the last remaining growth sector," in which each claims to be the pioneer in Canada. CN says it was in the field first because it bought the Montreal Telegraph Company, which in December 1846 sent the first telegram in Canada. CP says it was first since it predated CN by several decades in creating a telegraph division in 1886, nearly forty years before CN became a Crown corporation.

As early as 1931, CN and CP discussed merging their telecommunications operations, but did not begin doing so until the 1950s. In 1956, the two firms jointly introduced Telex, still their bread and butter, and in 1962, they jointly built a cross-Canada microwave network for telecommunications. Then in 1965, they integrated their sales forces, under the name CNCP Telecommunications, but still retained separate headquarters, with CN Telecommunications in Toronto and CP Telecommunications in Montreal.

Working for two masters could have been difficult for sales manager Jim McDaniel. Instead, he often played the two firms against each other to get what he wanted. "My favorite dodge was to tell CP I needed $50,000 for the sales department and that CN had already agreed and then phone CN and say CP had already given its approval," he says. It was this talent to persuade both firms that eventually led McDaniel, as sales manager for both CN Telecommunications and CP Telecommunications, to become their advertising spokesman until his retirement in 1983. "I used to tell CNT's and CPT's advertising managers and their separate advertising agencies about our new products and one day the CNT manager suggested I do the commercials." McDaniel soon developed a trademark with his crew-cut hair. "I let it grow in once at the suggestion of my wife's barber, but when people stopped me in the street to complain, I got it cut."

But while CN Telecommunications and CP Telecommunications cooperated on the sales front, there was friction behind the scenes that was harmful to aggressive innovation and marketing. The time-consuming process of getting clearance at both firms for new products blunted CNCP's competitive edge in a field where speed is essential to stay ahead of rivals. For example, CN and CP were ready to introduce "Infoswitch," a nationwide computer-controlled digital data switching network, in 1971, but this was delayed until 1975. It took those four years to get the go-ahead from both firms.

A similar serious delay occurred with the introduction of "Infotex," which allows word processors made by different firms to "talk" to each other. Its go-ahead was delayed from 1977 until 1979 because of the double mountain of red tape that had to be surmounted. It was finally introduced commercially in 1982. "If something was started at CPT, CNT would look at it negatively and vice versa," says Oskar Stubits, manager, technical services planning, at CNCP. "It was often harder selling the idea within the two organizations than outside. Costs were also double what they had to be because both firms' engineering departments would work separately on the same item."

Another incentive towards a complete merger was the prospect of better financial results. In the early 1970s, when both CP and CN reorganized their companies by profit centers, they were able to get a clear picture of their winners and losers. They found their telecommunications business was dropping as the telephone companies eroded the market through encouraging the public to make more long-distance calls. Consequently, they applied to the Canadian Radio-Television and Telecommunications Commission (CRTC) for permission to merge, and the CRTC, which favored increased competition to the monopolistic telephone companies, gave its approval in January 1981.

Despite the merger, CNCP is still a small player in the telecommunications business. It is estimated to have 35 percent of the 13 percent of the Canadian telecommunications industry that is not the monopoly of the telephone companies. Canada has nine major telephone companies of which the largest is Bell Canada, operating in Ontario, Quebec, and the Northwest Territories for a 60 percent share of the total market. In most of the other provinces, the telephone system is owned by the government. CN also owns two telephone companies—NorthwesTel, serving northern British Columbia, the Yukon, and part of the Northwest Territories, and Terra Nova Telecommunications, serving rural Newfoundland. CP does not own any telephone companies.

Although CNCP was originally in the business of sending telegrams, that operation is being phased out, with night telegrams now ended. Where CNCP sees its potential is in data communications, already close to a $1 billion business in Canada and growing at a healthy rate of 15 to 16 percent annually. Data communications is making possible the paperless "office of the future" in which repetitive tasks such as maintaining mailing lists and voluminous work such as filing will be replaced by storage and retrieval on a computer system, with individual worker terminals.

CNCP's merger gives it the muscle to be a strong competitor in this field. The problem, from CNCP's viewpoint, is selling the whizbang technology to managers and clerical workers whose jobs will be changed or eliminated as a result.

"Factories willingly spend more than $50,000 on equipment, such as trucks and forklifts for blue-collar workers, but will not spend more than a few thousand dollars on secretaries and managers for typewriters, calculators, and telephones," says Oskar Stubits. "The problem is that cost justification is easier with new plant equipment because a forklift truck replaces the cost of paying several workers to stack boxes. By contrast, it can't be proved that without office automation equipment such as word processors, sales volume would be less. Also, managers are concerned about their potential loss in status if they start to do what were formerly regarded as clerical functions."

CN and CP realized their merger would quickly poise them to be a major participant in the data communications market, but they first had to go through the painful process of integrating their telecommunications management. Because CN had the larger organization, it was decided to use its Toronto headquarters rather than CP's in Montreal. John Sutherland, formerly vice-president, telecommunications, at CP, was selected as president of CNCP. The president of CN Telecommunications remained with CN to look after its two telephone companies. There is a nine-man board of directors, with four each from CN and CP, plus Sutherland. The board's chairmanship rotates every two years between CN's and CP's presidents.

Sutherland, who was sixty in August 1983, brought a wealth of experience to his job. A native of Winnipeg, like many other CP executives, he worked at RCA, including a three-year stint as president of RCA Iran Ltd., which hired RCA to install broadcasting and military communications equipment. In 1974, he joined CP Telecommunications as its general manager. On his neatly organized office desk, he has an executive yo-yo and a decision maker that suggests to its user "yes, no, maybe, or pass the buck."

One of the biggest problems for Sutherland was deciding how much each firm would contribute financially to the partnership. "CP and CN had different practices regarding what they capitalized and the rate at which they depreciated plant, partly because CP had been a tax-paying corporation and therefore had different accounting practices, in order to avoid taxes, than CN," Sutherland says.

CP and CN consequently turned to the management consultant firm of Peat, Marwick & Co. to evaluate the difference between the value of the assets of the two companies. Peat Marwick's six-month study found that CP's telecommunications assets were worth $42 million less than CN's. To equalize the situation, under the merger terms CP Telecommunications agreed to make up the differential by paying for the partnership's first $42 million worth of new assets. This was done by 1981, and subsequent purchases have been made jointly.

The new organization spent eighteen months setting up an accounting system. "It was a nightmare because each firm charged up things differently," Sutherland says. Finally, he decided to set up an entirely new system rather than mesh CP's and CN's systems. A separate pension plan was also started.

Besides finances, Sutherland had to ascertain how much autonomy he would have since CN and CP differed in how much authority they gave subsidiaries. CN, as a Crown corporation, had to meet certain rules that CP did not. Ironing out the differences took half a year. "Each firm's guidelines were outdated as to the level of expenditures they could approve on their own," Sutherland says. "The ceiling of $25,000 had been established when a dollar was worth a dollar but by 1981, due to inflation, this was too low." Sutherland succeeded in getting CN and CP to allow him to sign contracts of up to $500,000.

In addition to carving out his authority, Sutherland had the task of building up an *esprit de corps* among the merged company's 4,200 employees. Since only 800 are at head office in Toronto, Sutherland traveled across Canada, holding daytime meetings with managers and evening question and answer sessions with employees and their spouses.

With CNCP's structural framework in place, Sutherland started to develop a "road map for the next five to ten years" for the company, with the introduction in May 1981 of what he calls the "blue book." It covers CNCP's strengths and weaknesses and where the company wants to be by 1986. Each company function, such as marketing and engineering, was involved in this analysis. In addition, employee relations, training, and promotion programs were appraised. The company is not looking just within its own ranks, but has also hired executive recruitment firms to raid its chief competitor, Bell Canada, for top talent. Such headhunting is common in the fast growing telecommunications industry.

To outsiders, there is a certain irony to the claims of CNCP, jointly owned by a mammoth Crown corporation and a giant private enterprise, about the problems of competing with the big telephone companies. CNCP executives, however, are deadly serious in casting themselves as David versus the Goliath of Ma Bell. "The telephone companies use their monopolistic power to cross-subsidize their different services and engage in predatory pricing," Sutherland says. "It makes our lives difficult." Difficult, but not impossible. Indeed, with the help of federal government rulings, it has become less difficult for CNCP. Its existence and position as a national telecommunications carrier has been given several major boosts by the government, with each chipping away at Bell's monopoly.

In 1953, the government allowed CNCP to build a separate regional microwave system to compete with Bell Canada. Then, in 1962, the government approved construction by CNCP of a national microwave system in competition with Trans Canada

Telephone, an unincorporated association of Bell Canada, eight other telephone companies (apart from those owned by CN), and Telesat Canada for nationwide long-distance operations. This did not have much of a negative impact on the phone companies. In 1978, CNCP employed 4,460 people and had revenues of $188 million. By contrast, that year Bell Canada alone employed 53,328 people and had revenue of $3 billion. According to a 1978 CRTC study:

The Trans Canada Telephone System's monopoly in basic telephone service resulted in the development of a local distribution network that gave them a significant advantage over CNCP in the provision of business services. All the services of the telephone companies are accessible to their customers as quickly and easily as dialing an ordinary telephone call. CNCP customers, on the other hand, must access CNCP services through separate individual circuits, leased from the telephone company at considerably higher cost.

For more than ten years CNCP negotiated unsuccessfully to interconnect its telecommunications network with those of the telephone companies for the business market only. This would enable CNCP to provide such business services as data communications, intercity private lines, and transmission of teleprinter messages and facsimiles on an equal basis with the phone companies. The failure of its negotiations prompted CP Telecommunications to file an application in June 1976 with the CRTC to require Bell Canada to interconnect CP's telecommunications network with its own in Ontario and Quebec. CN Telecommunications joined CP Telecommunications as a coapplicant in October 1977 at the request of Bell Canada. Their application only pertained to the provision of business services, not the public telephone market.

CP Telecommunications' application followed three years of legal preparations headed by one of CP's ace lawyers, C.R.O. (Bob) Munro. Munro was a former federal deputy minister of justice, a job also held by Donald Maxwell, CP's present vice-president of law, before he joined CP. CNCP also had its own four-person legal team. In addition to the legal brains trust, CN and CP were fortunate in having the support of more than forty user groups opposed to Bell's monopoly. In opposition, Bell mustered a long list of witnesses and leased 15,000 square feet of office space in Ottawa in which to prepare its case.

CP's, CN's, and CNCP's legal groundwork paid off when the CRTC, in what was hailed by the telecommunications industry as a landmark decision, ruled on May 17, 1979, that CNCP could interconnect with Bell Canada's network. A subsequent petition by Trans Canada Telephone System to the federal Cabinet to overturn the CRTC's decision was rejected on June 15, 1979.

The May 17, 1979 decision was celebrated "with considerable mirth" at the suite in the Hotel de la Chaudière in Hull, which CNCP had obtained in advance "in anticipation of the triumph of justice," says Joseph Schmidt, CNCP's vice-president of regulatory and government matters. "We exchanged congratulations and lifted more than one glass in celebration."

However, because of the fragmented jurisdiction over telecommunications in Canada, the victory over Bell Canada was just part of a series of legal battles by CNCP. The CRTC only regulates five telephone companies—Bell Canada, British Columbia Telephone Co., Terra Nova Tel in Newfoundland, and NorthwesTel in the Northwest Territories, as well as CNCP. In November 1981, the CRTC extended its 1979 Bell Canada decision to cover B.C. Telephone, but the other telephone companies are under regional jurisdiction. CNCP has begun individual lawsuits, starting with Alberta. "The divided jurisdiction gives rise to inconsistent political decisions and unpredictable supply patterns," Schmidt says. "It will have to be a province by province trench fight because the outcome in one province is not regarded as a precedent by another province."

In dollar terms, Schmidt says CNCP's interconnect victory brought it only about $10 million in new business in 1982. That did little harm to Bell Canada, since it amounted to less than 1 percent of Bell Canada's total revenue. According to an October 1982 survey by the Canadian Industrial Communications Assembly, an association of 190 business telecommunications users, only three of the sixty-three respondents used CNCP's interconnect services, and all three also used Bell Canada facilities. In addition, the survey found that the association's members thought Bell's interconnect services provided greater value, especially in maintenance and in making changes or additions. CNCP acknowledged its difficulty in wooing customers away from Bell Canada by applying to the CRTC in late 1982 for permission to charge rates 15 percent lower than those of Bell Canada.

Sometimes, CNCP has beat Bell Canada in innovation. Its "Infotex" network, enabling the transmission of documents, business letters, and sales reports around the world in seconds through "communicating" word processors, was introduced in March 1982, months before Bell's competitive "Teletex." In October 1982, CNCP again scooped the telephone companies by introducing a system that reduced certain types of business long-distance charges by as much as 35 percent. Trans Canada Telephone System did not introduce its system until 1983.

Not only was CNCP first with this technology, but it could lead eventually to its providing a competitive public long-distance service to Trans Canada Telephone System. This is already done in the United States with such firms as ITT, Southern Pacific Communications Co., and Microwave Communications providing long-distance service in competition with American Telephone and Telegraph (AT&T). If this were proposed in Canada, TCTS companies, which rely on long-distance calls to cross subsidize local service, would raise a storm. However, if such action were approved by the government, the public could expect lower, competitive rates. The financial damage might not be that great to Bell Canada. AT&T has, indeed, lost hundreds of millions of dollars worth of long-distance business, but it still amounts to only 1 to 2 percent of its total revenue.

Getting a head start with new "office of the future" technology like Infotex should help CNCP gain customers in the data communications end of the telecommunications business, which is now dominated by the phone companies with an estimated 80 percent market share. At the same time, CNCP has a 90 percent market share of the electronic messaging market with "Telex," for which it has fifty-thousand subscribers. Although Infotex would cut into the Telex market somewhat, Telex is expected to remain a cash cow for CNCP because of its appeal to small businesses.

Both CNCP and Bell Canada face competition not only from one another, but also from a long list of other companies. The potential competitors include the cable television companies, which already have many subscribers, IBM, which is co-owner of a national satellite service, and large banks and corporations that could build their own cheaper private networks. Even oil and gas companies are acquiring office technology firms.

However, Bell Canada has several advantages over CNCP and other rivals. Bell does its own research and development through one subsidiary, Bell-Northern Research, and much of its technology is acquired from another subsidiary, Northern Telecom Ltd. In addition, Bell, as Northern Telecom's largest shareholder, partakes in its profits. Because it is smaller, CNCP does less research and development than Bell, and its equipment is made by outside manufacturers. "We are not in the hardware business," Sutherland says.

One year after they linked forces officially through CNCP Telecommunications to become a major player in the booming data communications market, CN and CP joined together again to enter the similarly buoyant telephone interconnect equipment market by establishing Telecommunications Terminal Systems. The term "interconnect" means that telephone company subscribers can buy their own equipment, ranging from one phone to a company switchboard, and connect it to the telephone company's network for voice as well as data communication. However, again this only applies to the phone companies under the jurisdiction of the CRTC, which first permitted interconnect for Bell Canada's subscribers in August 1980 and subsequently extended its ruling to all the telephone companies under its authority.

The ruling touched off a bonanza. Over one hundred and fifty interconnect companies cropped up, including Bell Communications Systems Inc., a division of Bell Canada, established in 1981. Business reached $500 million by 1982 and is expected to climb to $1 billion by 1986. This sparked CN's and CP's interest and led to their partnership in Telecommunications Terminal Systems, which is a separate arrangement from CNCP Telecommunications. Telecommunications Terminal Systems is selling and renting telephone equipment and systems, made by outside suppliers, including Northern Telecom, whereas CNCP transmits information through an electronic network system. TTS is a national system, giving it a potential competitive edge over Bell Communications Systems Inc., which operates only in Bell Canada's territory of Ontario and Quebec.

Although Telecommunications Terminal Systems is jointly owned by CN and CP, CN claims credit for the idea. CN's ex-president, Robert Bandeen, says CN executives wanted to make TTS a CN business, but that he overruled them, saying CN could not be partners with CP in one telecommunications area and not in others. Still, the February 1982 press conference at the Westin Hotel made it clear that CN was first among equals.

The press conference was conducted by Charles Armstrong, then president of CN Holdings, the non-transportation arm of CN. At his side, sitting silently throughout the proceedings, was Ronald Riley, corporate vice-president at CP, who was made a director of Telecommunications Terminal Systems. In its early stages Douglas Campbell, general manager of all CN communications equipment, including its investment in CNCP, served the new firm as a part-time president. The chairmanship will rotate between CN and CP, starting with CN's Armstrong.

TTS also raided other high-technology firms for its initial senior management. General Manager Glenn Myers, was previously president of Datapoint Canada, a supplier of office switchboard equipment. National Sales Manager Michael Cannata was recruited from Xerox Canada, and National Operations Manager David Rae was previously in Bell Canada's service installation and maintenance division.

The creation of Telecommunications Terminal Systems and Bell Communications Systems Inc. has concerned rival interconnect firms who fear they could be locked out of the market because of the ties between TTS and BCSI as suppliers of equipment and CNCP and Bell Canada as transmitters of messages sent over that equipment. However, so far the government appears satisfied that TTS and BCSI have been at arm's length from their related companies.

In addition to telecommunications, CN's and CP's other big joint effort was their proposed massive $1 billion Metro Centre on the railway tracks in downtown Toronto, which, when it was suggested in 1968, would have been the biggest redevelopment project in North America.

By the time the project fizzled in 1974, it had CN and CP angry at each other, their hired outside planner angry at them, citizens' groups upset with the planner, and CN, CP, municipal government officials, and the city of Toronto's legal, planning, and development departments angry at one another. Instead of "catching the imagination and enthusiasm, not only of Torontonians, but of all Canadians interested in solutions to the urgent problems of housing, transportation, and urban renewal," as CP's then chairman, Norris Crump, predicted, Metro Centre came to be a symbol for the anti-development movement rolling across Canada.

The proposed 187-acre Metro Centre site was submarine shaped, running from Front Street on the north to the Gardiner Expressway on the south, and from Yonge Street on the east to Bathurst Street on the west. Jutting north from the main site were two blocks between Simcoe and John Streets, running between Front and King, which were also included. The railways did not actually own all the land involved. Most of it is owned by the Toronto Harbor Commission, which leases it to CN and CP. CP's owned and leased lands are in the eastern end of this parcel of land, while CN's are to the west towards Spadina Avenue. The proposed site included Union Station, which is jointly owned by CN and CP on land leased from the owner, the city of Toronto.

Metro Centre would have created a city within a city. In land size, it was equivalent to the existing downtown core of Toronto. It would have had twenty thousand housing residents and fifty thousand people working in the office buildings. As Jeremy Carver, a cancer researcher at the University of Toronto and a member of the Confederation of Resident and Ratepayers Associations (CORRA), which was opposed to the Centre, wrote in a newsletter at the time: "Having 70,000 people living and working in Metro Centre would be like placing Peterborough, Ontario between the rest of Toronto and the waterfront." The density would have been among the highest in the city, at three hundred and fifty people per acre. By comparison, the density in the luxurious Rosedale district of the city is twenty-seven people per acre.

In appearance, with its tall office and apartment buildings, Metro Centre would have dramatically changed Toronto's waterfront. Metro Centre had four main features: residential, commercial (office towers, stores, theaters, restaurants), communications center (offices and a transmission tower for the Canadian Broadcasting Corporation), and a new transportation terminal. The plans called for the demolition of Union Station, regarded by Torontonians as an architectural landmark, as part of a proposed relocation southward of the rail corridor. A new transportation terminal would have been built to the south of Union Station. The terminal would have been a hub for intercity and commuter rail traffic and would have also served as an inter-city bus depot. In addition, it would have contained a hotel, convention center, and trade mart.

The feasibility study for the Centre was done by Stewart ("Bud") Andrews, a Toronto planner whose firm, Community Development Consultants Ltd., had previously done studies for Habitat in Montreal and Flemingdon Park, an apartment-retail complex in northeast Toronto. The architect was John Andrews (no relation to Stewart), then a rising talent and later a leading Canadian designer. Bud Andrews asked John Andrews why he thought he was good enough to design Metro Centre and hired him when John Andrews, in turn, asked why he should take the job.

While Bud Andrews was the spokesman for the project, behind the scenes he was engaged in a power struggle with executives of Marathon Realty Co., CP's real estate arm, which had been formed just a few years earlier in 1963 and wanted to prove itself. Andrews mainly clashed with Stuart Eagles, then assistant general manager of Marathon. "He would tell me one thing and then do another," Andrews says. "He never wanted to be wrong, so he wouldn't commit himself to anything."

In addition, the alliance between CN and CP was an uneasy one. "You couldn't get two more competitive groups," Andrews says. "They were always making a big effort to upstage each other."

The proposed Centre quickly attracted a storm of criticism.

The long list of complaints included the lack of public involvement and consultation; the proposed demolition of Union Station; the strain that would be placed on the already overloaded Union Station subway stop; the long walking distance between the proposed transportation terminal and the subway station; the traffic and parking problems that the large number of occupants would create; the upper-price emphasis for the housing; the lack of schools; the barrier the project would create between existing downtown Toronto and the waterfront; and the project's style. As one opponent of the design said at a March 30, 1971 citizens' forum on the Centre: "Nobody else is going to want to use the place except the people who are there. And they're only going to want to get out again."

In addition to their dislike of the project, the Confederation of Resident and Ratepayers Associations (CORRA) came to mistrust Andrews, which made dialogue between them extremely difficult. "You could never trust a word Andrews said," Jeremy Carver says. "He was playing out two scenarios. One was the real exercise of negotiations with supporters on City Council and the other was his pretending to be open and willing to provide information in public. But when he was pressed for an answer in public, he would be evasive." Andrews counters that "never in the history of development had there been as much consultation with the public. I virtually lived in public forums."

In 1972 the proposal for the Centre went to the Ontario Municipal Board for consideration. Both Metro Centre and CORRA pulled out their top legal guns. Richard Rohmer, who has since become a best-selling fiction writer, represented Metro Centre. Ian Binnie, now with the federal Department of Justice, volunteered to represent CORRA. The two lawyers engaged in some pre-hearing jousting. On March 27, 1972, Rohmer wrote Binnie a list of nitpicking questions about CORRA, the queries including a request for a list of its members, where they lived, when their meetings about Metro Centre were held, and what the results were. Rohmer also asked for copies of related documents and minutes. The following day Binnie tartly replied that Rohmer's questions were "irrelevant" and that, therefore, he was not supplying the information.

Following the Ontario Municipal Board's approval of the

Centre, despite the reservations of Chairman J.A. Kennedy, civic action groups intensified their opposition through newsletters and public forums. The city's technical planning committee also criticized the isolated character of the development, resulting in the establishment of a working group, made up of various city department commissioners and the city's chief planner, to make recommendations on how to improve the Centre. The working group's report, made on November 4, 1974, said that Union Station should be retained, low income housing provided, and that Metro Centre, the downtown core, and the waterfront should not be isolated from one another. These suggestions were accepted by municipal government officials and it seemed the Centre would be built despite public protests.

Yet, on January 1, 1975, the project was halted. It was not defeated by civic action groups, but by the passage of time. During the six years of debate over the Centre, the real estate market had changed, with new downtown office towers making it unlikely that Metro Centre would get enough business tenants. All that remained of the grand design was the $5 million in architectural, consulting, and legal fees that CN and CP had to pay, the CN Tower, and a large residue of bitterness among some of the key participants, especially Andrews. "The main lesson I learned was never to get caught between two giants again," he says. "It was impossible for them to work naturally together on a real estate development."

The tower was originally to be jointly financed by CN and CP, but after Metro Centre was shelved, CP withdrew its funds and CN proceeded on its own. The needle shape was the second design selected for the tower. The first design called for three tubular columns at different heights, sculpted together with artistic joints, and a circular pod at the top. The design was killed when CP Chairman Norris Crump and CN Chairman Norman MacMillan viewed the four-foot model. "Crump puffed on his long cigar and said to MacMillan, 'Norman, I don't like it. Do you?' and MacMillan answered, 'I don't like it either' and that was the end of that," recalls Robert Bandeen, then a financial executive assigned to the project and a supporter of the design.

But while Metro Centre was shelved, it was not forgotten. In

1982, the idea was floated again by CN and Marathon, with construction slated to begin in 1984. Inflation had pushed the price tag from $1 billion to $2 billion, but the basic features of housing for twenty thousand people and several office towers were retained. However, the companies learned from their mistakes. There is now no proposal to demolish Union Station and there is greater emphasis on scaling the development to its surroundings and providing parkland. In addition, CN and Marathon have separate design teams for their portions of the project, rather than the joint management used for Metro Centre.

"Metro Centre was too big and assumed far too much change in relation to what existed," says Kenneth Greenberg, a city of Toronto urban designer dealing with the railway lands. "It treated a large area of the city as if it were a building. This new project accepts more of what exists and is a much more traditional and modest way of development, because it is being done in manageable bite-size pieces."

Although CN is publicly owned and CP is a private enterprise, the top executives at each company could probably be easily interchanged. They would be at home in each other's place because both companies are profit-center oriented, in many of the same types of businesses, and willing to join forces if it is of benefit to them.

· 14 ·

A For Sales, B Minus
For Profits

When it comes to talking about profit, Ian Sinclair, William Stinson, and their speechwriters, have a common idol. In 1980, Sinclair told a conference: "The first corporate obligation is to earn a profit. As Sir Winston Churchill once observed, 'It is a socialist idea that making profits is a vice. I consider the real vice is making losses.' I certainly agree with that."

A year later, Stinson, during a speech in Toronto, said: "The first responsibility of any business to the community is making a profit. As Sir Winston Churchill said: 'It is a socialist idea that making profits is a vice. I consider the real vice is making losses.'" So much for originality in speech writing at CP.

CP does live up to its "corporate obligation" of making a profit. But just because CP is Canada's largest company in terms of revenue does not mean that it has the best overall financial report card in either good times or bad.

In September 1982, *Fortune* magazine asked six thousand executives, corporate directors, and financial analysts to give their perceptions of the 1981 financial and corporate behavior reputations of the two thousand largest companies in the United States. The survey found that the most admired firms had the best profit margins (net income as a percentage of revenue), price-earnings multiples (the share price as a multiple of the earnings per share), and return on shareholders' equity (net income as a percentage of equity). CP's performance in each of these areas was considerably below the median of the ten U.S. firms ranked at the top of the survey, which included IBM, General Electric, and Eastman Kodak. CP's profit margin in

1981 was 3.9 percent of sales (versus the median of 10.7 percent among the top ten U.S. companies), its return on shareholders' equity, 12.4 percent (versus 18.2 percent), and its price-earnings multiple, 8.2 percent (versus 12 percent).

Measured by such indicators of corporate performance, CP also ranks well behind diversified American transportation companies and many Canadian and American conglomerates. While CSX in the United States and Molson's and Imasco in Canada had little change between 1981 and 1982 in profit margins, return on investment (net income as a percentage of assets), and return on shareholders' equity, CP and CPE saw their comparative performance more than halved. CP and CPE did do better, however, than such non-transportation conglomerates as Genstar Corporation and Jannock Ltd., which dropped from strong profits in 1981 to substantial losses in 1982.

On the transportation side, CP could argue that its financial performance was handicapped by the artificially low Crow's Nest Pass rate for shipping grain while the American railroads have been able to charge full rates. CN suffered the same handicap, yet did better in return on investment than CP in 1981. In addition, CP has diversified far more than the American railroads and is, therefore, less reliant on its rail operations for its profitability. Nevertheless, it has a transcontinental system, while there are no cross-country systems in the United States (although this could change if two large lines there—Norfolk Southern and the Atchison, Topeka and Santa Fe—merge, as predicted). CSX, Burlington Northern and Union Pacific only go partway across the United States, although they cover longer distances than CP—all run more than twenty thousand miles, whereas CP covers close to seventeen thousand miles.

On a sector by sector basis outside of rail, CP's subsidiaries sometimes outpace, sometimes are average, and sometimes are below average in profit margins for their respective industries. The winners include PanCanadian Petroleum and Great Lakes Forest Products. Cominco usually does better than most minerals companies, but is outdistanced by Teck Corporation and Rio Algom Ltd. Maple Leaf Mills fares less well than General Foods. CP Air does worse than Air Canada and sometimes better, sometimes worse, than Wardair.

Overall, while CP was buffeted by the 1982 economic slump, it was not battered as badly as such other long-established industrial giants as Massey-Ferguson and Inco, or as many of Canada's leading real estate companies were. Despite CPE's rating being lowered in 1982 by Moody's Investor Services (a major U.S. bond rating service), and CP reducing its dividends that year, the share prices of both companies remained steady following both moves. And, while CP's return on investment and profit margin trail those of its American diversified transportation counterparts, the company has often kept pace with the world's best-known conglomerate, International Telephone and Telegraph, in these areas.*

It could be argued that using data from the recessionary years alone casts an overly dim light on CP's performance. But disappointing indicators are not a recent phenomenon. In fact, over the last decade, investors would have made more on their money by investing it in guaranteed investment certificates, rather than CP shares whose dividend yield (the dividend as a percentage of the market price) declined from 4.5 percent in 1970, on the high price of the shares, to 3.3 percent in 1982. In addition, the 1982 high price of the shares of $41^7/8$ was $30 below the value in 1971 before a 5-for-1 split that year. And while not declining, the share price of CPE, which because it is not in transportation and thus is not subject to the same government regulations as CP, has remained relatively unchanged since it was listed in 1973. In 1982, the range was $19^3/8$–$12^7/8$, compared with $16^3/4$–$15 in 1973. Its dividend yield has gone from 3.5 percent in 1973 to 4.1 percent in 1982.

In view of this record, the question arises as to why investing in CP is so widespread among Canadians. The incentive appears to be CP's financing methods, which place a heavy emphasis on long-term debentures, collateral trust bonds (bonds secured by collateral, such as other securities), and equipment trust certificates (a type of security issued to pay for new equipment). When such securities are issued, they offer a then good rate of interest.

---

*See Appendix, Table 6.

But they tend to attract only cautious investors because the interest rate offered could turn out to be lower than the rates available on savings accounts or guaranteed investment certificates during the fifteen- to twenty-year life span of the CP issues. The conservative investor, however, is assured of a steady income and CP keeps down its financing costs.

Another attraction is the company's involvement in most economic sectors, which makes it an easy, one-step investment for shareholders looking to cash in on an overall economic recovery. Thus, in the week following CPE's announcement that its 1982 profit declined by $255 million from 1981, its share price remained unchanged, and despite CP's 1982 profit dropping by $297 million from 1981, its share price also stayed stable following the news.

CP and CPE have been turning more in recent years to new share issues both in Canada and through listings on the New York, London, and Amsterdam stock exchanges, which provide access to the international money market.

CP finances its acquisitions from corporate cash flow, the issuance of long-term debt through debentures, and on a term loan basis. Although large subsidiaries, such as Cominco and PanCanadian, are mostly self-financing, other subsidiaries require either guarantees of their debt or long-term financing through debentures or loans from Canadian Pacific Securities Ltd., CP's financing arm. CP Securities' debt, in turn, is guaranteed by CP. This source of financing also helps subsidiaries that otherwise could not raise money because poor market conditions in their industry make lenders reluctant to provide funds.

One of CP's biggest albatrosses is its involvement in industries that require both initial heavy capital expenditures and, later, high modernization bills. Companies usually plan such new developments to come on stream when they expect demand to be at a peak. Unfortunately for CP and crystal ball gazers at other corporations, the economy did not cooperate with their latest round of spending. So they are stuck with equipment capable of greater output at a time when markets are soft and inventories high.

CP has laid out a bundle in capital expenditures in recent years and it is committed to even heavier spending during the rest of this decade. The $7.6 billion (1982 dollars) CP plans to spend on railway improvements alone during the coming years is equivalent of what all its operations spent on capital expenditures between 1975 and 1981. Some of that spending set records at various subsidiaries. For example, Algoma Steel spent $264.7 million on upgrading its facilities in 1981, the highest amount it had laid out in a single year in a decade and as much as its combined expenditures in the previous four years.

Even though markets are weak, stopping the expenditures would leave the companies with outdated machinery. All they can do is slow down their spending and pray that when the work is completed, the economy will have recovered.

At the same time as it is coping with the dampening impact of its heavy capital spending spree, CP is also being squeezed by having gobbled up so many acquisitions during the same period of time. Between 1978 and 1982, CP and its subsidiaries spent more than $1.6 billion on takeovers, some of which were less tasty morsels than Great Lakes Forest Products and Algoma Steel, whose net incomes tripled and quintupled, respectively, between 1974, when they were bought, and 1981, prior to the depths of the recession. The least tasty of all was the $1.1 billion purchase of CIP—CP's biggest acquisition ever—with its 1982 loss of $101.8 million.

With the recent concentration on acquisitions of American companies and the extensive sales of its forest products to the United States, CP's revenues have been boosted by the conversion of its U.S. revenue into Canadian dollars. However, with markets soft, sales have not been as high as CP might have expected, and consequently, it has not benefited to the fullest from the conversion rate. Also, Great Lakes Forest Products was too cautious in 1981 when it entered into contracts through 1984 at rates of $1 U.S. to $1.18 Canadian. Great Lakes potentially had a lot to gain from this arrangement because it sells about 84 percent of its output to the United States. However, the company was not as prescient as it thought it was, because the conversion rate rose to a high of $1.24 later in 1981 and to $1.30 in 1982.

The twin massive spending programs on capital equipment and acquisitions have had their toll on CP's balance sheet, although it is still in the black. Debt as a percentage of total capitalization has risen from 34.02 percent in 1979 to 44.6 percent in 1982, and from 36.3 percent in 1979 at CPE to 44.7 percent in 1982. Skyrocketing interest rates made this debt load more onerous. What this financial report card means is that CP is experiencing some very rough times. And when a colossus like CP experiences rough times, it does not suffer alone. Its reactions can have severe consequences for many Canadian workers and their communities. In a speech in 1975, Ian Sinclair said there are "only three ways to increase return on investment: reduce the size of the investment, increase revenue, or decrease costs." In a recession, it is hard to increase revenue or return on investment, and shortsighted to cut back on investment needed to modernize the company. The only remaining option is cost reduction.

Despite its huge revenues, CP diligently cuts fat in its expenses, with results that range from penny pinching affecting just its own operations to ruthless closure of facilities that damage an entire community's economy. On the penny pinching side, most CP executives occupy modest offices. Algoma Steel's headquarters in Sault Ste. Marie, for example, are in a three-storey, non-descript building with sagging floors that used to be a hotel. CP Air's ex-chairman, Ian Gray, had a spartan, windowless office. Great Lakes Forest Products' chairman, Charles Carter, has a plainly furnished corner office overlooking the company's mill operations spewing forth steam. Pacific Forest Products' head-quarters in Victoria, located across from the Legislative Build-ings, used to be the headquarters of CP's British Columbia Coastal Ships. Again, the offices are simply furnished. Instead of works of art, Pacific Forest's president, William Sloan, has chosen a beautiful section of a massive Douglas fir tree, logged by the company, to decorate his office.

Pennies are also counted on a daily operations basis. For example, the Royal York Hotel switched from powder to liquid laundry detergent, which laundry workers say reduces monthly detergent bills by $2,000. The hotel also shaves costs by being self-sufficient as much as possible, rather than relying on outside contractors. It has what it claims is the only hotel glad iron press in North America that stacks napkins and pillowcases; it prints its own office forms, business cards, and menus; and an uphol-stery shop repairs bedspreads, furniture scratches, and burns.

All the shops are located in a warren of hidden passages in the hotel's basement. The hotel is also cutting down on its chinaware expenses. The Royal Doulton dishes designed for CP—white with blue trim and decorated with wheat sheaves—have been set aside for special occasions and Kosher food patrons. For general use, the hotel has switched to cheaper china made by CPE's Syracuse China subsidiary.

A similar close watch is kept over expenses in other CP divisions, particularly those requiring expensive equipment. For example, the average cost of freight car equipment has risen 300 percent since the mid-1970s and the financing costs have more than doubled. This has forced CP to be more creative in freight loading, ultimately with negative consequences for Quebec City and Halifax.

One way CP Rail can get its money's worth is through increasing intermodal traffic, in which trailers and containers without wheels are transferred from truck to rail to boat. CP is so convinced about the potential of intermodal that it has created an intermodal services division within CP Rail as a profit center within a profit center. The department has its own sales, marketing, pricing, and accounting staff and manages its own operations and terminals.

While other railways, notably Canadian National, are still relying on conventional boxcars, CP is enthusiastically developing containers. Because containers have no wheels, fit on a railway flatcar, and can be easily transferred to a truck, they provide the convenience of a boxcar, plus the door-to-door service of a truck trailer without the need for tracks to a customer's plant. They also put rail in direct competition with truck trailers, a rivalry CP has heightened by developing containers that are smaller and lighter than standard rail containers but can carry the same load. As a result, more containers and goods can be loaded on a train. But the innovation may hurt other CP businesses. CP's competitive drive is resulting in its competing against itself, with its trucking and other freight cars as potential victims.

In some instances, CP's thrust for improved profitability through cost reduction and consolidation can harm a community. Such is the case, according to Halifax officials, with CP

Ships forming a coordinated overseas container shipping service in 1981 with two major European shippers—Dart Containerline and Manchester Lines. Dart is 50 percent owned by the Société Générale de Belgique, which also has an interest in Genstar Corporation, whose co-chairman, Angus MacNaughton, is on CPE's board. Manchester is owned by the C.Y. Tung Shipping Group of Hong Kong, which used to own two-thirds of Dart Canada.

The 1981 consolidation followed CP Ships' switching its North American container shipping base from Quebec City to Montreal in 1978, since Montreal is closer to most shippers. That move put Quebec City out of the container business.

Containerized shipping is preferred by shippers to the conventional piecemeal handling of goods, because the merchandise is sealed at the point of departure and not touched until it reaches its destination. One invoice covers the transfer of the container from truck to rail to boat in Canada and then from rail to truck in Europe. Consequently, the high damages and pile of paperwork of the old system have been erased.

In CP's quasi partnership with Dart and Manchester, each company owns one of three former Dart vessels and all share ownership of a fourth. Each company, however, continues to sell cargo space on each boat independently. The Dart ships use the same number of crew members as the smaller ships formerly operated by CP Ships and Manchester, handle more than double the cargo, and consume less fuel per cargo ton.

The deal, therefore, provides each firm with economies of scale, as well as an estimated 40 percent of Canada–United Kingdom and continental freight conference trade. (A shipping conference is a group of shipping lines that decide to charge identical rates so that if one line is not sailing on a particular day, customers can use another member of the group that is sailing and be charged the same rates.) In addition to the advantages shared by all three lines, the deal has an extra benefit for CP. If shippers prefer to ship from the U.S. east coast rather than inland from Montreal, CP comes out all right because it owns a one-third interest in Dart's United States-to-Europe run.

There has been skepticism about just how competitive CP, Dart, and Manchester will be. "Despite their stated intentions to remain competitors, the three companies will be operating the same ships on the same schedule to the same ports at the same rates," *Marine News* wrote in August 1981. "The question is: will their customers still perceive them as competitors when the three companies are literally in the same boat?"

The shipboard pooling of the three lines also led to the consolidation of their operations at CP's Racine Terminal at the Port of Montreal. CP Ships had built the seventeen-acre terminal in 1977–78 in preparation for its move in November 1978 from the port at Quebec City. The terminal is being expanded to twenty-nine acres to handle the increased traffic resulting from the consolidated service. Previously, Dart had sailed from Halifax, and the switch resulted in Halifax losing 35 percent of its container traffic.

In addition to being able to charge Dart and Manchester rent for use of the Racine Terminal, CP had another vested interest in wanting Dart to shift to the inland port. Since CP Rail runs to Montreal but not to Halifax, CP would have lost out on additional revenue from rail freight operations if Halifax had been chosen as the operational center. CP stands to make a tidy sum on rail freight operations by shippers using the combined service, because the coordination agreement stipulates that shippers using ships of the three lines should send their goods overland by CP Rail as long as its rates are competitive with any rival railway.

Outside of the Maritimes, shippers' reaction has been split between those who fear the threeway consolidation will reduce competition and lead to higher rates and those who feel it will provide more stability and reliability. Smaller volume shippers are more at the mercy of the arrangement than big tonnage shippers who can afford to charter their own vessels or use ships that do not belong to shipping conferences; filling an entire ship with 400,000 tons of bulk goods like coal is more practical than using the eighty to one hundred containers that would be necessary for such a large quantity. Within the Maritimes, there has been concern that Atlantic region exporters would be placed at a disadvantage because their cost of shipping goods overland to Montreal is higher than to Halifax.

The decision to use the Racine Terminal naturally made the Port of Montreal people ecstatic and Halifax and Nova Scotia officials miserable. The move will cement Montreal's position as Canada's leading port for containerized shipping (the port ranks fourth in North America, after New York, Philadelphia, and Baltimore, in containerized shipping business), and while Vancouver is still Canada's leader in total traffic, Montreal port officials say containerized shipping is rapidly growing in volume. They predict their port will handle 500,000 containers by 1985, compared with 10,000 in 1968. The Port of Montreal's gain was Halifax's loss; previously Halifax had quintupled its share of container business handled at Canadian ports.

With major restructuring along the lines of the Dart consolidation and with "nickle and dime" cost-cutting moves in menu printing and other areas, CP has been able to ride out the recession. But the costs are not measured simply in dollars. For Canada, when a company the size of CP cuts back, the costs become apparent in unemployment figures in cities and towns from Halifax to Trail, British Columbia. For the company, the real costs are not so immediately apparent. But there are costs when a company puts its plans for growth on hold, for in the long run, lost or postponed opportunities can be even more damaging than immediate financial losses.

· 15 ·

Waiting For
Better Times

In 1982, it became impossible to open a major Canadian magazine without seeing a two-page advertisement by Canadian
Pacific Enterprises confidently predicting a bullish future for
itself. The advertising started after Robert Campbell became
vice-chairman of CPE in May 1982. The advertisements have
stoutly ignored CPE's sagging profits and have repeated the
company's credo that "it did not grow to its present stature by
accident. It made things happen. . . .This positive strategy has
paid off in the past, and will give Canadian Pacific Enterprises
the growth-edge in the future."

So far, however, there has been more talk than action. The
weak economy forced CP and CPE to put on hold their plans to
become still bigger, as well as to impose salary and hiring
restrictions, lay off employees, shut down various operations for
many weeks, and curb expansion plans.

A long, sad litany of stories in the newspapers show how much
CP and its workers—about 10 percent of whom lost their jobs or
suffered long layoffs—have been hurt as the economy sank into
quicksand:

1982

January 28   Algoma to close iron ore unit in July.

January 30   Cominco to lay off 900.

February 5   200 jobs to be lost in CP Air squeeze.

March 2   Algoma to lay off 310.

March 9   Cominco to close Trail and Kimberley facilities for at least one month.

March 16   Algoma lays off 150.

March 23   More layoffs at Algoma.

April 3   Algoma sets one-week shutdown of steel unit.

April 20   Cominco has first loss since 1932.

May 15   CP Rail to lay off 3,800 shopcraft workers for one month in summer.

May 24   CP Rail lays off 311 shopcraft workers indefinitely.

May 26   Third Algoma division told of possible layoffs.

June 12   Algoma posts layoff notices.

August 5   Canadian Pacific Enterprises reports $83.9 million decline in profits in first half of 1982.

August 10   Canadian Pacific has 56 percent drop in profits in first half of 1982.

September 23   CP Air to sell two of its four 747s and will lay off 800.

October 16   CP Rail to lay off 3,600 of its 4,300 repair shop workers from November 15 to January 14, 1983.

October 17   Great Lakes Forest Products to close two kraft pulp mills, affecting 1,760 workers.

October 23   CP Rail lays off 490 workers in British Columbia and Alberta.

November 5   Workers at Fording Coal agree to reduce work week from seven to six days due to slumping coal market.

November 6   Algoma Steel to cut back operation of iron ore and sinter plants in Wawa, Ontario, to every other week due to sagging demand.

               Canadian Pacific Enterprises reports sharp drop in net income for first nine months of 1982 of $9.1 million, compared with $104.3 million a year earlier.

November 9   Canadian Pacific's nine-month net income falls to $153.5 million, down $237.7 million from a year earlier.

November 12   Algoma to close its bar and strip mills, two of its oldest, in 1983 and will relocate their 130 employees. Two-week reduction in operations planned for late December.

December 1   Pine Point Mines plans temporary shutdown of Pine Point operations in Northwest Territories, starting January 2, 1983.

1983

February 4   Algoma Steel to reduce its salaried work force by 200 workers by June.

               Great Lakes Forest Products reports its 1982 profit was only 23 percent of its 1981 profit. In the fourth quarter of 1982, it had a $4.4 million loss, compared with an $18.8 million profit a year earlier.

February 5   Canadian Pacific Enterprises reports 1982 profit of $150 million, or $255 million less than it made in 1981.

February 10   Algoma Steel reports a $40.4 million loss in 1982, compared with a profit of $165 million in 1981.

AMCA International reports its profit dropped $22 million in 1982 from the $69 million it made in 1981.

February 15   Canadian Pacific reports 1982 net income of $188 million, compared with $485.6 million in 1981.

February 26   Fording Coal extends its one-day-a-week and week-long shutdowns at its Elkford, British Columbia, mine because of a 20 percent decline in contract volume expected to last through March 1984.

June 8   Algoma Steel announces the planned closure of a third mill in August 1983.

Historically, CP has reflected Canada's economic development, and today CP is representative of the dilemmas with which corporate Canada is wrestling. Conglomerates say the advantage of having a basketful of diversified companies is that when one company is having a rough time, the other members of the family pick up the slack. But the current recession pummeled all areas of the economy and CP's diversification turned out to be a millstone instead of a tonic. Its troubles show how Canada's economy crumbled across the board.

In view of the vulnerability shown by CP's transportation and natural resources business during the recession, with the notable exception of PanCanadian Petroleum, and the relative lack of acquisition opportunities left in Canada, CP will likely look for its future growth both in more recession-proof industries and in the United States.

Two logical areas of diversification with potential promise for CP are agribusiness and the financial sector, both of which have exhibited strong earnings growth. Canadian Pacific Enterprises has been engaged in agribusiness, a broad field that embraces agricultural products and equipment, through Maple Leaf Mills, Baker Commodities, and Corenco Corporation. And Baker's and Corenco's locations in the United States provide CPE with a vantage point for spotting other possible acquisitions.

CPE is also already involved in financial services through its ownership of Canadian Pacific Securities (money market operations and loans to CP companies) and Château Insurance (all types of insurance except life), and is now considering expanding into the mortgage and consumer finance field.

Expanding in agribusiness and financial services, both of which are already populated by many large firms, would maintain CP's tradition of being a major player in each industry it enters, while staying clear of being a monopoly in order to avoid arousing both public fury and possible anti-trust action by the government.

With the economy slowing down CP's acquisitions from the nearly non-stop Pac-Man pace of the 1970s, CP has turned its attention to completing the largest ever spending program on modernization of its facilities. The extensive upgrading of facilities is both good and bad for CP. On the plus side, it makes facilities more productive and capable of cashing in on the recovery expected by 1985. On the minus side, CP has been laying out millions of dollars to increase output and efficiency at a time when the economy and demand for its products have been at a forty-year low.

Apart from the $7.6 billion realignment and extension of its railway tracks through western Canada, a $430 million modernization of Great Lakes Forest Products' facilities is underway and work has begun on a $1 billion copper development in British Columbia by Cominco, which will be the largest in Canada and one of the largest of its type in the world. Investment analysts say this project alone could eventually double Cominco's earnings per share. Cominco further plans to develop a lead, zinc, and silver mine in a remote part of Alaska.

Fording Coal, another CP subsidiary, will open a $100 million thermal coal mine near Lethbridge, Alberta. With a potential output of three million tonnes a year, it will be one of the largest in North America. Fording will also manage another coal mine being planned near Edmonton from which Edmonton Power, the city-owned electrical utility, will generate power for the city. Big as these two projects are, they are dwarfed by a proposed third Fording mine near Red Deer, Alberta, which will cost $2.5 billion and is expected to produce 9.5 million tonnes of coal annually. The coal will fuel a new Alberta facility for producing electricity to be sold to the American western seaboard. The money received from the Americans will pay for the plant.

Marathon Realty has big plans, too, topped by the $2 billion redevelopment, in conjunction with Canadian National, of the railway lands blotting Toronto's waterfront. And Syracuse China, already one of the largest commercial chinaware manufacturers in the United States, is completing a 50 percent expansion of its New York State facilities.

CP has always been involved in industries that thrive on technological innovation costing millions of dollars. It can boast of many engineering feats, dating back to its construction in 1907 of the Spiral Tunnels through one of the steepest spots in the Rockies.* Cominco's Little Cornwallis Island mine, built in the shape of a barge and towed to the Arctic, is as spectacular an achievement in its own way as the spiral tunnels. Its cost was equally spectacular.

Like many other Canadian companies, CP has become a multinational corporation. Close to 16 percent of its assets are in the United States and 19 percent of its revenue is made there. Another 3 percent of its assets are in Europe, the Orient, and the Caribbean, and 3 percent of its revenue comes from these places. CP's goal is to have 25 percent of its assets in the United States, but recent acquisition attempts have been thwarted by angry American companies. However, that does not shut CP out from the American market, because expansion and acquisitions there by its subsidiaries have not met with similar resistance. And there is no reason why CP has to limit its outside Canadian expansion just to the United States. The listing in recent years of

---

*Despite the trains moving very slowly, there were still occasional runaways on a passage known as the "big hill." The spiral tunnels eliminated this problem by routing the train in a spiral formation through each of the mountains at either end of the "big hill."

CP and CPE on more overseas stock exchanges, as well as the New York, gives the two companies access to new sources of funds and a closer presence to acquisition opportunities outside of Canada and the United States.

CP is already aggressively pursuing overseas markets. For example, Fording Coal began a ten-year, $230 million contract in 1982 to ship coal to Taiwan. It also exports to Japan, Korea, and Brazil. AMCA International is building mooring facilities for India's and Brazil's national oil companies, as well as a pump-house structure for a Saudi Arabian power project. PanCanadian is exploring for oil in the North Sea and off the coast of China. Nine of Cominco's sixteen mines are outside Canada (in the United States, Greenland, Spain, Ireland, Australia, and South Africa). Maple Leaf Mills has flour mills throughout the Caribbean.

CP is also entering into more cooperative ventures with other firms, and this can be expected to continue because of the many advantages: partners may have greater expertise in particular areas, the risks can be shared, and the partner often buys what the joint enterprise makes. For example, Fording Coal is building its Lethbridge thermal coal plant with a Japanese firm, Idemitsu Kosan, the largest independent oil refiner and distributor in Japan, which is looking for substitutes for fuel energy. Maple Leaf Mills and Lever Brothers are partners in Maple Leaf Monarch Co., which has the largest multiseed processing plant in Canada, located in Windsor. PanCanadian Petroleum has a 35 percent interest in a world-scale methanol plant in Alberta, with the other 65 percent owned by Celanese Canada Inc. and Celanese Co. of America Inc.

Whatever moves CP makes over the rest of the decade will likely be made with caution and slow deliberation. The ravenous gobbling up of companies is a thing of the past, and CP will probably return to its more traditional pace of development.

CP is like an elephant—very big, plodding, and conservative. In its development of the riches on the lands it owned, CP has not been as enterprising as its critics would like it to be. Westerners resent what they view as undue slowness on the part of PanCanadian Petroleum in drilling on its vast land holdings. Today, CP is the proud owner of landmark office towers in Canada's major cities, on land where it used to have its rail yards, but it has often had to be shoved into removing these eyesore yards by municipal officials. CP was also a latecomer in moving into finished manufactured goods for the consumer products market, not shifting in this direction until the late 1970s when it first acquired Syracuse China and then Maple Leaf Mills.

For the next few years, CP will likely concentrate on putting its house in order. Its long-term debt is at a record level and its cash flow not as good as it used to be. This should limit any direct acquisitions, although that does not mean some of the purchase-happy subsidiaries, such as AMCA International, will not be in the market. Conversely, it is unlikely there would be any eager buyers for such big money-losing divisions as CP Ships and CP Air.

Whoever becomes CP's next chairman—Paul Desmarais, Robert Campbell, William Stinson, Stuart Eagles, or some unexpected dark horse—he will be forced to remain at a standstill, waiting for the return of better times for CP and for Canada.

Appendix

TABLE 1 Main Steps in Canadian Pacific's Growth

February	16, 1881	Canadian Pacific Railway Co. incorporated.	
November	7, 1885	Last spike on main line from Montreal to Vancouver driven at Craigellachie, B.C., five years in advance of contract date.	
	1882	Express service started (*with a horse and wagon*).	
	1886	First coast to coast telegraph transmitted.	
		Moved into steamship operations, starting on Pacific Ocean.	
	1887	First hotel (*the original Hotel Vancouver*) opened (CN *owns present Hotel Vancouver*).	
	1897	Purchased smelter (*the nucleus of Cominco*) at Trail, B.C.	
	1903	Atlantic steamship service started.	
	1906	Consolidated Mining & Smelting Co. (*now called Cominco Ltd.*) incorporated.	
	1925	CP Transport established.	
	1934	Highway trucking started.	
	1941	Pacific Logging (*now called Pacific Forest Products Ltd.*) established.	
	1942	CP Air founded.	
	1948	CP Air started international flights.	

1970	Telesat Canada (*launching of telecommunications satellites*) started in conjunction with CN and federal government.		
	Canadian Pacific Consulting Services established.		
1971	CanPac Leasing established.		
1972	CanPac International Freight Services established for movement of freight between Canada and foreign countries.		
1974	Acquired control of Algoma Steel Corp.		
	CanPac Waste Disposal Systems (*now CanPac Agri Products Ltd.*) established.		
1967–1974	Acquired more stock in Great Lakes Forest Products Ltd.; obtained control in 1974.		
1974	Château Insurance founded.		
1978	Railway passenger services turned over to Via Rail.		
	Acquired Syracuse China Corp.		
	Canellus International N.V. formed.		
1979	Marathon Realty bought Canadian Freehold Properties Ltd., a major Vancouver-based office building developer.		

218

1958 Smithsons Holdings Ltd., a major trucking firm, acquired.

Canadian Pacific Oil and Gas (*now Pan Canadian Petroleum Ltd.*) formed.

1959 CP Air got permission to operate transcontinental flights in Canada.

1960 $250 million dieselization of railway completed.

1962 Canadian Pacific Investments Ltd. (*now Canadian Pacific Enterprises Ltd.*) formed, as large-scale diversification launched.

1963 Canadian Pacific Hotels Ltd. established.

Marathon Realty Co. Ltd. founded.

1964 Canadian Pacific (*Bermuda*) Ltd. (*international deep sea shipping*) established.

An interest in Great Lakes Forest Products Ltd. first acquired.

1967 Canadian Pacific Investments Ltd. went public with sale of $100 million in convertible preferred shares (*the largest financed to that date in Canada*).

1968 Fording Coal Ltd. established.

1969 CanPac Minerals (*mineral exploration in Canada*) established.

1980 Bought Norin Corp. (*main asset Maple Leaf Mills Ltd.*)

Bought 9.4 percent of AMCA International Ltd. in addition to Algoma's holdings.

CN Telecommunications and CP Telecommunications merged.

AMCA International Ltd. bought Koehring Co., an international manufacturer of construction equipment.

1981 Paid $1.1 billion to acquire Canadian International Paper Co.

Polaris (*Cominco's zinc-lead mine*), the first of its type, opened in the Arctic.

Power Corp. of Montreal acquired 6.4 percent of Canadian Pacific Ltd., with option to increase its interest to 15 percent over ten-year period. Purchase made Power largest CP shareholder.

1982 AMCA gains control of Giddings and Lewis Inc., a major U.S. machine tool maker.

CP buys Moffatt Bros. Ltd., one of the Maritimes' largest trucking companies. This makes CP a transcontinental trucking operator with its own trucks; previously, it relied on interline agreements in parts of the Maritimes.

TABLE 2 Chronology of Senior Executives at Canadian Pacific Ltd.*

NAME	POSITION	YEAR
George Stephen	Chairman and President	1881–1888
William Van Horne	Chairman and President	1888–1899
Thomas Shaughnessy	President	1899–1918
	Chairman	1899–1922
Edward Beatty	President	1918–1942
	Chairman	1924–1943
D'Alton Coleman	President	1942–1946
	Chairman	1943–1946
William Neal	Chairman and President	1946–1947
G.A. Walker	Chairman	1947–1955
W.A. Mather	President	1947–1955
	Chairman	1955–1960
Norris "Buck" Crump	President	1955–1964
	Chairman	1960–1972
Robert Emerson	President	(*Oct.*) 1964–1966 (*March*)
Ian Sinclair	President	1966–1972
	Chairman	1972–1981
Frederick Burbidge	President	1972–1981
	Chairman	1981–
William Stinson	President	1981–

*Known as Canadian Pacific Railway Co. until 1971.

Chronology of Senior Executives at Canadian Pacific Enterprises Ltd.*

NAME	POSITION	YEAR
Norris Crump	President	1962–1966
	Chairman	1966–1971
F.V. Stone	President	1966–1968
Duff Roblin	President	1968–1974
Ian Sinclair	Chairman	1971–
William Moodie	President	1974–1979
Walter (John) Stenason	President	1979–1983
Paul Nepveu	Vice-Chairman	1979–1981
Robert Campbell	Vice-Chairman and Chief Executive Officer	1982–
Stuart Eagles	President	1983–

*Known as Canadian Pacific Investments Ltd. until 1980.

TABLE 3 Canadian Pacific: Major Segments
Total Number of Major Segments: 160*
(*All figures are for 1982: wholly owned unless otherwise noted*)

Canadian Pacific Ltd./Montreal
ASSETS $17,273 million

Canadian Pacific Enterprises Ltd./Calgary (*70.3% owned by Canadian Pacific Ltd.*)
ASSETS $12,017.5 million

Subsidiaries, Their Subsidiaries, and Affiliated Companies (*100% owned unless otherwise indicated*)

CNCP Telecommunications Ltd.
Toronto (*Head Office*)
50% Joint partnership with Canadian National

Telecommunications Terminals Systems
Toronto (*Head Office*)
Joint partnership with Canadian National
Interconnect supplier of telephone systems

CP Air
Vancouver
Canada's second largest airline
→ Transpacific Tours (*operates CP Air Holidays*)

Algoma Steel Corp. →
Sault Ste. Marie
Canada's third largest steel company 61.15%

Algoma Tube Corporation
Michigan
Threads, attaches couplings to and tests seamless tubings.

AMCA International Ltd.
(*formerly: Dominion Bridge Company*)
Montreal
34.94% by Algoma
16.38% by CPE → 39 subsidiaries

Cannelton Industries Inc.
West Virginia
Coal producer with 30 years of reserves
Supplies Algoma → Tilden Mine Michigan Iron ore mine 30%

Maple Meadow Mining Co.
West Virginia
Coal producer—to supplement Cannelton

Sault Marine Services Ltd.

Sault Windsor Hotel Ltd.

CP Rail
16,000 miles of rail

CP Ships
Montreal
Shipping to Europe
Owns Racine Terminal
at Port of Montreal

CanPac →
International Freight
Services Inc.
Services related to
movement of freight
between Canada and
foreign countries—

American
Overseas
Express
Containers Inc.
Delaware
Handles freight
for midwestern
United States.

Crossworld
Freight Ltd.
Toronto
International
freight
forwarding.

Canadian →
International
Paper Co.
Montreal
Canada's fourth largest
forest products company:
owns 1.4 million acres of
timberland—equivalent to
size of Prince Edward
Island.

Canadian Pacific →
Hotels Ltd.
Toronto
Owns, manages or leases
hotels in Canada, United
States, West Germany and
Israel

Restaurants at Calgary
Tower, Royal Bank Plaza
and Village Station in
Toronto, Granville Square
in Vancouver.

Château Flight Kitchens

Canadian Pacific Securities
Ltd.
Toronto
Financing arm of CPE and
its subsidiaries.

CP Daxion Inc.
Facelle Co. Ltd.
Masonite Canada Inc.
New Brunswick International
Ltd. 67%
Tahsis Co.

Casa Ponce de Leon
Mexico City
Jointly run airline catering service
with KLM Airlines.

Maple Shipping Co.
England
Ship brokerage.

Mendellsohn Commercial Ltd.
Montreal
Rail and air traffic customs matters.

Universal Container Services Ltd.
Montreal

Canellus International N.V.
(*Holding company*) →

Baker Commodities Inc.
Rendering plants in six southwest states; liquid bulk storage facilities in California and Korea.

CanPac Agriproducts Ltd.
Los Angeles

Corenco Corp.
Tewksbury, Mass.
Rendering plants in three northeast states and production of fruit preserves, jams and jellies (*through wholly owned subsidiary, Theresa Friedman & Sons, Inc.*)

Processed Minerals Inc.
Hutchinson, Kansas
Salt production, white silicate used in making ceramics, plastics and coatings.

Syracuse China Corp.
Plants in Syracuse, N.Y. and Joliette, Quebec.
Chinaware for hotels, restaurants, nursing homes, company cafeterias, hospitals.

Château Insurance Co.
Toronto 99.98%
All insurance, except life, for CP companies.

Cominco Ltd.
Vancouver 54.34%
Canada's leading lead and zinc producer. → 30 subsidiaries

Canadian Pacific → Canadian Pacific (Bermuda) Ltd. Chartered ocean-going tankers and bulk carriers.

Arion Insurance Co. Bermuda

Arion Shipping Corp. Liberia

Milanian Maritime Services Ltd. 75%

Fording Coal Ltd. Calgary 60% 40% owned by Cominco Ltd.

Great Lakes Forest → Products Ltd. Thunder Bay, Ont. 54.28% Newsprint: pulp, lumber, chemicals.

Lake Superior Newsprint Co. Chicago Servicing of newsprint contracts

Lake Superior Pulp & Paper Inc. Chicago Sale of kraft pulp.

Maple Leaf Mills → Ltd. Toronto Food products, grain elevators, production of poultry.

Barbados Mills Ltd.

Corporate Foods Ltd. Toronto 62% Breads. Brand names: "Toastmaster," "Dempsters," "Gainsborough."

Eastern Bakeries Ltd. Saint John, New Brunswick Bread, rolls, cake and sweet goods. Brand names: "Butter Nut," "Sunny Bee," "Fun Buns."

East Caribbean Flour Mills Ltd. Kingston, St. Vincent 40%

Gordon Young Ltd. Toronto Rendering

Maple Leaf Monarch Co. Windsor, Ontario 50% Vegetable, oil mill and refinery.

Canadian Pacific Consulting Services Ltd. Engineering, economic research and management consulting services on transportation, communications, hotel and resource development.

Canadian Pacific → Express and Transport Ltd.

Bulk Systems Ltd.

Canpar (*Parcel Delivery Service*)

DeLuxe Moving & Storage Ltd.

McGavin Foods Ltd.
Vancouver
(40% equity and 50% voting interest)
Bread, rolls, cakes.
Brand names: "McGavin," "Toastmaster."

Midland Simcoe Elevator Co.
Midland, Ontario

Rothsay Concentrates
Moorefield, Ontario 99%
Rendering company.

Stillmeadow Farms Ltd.
Elora, Ontario
Chicken products.

Marathon Aviation Terminals
Toronto 76%
Aircraft hangars, cargo facilities, flight kitchens at Toronto, Dorval, Mirabel and Edmonton airports.

New Brunswick Cold Storage Co.

Marathon Realty Co. Ltd.
Toronto →
Office, shopping center and industrial park development in Canada and United States.
Major projects include Downtown West and University Place in Toronto, Place du Canada

Express Airborne Ltd.

Highland Transport Ltd.

Moffatt Bros. Ltd.

Smith Transport Ltd.

Zot Transportation Ltd.

Incan Ships Ltd. 38%
Transports forest products across Lake Superior in a rail barge operation.

Intertank Inc.
Quebec City
Bulk liquid storage

Soo Line Railroad Co. Minneapolis 55.7% 4,400 miles of rail in midwestern United States. →

Minneapolis Northfield and Southern Railway

in Montreal, Palliser Square and PanCanadian Plaza in Calgary, Granville Square in Vancouver, 55 Park Place in Atlanta and 595 Market St. in San Francisco.

Pacific Forest Products Ltd. Victoria Logging and sawmills →

Chemanus Towing Co. Ltd. Tugboats for B.C. logging industry

Marina

Mayo Forest Products Nanaimo, B.C. 60% Serves Japanese market

Victoria Plywood Ltd. Victoria

Toronto, Hamilton and Buffalo Railway Co. 111 miles of rail between Toronto–Hamilton and Buffalo–Niagara Falls, N.Y.

PanCanadian Petroleum Ltd. Calgary 87.08% Canada's largest independent producer of crude oil and natural gas. Active in coal exploration. Oil and natural gas rights in United States, Australia, and North Sea. →

Canadian Pacific Oil and Gas of Canada Ltd. *(Oil and gas rights in the United Kingdom)*

Canadian Pacific Oil and Gas Nederland *(North Sea operations)*

Minerals Ltd.

Joint venture with Scurry-Rainbow Oil Ltd. in oil and gas exploration in Saskatchewan.

PanCanadian Gas Products Ltd. *(Has 50% interest in a natural gas liquids extraction plant in Alberta, operated by Dome Petroleum)*

Toronto Terminals
Railway Co.
Toronto 50%
Joint operations with
Canadian National of
Toronto's Union
Station.

Steep Rock Iron
Mines Ltd.
Toronto 79.44%
Iron ore

$\longrightarrow$

Panarctic Oils Ltd.
Calgary
(16.75% owned by Cominco and Pan Canadian)

Syncrude Canada Ltd.
Calgary 4%
Oil sands development

Don Park Homesites Ltd.

Sanjo Iron Mines Ltd.

Steerola Explorations Ltd.

*CP also has a majority or
minority interest in 112 smaller
firms, according to Statistics
Canada's Report on
Inter-Corporate Ownership.

Note: Re total count: Fording
Coal Ltd. *(listed under CPE
Ltd. and Cominco Ltd.)* and
Panarctic Oils Ltd. *(listed
under PanCanadian Petroleum
Ltd. and Cominco Ltd.)* have
each been counted only once.

AMCA International Ltd.
(formerly Dominion Bridge Company)

	Subsidiaries
AMCA Netherlands B.V. Amstelveen, The Netherlands	International financial services
Atomaster Bowling Green, Kentucky	Portable heaters
Koehring-Bantam Waverly, Iowa	Hydraulic excavators
Koehring Benton-Harbor Benton Harbor, Mich.	Hydraulic valves and cylinders
Koehring-Bomag Boppard, West Germany and Springfield, Ohio	Compaction and stabilization equipment
Koehring-Canada Brantford, Ont.	Pulpwood, harvesting, and paper mill machinery
Cherry-Burrell Cedar Rapids, Iowa	Food and beverage processing and packaging machines
Koehring-Clyde Duluth, Minnesota	Cranes
Koehring Construction Equipment Toronto	Forklifts, trowels, and alternators
Continental Screw New Bedford, Mass.	Fasteners
DESA Park Forest, Ill.	Chain saws, construction, and do-it-yourself tools
Dominion Bridge Company Montreal	Industrial steel products

Dominion Bridge-Sulzer Lachine, Que. *(Joint venture with Sulzer Bros. Ltd. of Switzerland)*	Steel products for electrical utility applications
DB Engineers and Constructors Montreal	Engineering and construction
DB McDermott Halifax	Offshore engineering and construction services
Koehring-Excavators Milwaukee	Excavators and cranes
Fenn Manufacturing Newington, Connecticut	Aerospace components
Koehring-Finance Brookfield, Wisc.	Financing for buying company products
Giddings and Lewis Inc. Fond du Lac, Wisc.	Machine tools
Koehring-Husco Waukesha, Wisc.	Control valves
IMODCO Los Angeles	Offshore marine terminals
Janesville Products Norwalk, Ohio	Automotive parts
JESCO Inc. Fulton, Miss.	Construction services
Koehring Co. Brookfield, Wisc.	Construction equipment
Litwin Cos. *(Litwin U.S. – Houston* *Litwin Europe – Puteaux, France)*	Construction services
Koehring-Lorain Chattanooga, Tennessee	Cranes

Manitoba Rolling Mills Selkirk, Man.	Steel products
Koehring-Menck Ellerau, West Germany	Pile driving equipment
Midland Screw Chicago	Fasteners
Monroe Forgings Rochester	Alloy metal forged rings, bars, and discs
Koehring-Morgan Alliance, Ohio	Cranes and oil field equipment
ORBA Corp. Fairfield, New Jersey	Dry bulk materials
Koehring-Pegasus Troy, Michigan	Valves
Koehring-Provincial Niagara Falls, Ont.	Cranes
ROTEK Aurora, Ohio	Industrial bearings systems
Span Holdings Nassau, Bahamas	International purchasing, marketing, consulting
Koehring-Speedstar Enid, Oklahoma	Well drilling machines
Varco-Pruden Memphis, Tennessee	Pre-engineered non-residential buildings
Wiley Manufacturing Port Deposit, Maryland	Barges, dredges, and tunnel fabrication

Cominco Ltd.
Subsidiaries and Sub-Subsidiaries

SUBSIDIARIES		SUB-SUBSIDIARIES
Arvik Mines Ltd.	Includes Polaris Project on Little Cornwallis Island and leases on nearby land.	
Bethlehem Copper Corp. British Columbia		
Bathurst Norsemines Ltd. Northwest Territories (43.8%) Option to increase to 65%	Zinc, lead, copper and silver lands.	
Brazil Diamante (*Eiendoms*) Beperk South Africa (50%)	Diamond mining.	
The Canada Metal Co. Ontario (50%)	Metal products.	Carter White Lead Co. Lead oxide facilities across Canada. Owned by The Canada Metal Co.
Cominco American Inc. Spokane, Washington	U.S. mineral exploration.	
Cominco Australian Pty Ltd.	Tungsten, copper, lead and zinc development.	Aberfoyle Ltd. Australia Tungsten and copper mining across Australia. 47% owned by Cominco Australian Pty Ltd. Que River Tasmania Lead and zinc projects. 90% owned by Aberfoyle Ltd.

Cominco Binani Zinc Ltd. Southwest India (40%)	Zinc production.
Cominco Electronics Materials Inc. Spokane, Washington	Semi conductors, high priority metals.
Cominco Europe Ltd. London, England	Management of European interests.
Cominco Holdings NV Europe	Exploration and marketing interests in Europe. Exploracion Minera International Spain 47% owned by Cominco Holdings NV
Cominco U.K. Ltd. Cominco G.m.b.H.	Marketing of products in United Kingdom. German subsidiary.
Fording Coal Ltd. Calgary (40%)	
Greenex A/S Copenhagen (63%)	Zinc and lead mining in Greenland.
Mazak Ltd. United Kingdom (50%)	Largest zinc alloy producer in United Kingdom.
Mitsubishi Cominco Smelting Co. Ltd. Japan (45%)	Lead smelter Supplied by Cominco's subsidiary, Pine Point Mines.
Pacific Coast Terminals Co. Ltd. (78%)	Warehouse, dock and bulk loading facilities in British Columbia.
Panarctic Oils Ltd. Calgary (8%; 16.75% owned by Cominco and Pan Canadian)	

Pine Point Mines Ltd. Northwest Territories (69%)	
Rycon Mines Ltd. Northwest Territories (46%)	
Tara Exploration & Development Co. Ireland (17.4%)	Zinc-lead mine.
Valley Copper Mines Ltd.	Copper mine in British Columbia.
Vestgron Mines Ltd. (63%)	Includes mining operations in Greenland.
Western Canada Steel Ltd.	Steel production. Hawaiian Western Steel Ltd. 51% owned by Western Canada Steel Ltd.
West Kootenay Power & Light Co. Ltd.	Operates Cominco's hydro electric plants. Utility power distribution in southern British Columbia.

Other Canadian Pacific Holdings

COMPANY	LOCATION	PERCENTAGE OF OWNERSHIP
Energy and Mineral Resources		
Ardley Coal Ltd.	Alberta	40.0
Bankeno Mines Ltd.	Alberta	8.8
Bethalta Resources Ltd.	Alberta	98.0
C.L.T. Quebec Exploration	Quebec	100.0
Canep (*Canadian Energy Projects Ltd.*)	Quebec	20.0
CanPac Minerals Ltd.	Alberta	60.0
Canpotex	Saskatchewan	20.0
Caribou Chaleur Bay Mines Ltd.	Ontario	22.5
Cascade Pipe Line Ltd.	British Columbia	90.0
Cascade Water Power and Light Co.	British Columbia	100.0
Coast Copper Co.	British Columbia	94.7
Commercial Solids Pipe Line Co.	Ontario	50.0
Confederated Copper Extraction Ltd.	British Columbia	100.0
Crest Copper Ltd.	British Columbia	23.3
Dynamic Power Corp.	Alberta	100.0
The George Gold-Copper Mining Co.	British Columbia	82.6
Ingenika Mines Ltd.	British Columbia	35.0
International Iron Ores Ltd.	Quebec	11.3
Kamcon Mines Ltd.	Northwest Territories	43.8
Kootenay Engineering Co. Ltd.	British Columbia	100.0
Kremzar Gold Mines Ltd.	Ontario	100.0

Other Canadian Pacific Holdings

COMPANY	LOCATION	PERCENTAGE OF OWNERSHIP
McDame Exploration Ltd.	British Columbia	100.0
Mexicanus Explorations Ltd.	Mexico	100.0
Minago Mines Ltd.	British Columbia	99.7
Nova Beaucage Mines Ltd.	Ontario	25.3
Okanagan Water Power Co.	British Columbia	100.0
Otterburn Mines Ltd.	British Columbia	95.0
PanCanadian Gas Products Ltd.	Alberta	100.0
PanCanadian Kerrobert Pipeline Ltd.	Alberta	50.0
Princeton Gold Mines Ltd.	Ontario	25.3
Ptarmigan Mines Ltd.	Northwest Territories	91.2
Redcon Gold Mines Ltd.	Ontario	14.5
Ryan Gold Mines Ltd.	Alberta	40.9
Rycon Mines Ltd.	British Columbia	60.0
South Kootenay Water Power Co.	British Columbia	100.0
Stillings Petroleum Canada Ltd.	Alberta	50.0
Sunloch Mines Ltd.	British Columbia	84.2
Sunro Mines Ltd.	British Columbia	48.5
TransCanada Pipelines Ltd.	Alberta	14.1
United Pemetex Ltd.	British Columbia	12.5

Food and Related Items

Adanac Poultry Ltd.	Ontario	100.0
Alberta Stock Yards Co. Ltd.	Alberta	99.4

Alberta Fresh Produce Ltd.	Alberta	11.0
Berwick Bakery Ltd.	Nova Scotia	100.0
Boulangerie Doyon Inc.	Quebec	25.0
Buns Master Bakeries Inc.	Alberta	16.7
Durivage Inc.	Quebec	25.0
Hagersville Elevators Ltd.	Ontario	100.0
Hillcrest Farm Ltd.	Newfoundland	100.0
Huche Sans Pareille 1969 Inc.	Quebec	25.0
Maple Leaf Investments Ltd.	Ontario	100.0
Maple Leaf Properties Ltd.	Ontario	100.0
Pinecrest Foods Ltd.	Alberta	50.0
Robin Le Pain Moderne Inc.	Quebec	25.0
Toronto Elevators Ltd.	Ontario	100.0
Woodstock Feed Co. Ltd.	Ontario	100.0

Forestry

Commandant Properties Ltd.	Quebec	100.0
Ladysmith Log Sorting Ltd.	British Columbia	50.0
Sooke Forest Products Ltd.	British Columbia	49.0

Real Estate and Hotels

Burnside Development Co.	Nova Scotia	100.0
C.C.C.L. Properties Ltd.	Ontario	33.3
Calgary Centennial Tower Ltd.	Alberta	100.0
Calgary Tower (1975) Ltd.	Alberta	97.0
Château Talbot London Ltd.	Ontario	50.0
Downtown West Plaza Ltd.	Ontario	100.0
Foundation Scottish Properties Ltd.	Quebec	100.0
Hawathaland Hotels Ltd.	Ontario	40.0
Manar Properties of Alberta Ltd.	Alberta	75.0

Other Canadian Pacific Holdings

COMPANY	LOCATION	PERCENTAGE OF OWNERSHIP
Metro Centre Developments Ltd.	Ontario	50.0
Pitt Street Developments Ltd.	Ontario	100.0
Place Montreal Inc.	Quebec	100.0
Project 200 Investments Ltd.	British Columbia	33.3
Project 200 Properties Ltd.	British Columbia	25.0
Vanisle Land Development Ltd.	British Columbia	100.0
Village Green Mall Ltd.	British Columbia	100.0
Vye Investments Ltd.	British Columbia	100.0
Transportation		
Atlantic and Northwest Railroad Co.	Quebec	100.0
Brunterm Ltd.	New Brunswick	100.0
CHEP Inc. *(loading pallets)*	Quebec and Ontario	50.0
Calgary and Edmonton Railway Co.	Alberta	100.0
Canadian Pacific Air Lines Repairs Ltd.	British Columbia	100.0
Canadian Pacific Transport *(Saskatchewan)* Ltd.	Saskatchewan	100.0
CanPac International Freight Services Inc.	Quebec	100.0
CanPac Shipmanagement (Hong Kong) Ltd.	Hong Kong	100.0
Dominion Atlantic Railway Co.	Quebec	100.0
Edmunds Transport Ltd.	Ontario	100.0
Esquimalt and Nanaimo Railway Co.	British Columbia	100.0
Grand River Railway Co.	Quebec	100.0
Intermediate Terminals Warehouses Ltd.	Ontario	100.0
Kingston and Pembroke Railway Co.	Quebec	100.0
Lake Champlain and St. Lawrence Junction	Quebec	100.0

Lake Erie and Northern Railway Co.	Quebec	100.0
Manitoba and North Western Railway Co. of Canada	Manitoba	100.0
Massawippi Valley Railway Co.	Quebec	93.0
Matac Cargo Ltd.	Quebec	50.0
Montreal and Atlantic Railway Co.	Quebec	100.0
New Brunswick and Canada Railway Co.	New Brunswick	100.0
Normans Transport Ltd.	Quebec	99.6
Ontario and Quebec Railway	Ontario	100.0
Pacific Coast Terminals Co.	British Columbia	78.3
Quebec Central Railway Co.	Quebec	100.0
Quebec and Western Railway Co.	Quebec	100.0
St. Lawrence Ottawa Railway Co.	Quebec	100.0
Shawinigan Falls Terminal Railway Co.	Quebec	50.0
Smith Transport International Ltd.	Ontario	100.0
Smith Transport U.S. Ltd.	Ontario	100.0
Southern Algoma Railway Co.	Ontario	100.0
Toronto Grey and Bruce Railway Co.	Ontario	67.0
Transport Terminals Ltd.	Quebec	100.0
Unitank Ltd.	Quebec	50.0
United Cargo Corp. (*Canada*) Inc.	Ontario	100.0
West Ontario Pacific Railway	Ontario	100.0

Investments

COMPANY	PERCENTAGE OF SHARES
MICC Investments Ltd.	3.92
Royal Trustco Ltd.	6.70
Telesat Canada	3.80
Union Carbide Canada Ltd.	8.24

Miscellaneous

COMPANY	DESCRIPTION	LOCATION	PERCENTAGE OF OWNERSHIP
Baram Ltd.	Warehousing	New Brunswick	100.0
C.P.T.A. Participants Ltd.	Holding company	Ontario	100.0
Canborough Ltd.	Holding company	Ontario	10.0
Compagnie d'investissement Long Champ Inc.	Holding company	Quebec	100.0

Major Desmarais Group Holdings

COMPANY	COMPANY'S 1982 ASSETS *(Those Available)*	PERCENTAGE INTEREST HELD BY DESMARAIS GROUP
Bentall Properties Ltd.	$ 275 million	30.0
Canada's Wonderland Ltd. *(Amusement park near Toronto)*	–	25.0
Canadian Pacific Ltd.	$ 17.0 billion	11.73
Consolidated-Bathurst Inc.	$ 1.6 billion	40.0
Delta Hotels Ltd. *(Canada's fastest growing hotel chain)*	–	30.0
Great-West Life Assurance Ltd. *(Canada's third largest life insurer)*	$ 6.7 billion	50.2
Investors Group	$ 1.5 billion	99.2
La Presse Ltée *(Leading French language newspaper)*	–	100.0
Montreal Trustco *(Canada's sixth largest trust company)*	$ 1.6 billion	50.2
PCL Construction Ltd.	$342.5 million	15.0
Pargesa Holdings SA Geneva, Switzerland	$2 + billion*	10.0
Power Corp. of Canada	$959.1 million	68.9

Sources: Statistics Canada
       Inter-Corporate Ownership;
       Financial Post 500

*Pargesa controls more than $2 billion in assets, including Paribas Suisse, a major Swiss bank specializing in oil trade financing; Copeba, a Belgian financial holding company; and Groupe Bruxelles Lambert, Belgium's second largest industrial and financial group.

TABLE 4 Directors of Publicly-Owned Canadian Pacific Companies by Position, Other Directorships, Clubs, Awards, and Activities

(for purposes of this table

Panarctic Oils Ltd., in which CP has a significant minority interest,

is included in the CP and subsidiaries column)

Name and Location	Position	CP and Subsidiaries Directorships and Subsidiary Titles	Other Positions and Directorships	Clubs	Awards	Professional and Community Activities
Adams, Senator Willie (*Ottawa*)		Director: Panarctic Oils Ltd.				
Allison, Russell S. (*Willowdale, Ont.*)	Executive Vice-President, CP Rail	President and Director: Toronto, Hamilton and Buffalo Railway Co. Director: Algoma Steel Corp.; Canadian Pacific Consulting Services Ltd.; CP Hotels Ltd.; The Toronto Terminals Railway Co.				Past President: Canadian Lung Association
Anderson, Myles Norman B.Sc. (*Vancouver*)	Chairman and Chief Executive Officer, Cominco Ltd.	Director: Aberfoyle Ltd.; Canadian Pacific Enterprises; Cominco Ltd.; Cominco American Inc.; Cominco Australian Pty. Ltd.; Cominco Binani Zinc Ltd.; Fording Coal Ltd.; Hawaiian	Director: Toronto Dominion Bank	Shaughnessy Golf and Country; Vancouver		Member: Alberta Professional Engineers; American Institute of Mining, Metallurgy and Petroleum Engineering; British Columbia

			Professional Engineers; Business Council on National Issues; Canadian Coal Association; Canadian Institute Mining and Metallurgy; Canadian Mining Association; Employers' Council of British Columbia
		...western Steel Ltd.; Fine Point Mines Ltd.; Tara Exploration & Development Co.; Vestgron Mines Ltd.; West Kootenay Power & Light Co.	
Andriuk, John (*Calgary*)	Sr. Vice-President, Dome Petroleum Ltd.	Director: Panarctic Oils Ltd.	
Armstrong, Robert Douglas B. Com., F.C.A. (*Don Mills, Ont.*)	Past Chairman and Chief Executive Officer, Rio Algom Ltd.	Director: Algoma Steel Corp.; Marathon Realty Co. Ltd.	Toronto: Granite; Rosedale; Toronto
Ayers, M.J. (*Victoria, B.C.*)	Vice-President Development and Administration and Corporate Secretary, Pacific Forest Products Ltd.	Director: Pacific Forest Products Ltd.	

Name and Location	Position	CP and Subsidiaries Directorships and Subsidiary Titles	Other Positions and Directorships	Clubs	Awards	Professional and Community Activities
Barber, Lloyd Ingram B.A., B. Comm., M.B.A., Ph.D. (*Regina, Sask.*)	President and Vice-Chancellor, University of Regina	Director: Canadian Pacific Ltd.	Director: Bank of Nova Scotia; Burns Foods Ltd.; Husky Oil Ltd.; Molson Companies; Muir Barber Ltd.; SED Systems Ltd.; Sinco Development	Assiniboia; Faculty (*Regina*); Masons; Regina Beach Yacht; Regina Officers Mess; United Service Institute	Q.C.; Officer of the Order of Canada; Canadian Council Pre-Doctoral Fellowship; Centennial Medal; Ford Foundation Dissertation Grant; Honorary Indian Chief (*Saskatchewan*); Vanier Medal	Honorary Lieutenant-Colonel 16 Service Battalion (M) President: Association of Universities and Colleges of Canada Director: Regina United Way Member: Canadian Economic Association; American Economic Association Author and co-author: Report of the Royal Commission on Government Administration (*Saskatchewan*) 1965; author of Brief to Carter Commission for Retail Merchants Association of Canada

	Position	Directorships	Clubs	Honours	Memberships
Barclay, Kenneth Stuart B. Com. (*Hanover, N.H.*)	Chairman, President and Chief Executive Officer, AMCA International Ltd. *(formerly: Dominion Bridge Ltd.)*	Director: AMCA International Ltd.	Bahamas: Lyford Cay, Nassau; Montreal: Forest and Stream; Pennsylvania: Laurel Valley and Rolling Rock; Ligonier		
Bata, Thomas J. (*Don Mills, Ont.*)	Chairman, Bata Industries Ltd.; Bata Financial Corporation of Canada Ltd.	Director: CP Air	England: Keston Flying; Royal Automobile New York: Canadian Ottawa: Rideau Toronto: Granite; National; Royal Canadian Yacht; Toronto Flying	Companion of the Order of Canada; Fellow, International Academy of Managers; International Business Executive of 1982 *(First recipient of Canadian Council International Chamber of Commerce annual award)*	Honorary Governor, Trent University Chairman: Committee on Development for Business and Industry to OECD *(Organization for Economic Co-operation and Development)* Director: French Chamber of Commerce in Canada; Canadian Executive Service Overseas; International Chamber of Commerce *(Canadian Council)*

Name and Location	Position	CP and Subsidiaries Directorships and Subsidiary Titles	Other Positions and Directorships	Clubs	Awards	Professional and Community Activities
						Member: Advisory Council, National Ballet of Canada; Canadian Economic Policy Committee; Canadian Institute of International Affairs; Chief Executives Forum; Founding Member, Young Presidents Organization; Founding Member and Chairman, Canada–India Business Council
Becker, George (*Fond du Lac, Wisconsin*)	Chairman, Giddings and Lewis Inc.	Director: AMCA International Ltd.				
Beddome, John (*Calgary*)	Group Vice-President Exploration and Production, Dome Petroleum Ltd.	Director: Panarctic Oils Ltd.				

Bélanger, Michel (*Montreal*)	Chairman, President and Chief Executive Officer, National Bank of Canada	Director: CIP Inc.	Director: Mortgage Insurance Co. of Canada; Power Corp. of Canada; Simpsons-Sears Ltd.	Montreal: Mount Royal; St. Denis, St. James's	Director: C.D. Howe Research Institute Member: Régie de la Place des Arts
Bélisle, J.D. (*St. Lambert, Que.*)	Executive Vice-President, Canadian Pacific Consulting Services Ltd.	Director: Canadian Pacific Consulting Services Ltd.			
Bell, Ronald (*Calgary*)	Vice-President Drilling, Petro-Canada	Director: Panarctic Oils Ltd.			
Benson, K.S. (*Vancouver*)	Corporate Secretary, Cominco Ltd.	Director: Cominco Ltd.			

Name and Location	Position	CP and Subsidiaries Directorships and Subsidiary Titles	Other Positions and Directorships	Clubs	Awards	Professional and Community Activities
Bentall, Harold Clark BASc., P.Eng. (*Vancouver*)	Chairman, The Bentall Group Ltd.	Director: Cominco Ltd.	Chairman: Dominion Construction Co. Director: British Columbia Forest Products Ltd.; Finning Tractor and Equipment Co. Ltd.; Scott Paper Ltd.; The Toronto Dominion Bank Trustee: Toronto Dominion Realty	Royal Vancouver Yacht; Shaughnessy Golf and Country		
Bowles, C.R. C.A. (*Thunder Bay, Ont.*)	Executive Vice-President, Great Lakes Forest Products Ltd.	Director: CP Hotels Ltd.; Great Lakes Forest Forest Products Ltd.				
Boyd, K.G. (*Victoria, B.C.*)	Executive Vice-President, Pacific Forest Products Ltd.	Director: Pacific Forest Products Ltd.				

Brawn, Robert G. B.Sc. (*Calgary*)	Chairman and Chief Executive Officer, Bankeno Mines Ltd.	Director: Arvik Mines Ltd. (Cominco); CP Air; Panarctic Oils Ltd.	Vice President: Calgary Chamber of Commerce Director: Canadian Chamber of Commerce; Canadian Foremost Ltd.; Challenger International Services Ltd.; Coast Copper Co. Ltd.; Lariat Oil and Gas Ltd.; Queenston Gold Mines Ltd.; Turbo Resources Ltd.; Turbo and Challenger subsidiary companies	Calgary Petroleum; Rotary	Director: Association of Professional Engineers (*Alberta*); Independent Petroleum Association of Canada; Young Presidents' Association Member: Dean's Advisory Committee, Faculty of Business Administration and Commerce, University of Alberta; Canada West Federation
Bromley, James D. (*Vancouver*)	Vice President Pacific Region, CP Rail	Director: Pacific Forest Products Ltd.			

Name and Location	Position	CP and Subsidiaries Directorships and Subsidiary Titles	Other Positions and Directorships	Clubs	Awards	Professional and Community Activities
Burbidge, Frederick Stewart B.A., LL.B. (*Montreal*)	Chairman and Chief Executive Officer, Canadian Pacific Ltd.	Director: AMCA International Ltd.; Canadian Pacific Ltd.; CNCP Telecommunications; CP Air; CP (*Bermuda*) Ltd.; Canadian Pacific Enterprises Ltd.; Canadian Pacific Steamships Ltd.; Canadian Pacific Transport Co. Ltd.; Cominco Ltd.; Marathon Realty Co. Ltd.; PanCanadian Petroleum Ltd.; Soo Line Railroad Co.; Toronto, Hamilton and Buffalo Railway Co.	Director: Bank of Montreal; C.I.L. Inc.	Montreal: Canadian Railway; Mount Royal; St. James's; Traffic Ottawa: Royal Ottawa Golf		Governor: Bishop's College School Honorary Vice-President: Boy Scouts of Canada (*Quebec*) Advisory Council: Board of Trade (*Montreal*); Chamber of Commerce; Minister of Industry, Trade and Commerce; General Council of Industry (*Quebec*) Director: Royal Victoria Hospital Foundation Member: Citizens' Advisory Board, The Salvation Army
Burnet, Frederick Ewart B.Sc. (*Vancouver and Spokane, Wash.*)	Former President and Chairman, Cominco Ltd., Cominco American Inc.	Director: Cominco American Inc.; Cominco Ltd.; Hawaiian Western Steel Ltd.; West Kootenay Power & Light Co. Ltd.	President: Taku Vessel Co.; Tara Exploration & Development Company Ltd.	Spokane, Wash.: City; Empire; Spokane Golf & Country		Director: Canadian Institute Mining and Manufacturing Clubs, Vancouver University; Centre for Resource Studies, Queen's University;

Burns, James William B. Comm., M.B.A. (*Montreal*)	President, Power Corp. of Canada	Director: Canadian Pacific Ltd. Chairman and Director: The Great-West Life Assurance Co. President and Director: Trans Canada Corporation Fund; Shawinigan Industries Ltd. Director: Bathurst Paper Ltd.; Consolidated Bathurst Inc.; Domglas Inc.; The GSL Group Inc.; Genstar Ltd.; Montreal Trust Co.	Vancouver: Shaughnessy Golf & Country Montreal: Mount Bruno; Mount Royal Toronto: Albany Winnipeg: St. Charles Country; Manitoba	Honorary Lieutenant Colonel, Queen's Own Cameron Highlanders in Canada	Mining Association, Canada; NW Mining Association; Professional Engineers (*Montreal*); Professional Engineers (*British Columbia*) Member: American Mining Congress; American Institute Mining Engineers Member, Board of Directors: Council for Business and the Arts in Canada; Ducks Unlimited (*Canada*); The Arthritic Society Director: The Investors Group Member of the Conference Board in Canada (*Ottawa*) Trustee: The Conference Board (*New York*); North American Wildlife Foundation Member: Canadian Council Christians and Jews

Name and Location	Position	cp and Subsidiaries Directorships and Subsidiary Titles	Other Positions and Directorships	Clubs	Awards	Professional and Community Activities
Campbell, Robert W. (*Calgary*)	Vice-Chairman and Chief Executive Officer, Canadian Pacific Enterprises Ltd.	Chairman and Director: PanCanadian Petroleum Ltd. Director: Algoma Steel Corp.; AMCA International Ltd.; Canadian Pacific Ltd.; Canadian Pacific Enterprises Ltd.; CIP Inc.; Canadian Pacific Securities Ltd.; Cominco Ltd.; Great Lakes Forest Products Ltd.; Maple Leaf Mills Ltd.; Panarctic Oils Ltd.	Director: Bank of Canada (*1970–82*); Celanese Canada Inc.; Crown Trust Co.; Industrial Development Bank; Natural Resources Growth Fund; Syncrude Canada Ltd.; Transcanada Pipelines Ltd.; Westinghouse Canada Ltd.			
Cardy, A. Gordon, B. Com. (*Toronto*)	Chairman and President, Canadian Pacific Hotels Ltd.	Director: Canadian Pacific Hotels Ltd.	Director: Cochrane-Dunlop Hardware Ltd.	Good-fellowship; Kiwanis (*Director*); Lambton Golf and Country	Knight of the Military and Hospitaller Order of St. Lazarus of Jerusalem (K.L.J.); Military Cross (M.C.)	
Carter, Charles J. (*Thunder Bay, Ont.*)	Chairman of the Board and President, Great Lakes Forest Products Ltd.	Director: Great Lakes Forest Products Ltd.; Pacific Forest Products Ltd.				

			Director: National Council YMCA's
Chambers, R.E. (*Thunder Bay, Ont.*)	Executive Vice-President, Great Lakes Forest Products Ltd.	Director: Great Lakes Forest Products Ltd.	
Cleghorn, J.E. (*Vancouver*)	Vice-President, Royal Bank of Canada	Director: Pacific Forest Products Ltd.	
Clough, J.P.T. (*Montreal West*)	Vice-President Finance and Accounting, Canadian Pacific Ltd.	Director: CHEP Canada Inc.; CNCP Telecommunications; CanPac Car Inc.; CanPac Terminals Ltd.; Canadian Pacific Consulting Services Ltd.; Canadian Pacific Express and Transport Co. Ltd.; Canadian Pacific Securities Ltd.; The Shawinigan Falls Terminal Railway Co.; The Toronto, Hamilton and Buffalo Railway Co.; The Toronto Terminals Railway Co.	

Name and Location	Position	CP and Subsidiaries Directorships and Subsidiary Titles	Other Positions and Directorships	Clubs	Awards	Professional and Community Activities
Cohen, Albert D. (*Winnipeg*)	President and Chief Executive Officer, General Distributors of Canada Ltd.	Director: PanCanadian Petroleum Ltd.	Chairman and Chief Executive Officer: Sony of Canada Ltd. Chairman, Executive Committee: Cam-Gard Supply Ltd.; Metropolitan Stores of Canada Ltd.	Glendale Country; Winnipeg Winter		Board Member: Du Maurier Council of The Performing Arts; Manitoba Theater Center (*Past President*); Metric Commission (*Past Member of the Board*); The Paul H.T. Thorlakson Research Fund (*Past President*); Winnipeg Clinic Research Institute (*Past President*)
Colussy, Dan Alfred M.B.A. (*Vancouver*)	President and Chief Operating Officer (*as of November 1982*), CP Air Ltd. Recent President of Pan American Airlines, Inc.	Director: CP Air Ltd.		Travelsphere		

Corner, Dick (Toronto)	Executive Vice-President, Maple Leaf Mills Ltd.	Director: Maple Leaf Mills Ltd.			
Craig, David B. (Calgary)	President, Inco Energy Resources Ltd.	Director: Panarctic Oils Ltd.			
Crump, Norris Roy M.E., D.Eng.,* LL.D.,* D.Sc.,* D.C.L.* *Honorary (Calgary)	Retired Chairman, Canadian Pacific Ltd. (1972)	Honorary Director: Soo Line Railroad Co.	Mount Stephen (Honorary Membership); Ranchmen's	Companion of the Order of Canada (C.C.); Knight of Grace from Order of St. John of Jerusalem	Life member, Engineering Institute Canada Honorary Member: American Society of Mechanical Engineers; Advisory Committee of School of Business Administration, University of Western Ontario
Dale, Robert Gordon (Toronto)	Chairman and Chief Executive Officer, Maple Leaf Mills Ltd.	Director: Corporate Foods Ltd.; Eastern Bakeries Ltd.; Maple Leaf Mills Ltd.; McGavin Foods Ltd.; McGavin Toastmaster Ltd.; Norin Corp.	Badminton and Racquet; Empire; National; Rosedale Golf	Companion of the Distinguished Service Order (D.S.O.); Distinguished Flying Cross; Hon. Lt. Col. Canadian Armed Forces	Board of Governors: Canadian Corps of Commissionaires; Chairman, Executive Committee: Trinity College, University of Toronto Advisory Council:

Name and Location	Position	CP and Subsidiaries Directorships and Subsidiary Titles	Other Positions and Directorships	Clubs	Awards	Professional and Community Activities
						Faculty of Administrative Studies, University of Toronto
						Advisory Board: Bloorview Children's Hospital
						Board of Trustees: United Community Fund of Greater Toronto
						Board of Trade: Metropolitan Toronto
de Billy, Jacques (*Quebec City*)	Partner, Gagnon, de Billy, Cantin, Martin, Beaudoin & Lesage (*law firm*)	Director: CIP Inc.	Alltrans Canada Inc.; Great Lakes Reinsurance Co.; Munich Reinsurance Co. of Canada; Roins Holding Ltd.; Royal Insurance Co. of Canada; Toronto Dominion Bank; Union Carbide Canada Ltd.; United Accumulative Fund Ltd.; Western Assurance Co.			

DeMone, R.S. (*Oakville, Ont.*)	President and Chief Operating Officer, Maple Leaf Mills Ltd.	Director: Baker Commodities Inc.; Canellus Inc.; CanPac Agri Products Ltd.; Canadian Pacific Securities Ltd.; Château Insurance Co.; Great Lakes Forest Products Ltd.; Maple Leaf Mills Ltd.; Processed Minerals Inc.; Rothsay Concentrates Co. Ltd.; Steep Rock Iron Mines Ltd.	Director: Home Capital Funds, Inc.	
Desmarais, Paul, B. Com. LL.D.* *Honorary (*Montreal*)	Chairman of the Board and Chief Executive Officer, Power Corp. of Canada Ltd.	Director: Canadian Pacific Ltd.	Chairman of Executive Committee: Consolidated Bathurst Inc. Directorships: Compagnie financière de Paris et des Pays-Bus; Consolidated Bathurst Inc.; Domglas Inc.; Gabriel Holdings Ltd.; Gelco Enterprises Ltd.; Gesca Ltée; Great-West Life Assurance Co.; Hilton Canada Ltd.;	Montreal: Mount Royal Ottawa: Rideau Toronto: Toronto United States: (*Delray Beach*) St. Andrews; (*New York*) The "21" Club; (*Palm Beach*) Bath and Tennis;	Officer of the Order of Canada (O.C.)	Chancellor: Memorial University of Newfoundland Member: Business Council on National Issues; Canada-China Trade Council; Canadian Executive Service Overseas; Chamber of Commerce (*Montreal*); Chamber of Commerce (*Province of Quebec*); Clinical Research Institute of Montreal; The Fraser Institute; C.D. Howe Research Institute;

Name and Location	Position	CP and Subsidiaries Directorships and Subsidiary Titles	Other Positions and Directorships	Clubs	Awards	Professional and Community Activities
			The Investors Group; Les Journaux Trans-Canada Ltée.; Katenac Holdings Ltée.; Montreal Trust Co.; Power Corp; Prades Inc.; La Presse Ltée; Prime Investors Ltd.; The Seagram Co.	*(Palm Desert)* Eldorado Country		Hudson Institute; Institute of Cardiology *(Montreal)*; Institute for Research on Public Policy; Montreal Museum of Fine Arts; Quebec-Labrador Foundation Inc.
Dillabough, J.A. *(Calgary)*	Vice-President Production, Canadian Hunter Exploration Ltd.	Director: Panarctic Oils Ltd.				
Dingman, Michael D. *(Hampton, N.H.)*	President, The Signal Companies Inc.	Director: AMCA International Ltd.				
Douglas, Roderick, P. B.Sc. *(Vancouver)*	Senior Vice-President, Operations, Cominco Ltd.	President and Chief Executive Officer: Pine Point Mines Ltd. Director: Fording Coal Ltd.; Hawaiian Western				Board Member: Northern Addiction Services; Stanton Yellowknife Hospital

		Steel Ltd.; Panarctic Oils Ltd.; Western Canada Steel Ltd.			Director: Canadian Institute of Mining; Chamber of Mines (*Northwest Territories*); Professional Engineers of British Columbia
Dufour, Marcel (*Montreal*)	Secretary, CIP Inc.	Director: CIP Inc.			
Duthie, R.G. (*Vancouver*)	Corporate Director	Director: Cominco Ltd.; Pine Point Mines Ltd.	Director: Teck Corp.		
Eagles, Stuart Ernest B.Sc. (*Toronto*)	President, Canadian Pacific Enterprises Ltd.		Director: MICC Investments Ltd.; Mortgage Insurance Company of Canada	Canadian; National (*Board of Directors*)	Governor: Acadia University; President: Canadian Institute of Public Real Estate Companies; Director: Chamber of Commerce (*Ontario*); Member: American Statistical Association; Board of Trade; International Council of Shopping Centres; Ontario Business Advisory Council

Name and Location	Position	CP and Subsidiaries Directorships and Subsidiary Titles	Other Positions and Directorships	Clubs	Awards	Professional and Community Activities
Fargey, Harold T. B.A. Sc. *(Toronto)*	Executive Vice-President, Cominco	Director: The Canada Metal Co. Ltd.; Cominco Ltd.; Pine Point Mines Ltd.		Engineers		Member: Canadian Institute Mining and Metallurgy
Farquharson, G. *(Toronto)*	President, Strathcona Mineral Services Ltd.	Director: Pine Point Mines Ltd.				
Field, M.J. *(Chicago)*	Chairman and Chief Executive Officer, Marathon U.S. Holdings Inc.	Director: Marathon Realty Co. Ltd. Chairman: Marathon Development California Inc.; Marathon Development Georgia Inc.; Marathon Development Oregon Inc. Director: Marathon U.S. Holdings, Inc.; Marathon U.S. Realties, Inc.				Fellow of the Royal Institute of Chartered Surveyors *(F.R.I.C.S.)*
Finlayson, Jock Kinghorn *(Toronto)*	Past President, The Royal Bank of Canada	Director: PanCanadian Petroleum Ltd.	Director: Hall Corporation Shipping Ltd.; Macdonald Tobacco Inc.; R.J.R. Macdonald Inc.; Miron Inc.; Orion	Montreal: Forest and Stream; Mount Bruno; Mount Royal		

	Bank Ltd., London, England; Orion Bank Ltd., Nassau; Roins Holding Ltd.; Royal Bank of Canada; Royal Bank & Trust Co., New York; Royal Bank of Canada Trust Corporation Ltd., London, England; Royfund Ltd.; Roymor Ltd.; Roy National Ltd.; Royal West Banking Corp. Ltd. Nassau; Royal West Trust Corp. *(Bahamas)* Ltd.; Royal Insurance Group *(Canada)*; Sun Life Assurance Co. of Canada; United Corporations Ltd.; The Western Assurance Co.		London, England: Overseas Bankers Toronto: Granite; Toronto; York
Fisher, G.T. *(Montreal)*	President, Canadian Pacific Consulting Services Ltd.	Director: Canadian Pacific Consulting Services Ltd.	

Name and Location	Position	CP and Subsidiaries Directorships and Subsidiary Titles	Other Positions and Directorships	Clubs	Awards	Professional and Community Activities
Flenniken, Cecil S. (*Montreal*)	President and Chief Executive Officer, CIP Inc.; Vice-Chairman and Chief Executive Officer, Tahsis Co. Ltd.	Director: CIP Inc.; Facelle Co. Ltd.	Director: Toronto Dominion Bank	Montreal: Mount Royal; St. Denis; St. James's Ottawa: Rideau		Member: Executive Board Canadian Pulp and Paper Association
Fortier, L. Yves B.A., B.C.L., B.Lit. (*Montreal*)	Partner, law firm of Ogilvy, Renault	Director: Maple Leaf Mills Ltd.	Director: Jannock Ltd.; Lemoine Mines Ltd.; Manufacturers Life Insurance Co.; Mines Patino (*Quebec*) Ltd.; Patino Mining Investments Ltd.; Les Enterprises J. René Ouimet Ltée.; Westinghouse Canada Inc.; Westroc Industries Ltd.	Canadian (*Past President*); Hermitage Golf and Country; Montreal Badminton and Squash; University	Q.C.	Governor: Hôpital Marie-Enfant; McGill University; Montreal General Hospital; Montreal Neurological Institute Governor and Director: National Theatre School of Canada Regional Vice-President: Association of Canadian Clubs Director: Canadian Association Rhodes Scholars; Canadian Olympic Association;

Name	Position	Directorships		Clubs	Professional	Other
Fox, J. *(Calgary)*	Vice-President Engineering and Special Projects, CP Rail	Director: Canadian Pacific Consulting Services Ltd.				Montreal Neurological Institute; Montreal YMCA; National Youth
Galt, Thomas M. B. Comm. *(Toronto)*	Chairman and Chief Executive Officer, Sun Life Assurance Co. of Canada	Director: Canadian Pacific Enterprises Ltd.	Chairman and Director: Sun Life Assurance Co. of Canada *(U.K.)* Ltd.; Sun Life Assurance Co. of Canada *(U.S.)* Director: Bank of Montreal; Canron Ltd.; Stelco Inc.; Sun Life Assurance Co. of Canada; Stelco Inc.; Textron Canada Inc.	Montreal: Mount Bruno; Mount Royal; Montreal Skeet; St. James's Ottawa: Royal Ottawa Golf Toronto: Toronto; Toronto Golf; York Scotland: Royal and Ancient Golf Club of St. Andrews;	Fellow of the Society of Actuaries *(F.S.A.)*; Fellow of the Canadian Institute of Actuaries	Director: American Council of Life Insurance; Toronto Symphony Orchestra

Name and Location	Position	CP and Subsidiaries Directorships and Subsidiary Titles	Other Positions and Directorships	Clubs	Awards	Professional and Community Activities
Geller, John Arthur (*Toronto*)	Partner, law firm of Campbell, Godfrey & Lewtas	Director: Algoma Steel Corp., Ltd.; CP Air Ltd.; Maple Leaf Mills Ltd.	Director: Crown Trust Company; IBM Canada Ltd.; Leitch Transport Ltd.; Pilkington Glass Industries Ltd.	National; Toronto	Q.C.	Member: Canadian Bar Association; County of York Law Association; International Commission of Jurists
Giegerich, H.M. (*Yellowknife, N.W.T.*)	Vice-President, Northern Group, Cominco Ltd.	Director: Pine Point Mines Ltd.				
Gratton, Robert (*Outremont, Quebec*)	Chairman, President and Chief Executive Officer, Montreal Trust Co.	Director: Marathon Realty Co. Ltd.	Director: Allstate Insurance Companies of Canada	Mount Royal; Saint Denis; Saint James's		Chairman: Youth Orchestra (*Quebec*) Director: Canadian Institute of International Affairs; Société générale de financement

Name	Position		Directorships	Designation	Clubs	Memberships
Gray, Ian A. (*Vancouver*)	Chairman and Chief Executive Officer, Canadian Pacific Air Lines Ltd. (CP Air)	Director: CP Air Ltd.	Director: IBM Canada Ltd.			Past President: Engineering Institute of Canada
Hamilton, John B. (*Toronto*)	Senior Law Partner, Hamilton, Torrance, Stinson, Campbell, Nobbs and Woods	Director: CP Air Ltd.	President and Director: Hamilton Paint & Varnish Works Ltd. Director: Acher Daniels Midland (*Canada*) Ltd.; Abbey Glen Property Corp.; Dominion Helicopters Ltd.; Genstar Corp.; Skyline Hotels Ltd.	Q.C.	Albany; Royal Canadian Yacht Club; St. George's Golf	Governor: Etobicoke General Hospital Member: Air Transport Association; Canadian Bar Association; Law Society of Upper Canada
Hankinson, J.F. (*Montreal*)	Vice President Finance and Accounting, Canadian Pacific Enterprises Ltd.	Director: Canadian Pacific Securities Ltd.				

Name and Location	Position	CP and Subsidiaries Directorships and Subsidiary Titles	Other Positions and Directorships	Clubs	Awards	Professional and Community Activities
Heffernan, Gerald R. (*Whitby, Ont.*)	President, Co-Steel International Ltd. and Lake Ontario Steel Co. Ltd.	Director: Steep Rock Iron Mines Ltd.		Oshawa Golf		Member: American Mining Institute; Canadian Institute of Mining; Royal Automobile Club
Hetherington, Charles R. B.S., M.S., Sc.D. (*Calgary*)	President and Chief Executive Officer, Panarctic Oils Ltd.	Director: Panarctic Oils Ltd.	President: Chas. R. Hetherington & Co. Ltd.; Cancrude Oil & Gas Co. Ltd. Director: Greyhound Lines of Canada Ltd.; Hetherington Panches Ltd.	Calgary Golf and Country; Calgary Petroleum; Calgary Polo; El Dorado Country; El Dorado Polo; Glenmore Racquet; Mount Pleasant Racquet		Member: American Chemical Society; American Gas Association; Canadian Gas Association
Hill, Richard M. (*Inuvik, N.W.T.*)	Arctech Resource Management Services	Director: Panarctic Oils Ltd.				

Hogarth, Richard M. (*Toronto*)	Associate, Cassels, Blaikie and Co. Ltd. (*stockbrokers*)	Director: Steep Rock Iron Mines Ltd.	Director: Cullaton Lake Gold Mines Ltd.; Noble Mines and Oils Ltd.; Nufort Resources Ltd.
Horte, Vernon L. (*Calgary*)	President, V.L. Horte Associates Ltd.	Director: PanCanadian Petroleum Ltd.	
Hougen, R. (*Whitehorse, Yukon*)	Chairman of the Board, Canadian Satellite Communications Inc.; President, Hougens Ltd.	Director: Cominco Ltd.	
Hunkin, R.G. (*Beaconsfield, Quebec*)	President and Chief Executive Officer, Roy Lease Ltd.	Director: Canadian Pacific Securities Ltd.	President: Roy Marine Leasing Ltd.

Name and Location	Position	cp and Subsidiaries Directorships and Subsidiary Titles	Other Positions and Directorships	Clubs	Awards	Professional and Community Activities
Jiskoot, Allard *(Baarn, Netherlands)*	Past Chairman of the Board of Managing Directors, Pierson, Heldring & Pierson, N.V. Banking firm; formerly Adolph Boissevain & Co. Introduced CP shares on Amsterdam Stock Exchange in 1883.	Director: cP Air Ltd.; Canadian Pacific Ltd.				Grandfather, J.L. Pierson, traveled to Canada to meet Sir William Van Horne and wrote a book on him and Canadian Pacific
Jones, J.R. *(Thunder Bay, Ont.)*	President, Lakehead Newsprint Ltd.	Director: Great Lakes Forest Products				
Joplin, Albert Frederick B.Ap.Sc. *(Hamilton, Bermuda)*	President and Chief Executive Officer, Canadian Pacific *(Bermuda)* Ltd.	President: CanPac Shipmanagement (Hong Kong) Ltd. President and Director: Arion Shipping Corp. Director: Arion Insurance Co. Ltd.; Canadian	Director: Britannia Steamship Insurance Association Ltd.; Expo Oil, N.L.; Shaw Industries Ltd.	Canadian Railway; Hamilton Rotary; Mid Ocean; Mount Stephen; Royal	Order of St. John	Association of Professional Engineers, Province of British Columbia; Canadian Society for Civil Engineers; North America Society, Corporate

Name	Position	Directorship	Other directorships / companies	Clubs	Other affiliations
Kelsey, D.J. (*Vancouver*)	Consultant and Corporate Director	Director: Cominco Ltd.	Pacific Consulting Services Ltd.; Canadian Pacific International Freight Services Ltd.	Montreal Golf, Traffic	Planning; Railway Association
Kenny, J.D. (*Pierrefonds, Quebec*)	Comptroller, Canadian Pacific Enterprises Ltd.	Director: CP Hotels Ltd.; Commandant Properties Ltd.			
Kerr, James W. (*Toronto*)	Consultant and Director, Trans Canada Pipelines Ltd.; formerly Chairman and Chief Executive Officer 1968–1979	Director: Maple Leaf Mills Ltd.	Director: Bell Canada; Canadian Imperial Bank of Commerce; Great Lakes Gas Transmission Co.; International Minerals and Chemical Corp. (Canada) Ltd.; Lehndorff Corp.; Manufacturers Life Insurance Co.; Northern Telecom Ltd.	Montreal: Mount Royal; Ottawa: Rideau; Toronto: Rosedale Golf; Toronto; York	Governor: The Ontario Research Foundation; The Queen Elizabeth Hospital; Deputy Chairman, Board of Trustees: Timothy Eaton Memorial Church (*Toronto*); Honorary President: International Gas Union; Director: McMaster University Medical Centre Foundation

Name and Location	Position	CP and Subsidiaries Directorships and Subsidiary Titles	Other Positions and Directorships	Clubs	Awards	Professional and Community Activities
King, Donald *(Mississauga, Ont.)*	President, Marathon Realty Co. Ltd.	Director: Marathon Aviation Terminals; Marathon Realty Co. Ltd.; Marathon U.S. Holdings, Inc.				
Kissick, W. Norman *(Agincourt, Ont.)*	President and Chief Executive Officer, Union Carbide Canada Ltd.	Director: Great Lakes Forest Products Ltd.				
Klein, R. *(Montreal)*	General Manager Research, Canadian Pacific Ltd.	Director: Canadian Pacific Consulting Services Ltd.				
Lamb, Laurence J. *(Toronto)*	Chairman, President and Chief Executive Officer, Steep Rock Iron Mines Ltd.	Director: Steep Rock Iron Mines Ltd.				

Name	Position	CIP	Director (other)	Clubs		Other
Lambert, Allen T. (*Toronto*)	Deputy Chairman, London Life Insurance Co.; Past Chairman, Toronto Dominion Bank (*1961–1976*)	Director: cip Inc.; Tahsis Co.	Director: Dome Mines Ltd.; Hiram Walker—Gooderham & Worts Ltd.; Hiram Walker Resources Ltd.; Hudson Bay Mining & Smelting Co. Ltd.; Rolls Royce Holdings North America Ltd.	Granite; Rosedale Golf; Toronto; Toronto Golf; Toronto Hunt		
Leitch, Mervin (*Calgary*)	Former Energy Minister of Alberta; Partner, law firm of Macleod Dixon	Director: Canadian Pacific Enterprises	Director: Chieftain Development Co. Ltd.		Q.C.	
Leman, Paul H. (*Montreal*)	Retired Vice-Chairman, Alcan Aluminium Ltd.	Director: cip Inc.	Director: Alcan Aluminium Ltd.; Bell Canada; Credit Foncier; Fiduciares de la Cité et du District de Montréal Ltée.	Mount Bruno Golf; Mount Royal	Q.C.	Trustee: National Museum of Canada

Name and Location	Position	CP and Subsidiaries Directorships and Subsidiary Titles	Other Positions and Directorships	Clubs	Awards	Professional and Community Activities
Love, G. Donald B.E. (*Edmonton*)	Chairman and President, Chief Executive Officer, Oxford Development Group Ltd.	Director: PanCanadian Petroleum Ltd.		Edmonton: Griffith Island; Derrick Golf	Gold Executive (*Engineering Award*)	
MacKimmie, Ross Anderson LL.B., LL.D. (*Calgary*)	Senior Partner, law firm of MacKimmie, Matthews	Director: Cominco Ltd.; Pine Point Mines Ltd.	Chairman: Alberta Natural Gas Co. Advisory Board (*Calgary*): National Trust Co. Ltd. Director: Alberta & Southern Gas Co. Ltd.; Hatleigh Corp.; Northern Canadian Oils Ltd.; Pacific Gas Transmission Co.; Sulpetra Ltd.	Calgary Golf and Country; Calgary Petroleum; Glencoe; Ranchmen's (*Calgary*)	Q.C.	Chairman, Board of Governors: University of Calgary Member: American Bar Association; Canadian Bar Association; College of Trial Lawyers; Law Society of Alberta; Law Society of England; YMCA
Macnamara, John M.Sc. Ph.D. (*Sault Ste Marie Ont*)	Chairman and Chief Executive Officer,	Director: Algoma Steel Corp., Ltd.; AMCA International Ltd.; Canadian Pacific	Director: Redpath Industries Ltd.	Sault Ste. Marie Golf		Past Chairman: National Open Hearth and Basic Oxygen Society

	Algoma Steel Corp., Ltd.	Enterprises Ltd.; Cannelton Industries, Inc. (*West Virginia*)			Director: American Iron & Steel Institute; International Iron & Steel Inst.; Metallurgy Society, New York; Plummer Memorial Hospital
MacNaughton, Angus Athole C.A. (*San Francisco*)	President and Chief Executive Officer, Genstar Corp.	Director, Canadian Pacific Enterprises Ltd.	Director: Canada Permanent Mortgage Corp.; Canadian Commercial Corp.; Dart Containerline Inc.; Royal Trust Co. Ltd.; Sun Life Assurance Co. of Canada	Badminton and Squash (*Montreal*); Canadian; Mount Royal; Pacific Union; St. James's; World Trade	Board of Governors: Lakefield College School
Madill, J. Wallace (*Calgary*)	General Manager, Alberta Wheat Pool	Director: Fording Coal Ltd.; FanCanadian Petroleum Ltd.	Bank of British Columbia; Transalta Utilities Ltd.		
Magee, Brian A. (*London, England*) (*office in Toronto*)	Deputy Chairman, Markborough Properties Ltd.	AMCA International Ltd.	Honorary Chairman: A.E. LePage Ltd. Director: Casualty Co. of Canada;	London, England: M.C.C. Nassau (*Bahamas*): Lyford Cay	Military Cross; Fellow of Canadian Institute of Realtors	Past Trustee and Chairman: Building and Planning Commission, Toronto General Hospital

Name and Location	Position	CP and Subsidiaries Directorships and Subsidiary Titles	Other Positions and Directorships	Clubs	Awards	Professional and Community Activities
			Delta Hotels Ltd.; The Dominion of Canada General Insurance Co.; E-L Financial Corp. Ltd.; Empire Life Insurance Co.; The Mercantile Bank of Canada; Rawson Trust Co. Ltd. *(Nassau)*; Span Holdings Ltd. *(Nassau)*; Span International Ltd. *(Nassau)*	Palm Beach, Fla.: Lost Tree Quebec: Ristigouche Salmon Toronto: Granite; National; Rosedale Golf; Toronto Racquet		Past President and Honorary Life Member: Toronto Real Estate Board Past Director: Canadian National Sportsmen Show Honorary Life Member: Canadian Real Estate Association Member: Advisory Council York University
Maitland, J.D. *(West Vancouver)*;	Chairman, Hastings West Investment Ltd.	Director: Marathon Realty Co. Ltd.	Director: Dillingham Corp. Canada Ltd.; International Land Corp. Ltd.			
Marcolin, Albert V. *(Trail, B.C.)*	Vice President, British Columbia Group, Cominco Ltd.	Director: Canada Metal Co. Ltd.; Pine Point Mines Ltd.; West Kootenay Power and Light Co. Ltd.		Canadian *(Vancouver)* Union *(Victoria)*		Canadian Institute of Mining and Metallurgy

Martin, Hugh A. (*Vancouver*)	President, Western Construction & Engineering Research Ltd.	Director: CP Air Ltd.; PanCanadian Petroleum Ltd.	Chairman: Canadian Dredge & Dock Co. Ltd.; Marwell Dredging Ltd. President: Hampshire House Holdings Ltd.; Marwest Hotels Ltd. Director: PeBen Oilfield Services Ltd.; Westin Hotels Inc.	Capilano Golf and Country; Shaughnessy Heights Golf; The Vancouver and Terminal City	Chairman: Community Planning Association of Canada (*British Columbia Branch*) Former Campaign Chairman: Federal Liberal Campaign Patron: Lester B. Pearson College of the Pacific; Vancouver Oral Centre for Deaf Children
Matthews, Donald C. M.Sc. (*Calgary*)	President and General Manager, Highland Stock Farms Ltd.	Director: Canadian Pacific Ltd.		Ranchmen's	Centennial Medal 1967 Board of Governors and Senate: University of Calgary President and Charter Director: Canadian Agriculture Hall of Fame Director: Canadian Cattlemen's Association

Name and Location	Position	cP and Subsidiaries Directorships and Subsidiary Titles	Other Positions and Directorships	Clubs	Awards	Professional and Community Activities
						Member: Agriculture Institute (Canada); American Genetics Association; Canadian and American Society, Animal Production; Cattle Breeders Association
Mauro, Arthur V. B.A., LL.M. (Winnipeg)	Executive Vice President, The Investors Group	Director: Canadian Pacific Hotels Ltd.	Director: Federal Industries Ltd.; Great West Life Assurance Co.; Investors Group; Investors Syndicate Ltd.; Montreal Trust Co.; Pacific Western Airlines		Knight of St. Gregory (K.S.G.); Q.C.	Chairman of Board: St. Paul's College President: Winnipeg Art Gallery Member: Manitoba Bar Association
Maxwell, Donald Spencer B.A. (Ottawa)	Vice President Law and General Counsel, Canadian Pacific Ltd.	Director: Château Insurance Co.; Soo Line Railroad Co.		Le Cercle Universitaire; Montreal Amateur Athletic Association; Rideau; Royal Ottawa Golf		Member: Canadian Bar Association; Law Society of Upper Canada

Maxwell, John S. *(Montreal)*	Executive Vice President Finance, CIP Inc.; Vice President, Facelle Co. Ltd.; Masonite Canada Ltd.	Director: CIP Inc.; NBIP Ltd.; Tahsis Co.	
McCleery, John A. *(Toronto)*	President, J.A. McCleery Ltd.	Director: Maple Leaf Mills Ltd.	Chairman: John Leckie Ltd. Director: DRG Ltd.; Sarco Canada Ltd.; Zurich Life Insurance Co. of Canada	Fellow of the institute of Chartered Accountants (F.C.A.)	Governor: Ontario Bible College Honorary Governor: YMCA of Metropolitan Toronto President: North York General Hospital Foundation Treasurer and Director: Tippet Foundation
McDonald, James Albert *(Montreal)*	Vice President Industry Relations, Canadian Pacific Ltd.	Chairman of the Board: Canadian Pacific Consulting Services Ltd. Chairman and Chief Executive Officer: Canadian Pacific Terminals Director: CHEP Canada Inc.; CanPac	Director: Business Linguistics Centre	Montreal Indoor Tennis; Mount Royal Country; University *(Montreal)*	Royal Commissions: Turgeon; Gordon; McPherson Chairman of the Board: Servicios de Consultorio Pacifico Can., S.A.

Name and Location	Position	CP and Subsidiaries Directorships and Subsidiary Titles	Other Positions and Directorships	Clubs	Awards	Professional and Community Activities
		International Freight Services Ltd.; CanPac Terminals Ltd.; Canadian Pacific Steamships Ltd.; Central Terminal Railway Co.; The Toronto, Hamilton & Buffalo Railway Co.				Co-Chairman, Steering Committee: Canadian Chamber of Commerce Member: Canada-U.S. Advisory Committee; Corporate Affairs Committee; Ottawa Liaison Committee
McGill, Beverly John *(Toronto)*	Former Chairman, Canadian Pacific Hotels Ltd.	Director: Canadian Pacific Hotels Ltd.	Director: Old Brewery Mission Inc. *(Montreal)*	The Little Club; Delray Beach		Freemason; Shriner
McLaughlin, W. Earle B.A., LL.D. *(Montreal)*	Former Chairman of the Board, The Royal Bank of Canada	Director: Algoma Steel Corp. Ltd.; Canadian Pacific Ltd.; Canadian Pacific Enterprises Ltd.	Chairman: Sun Alliance Insurance Co. Trustee: Sun Alliance & London Insurance Group, Canadian Staff Pension Plan	Engineers; Forest and Stream Bermuda: The Mid-Ocean Montreal: Montreal;	Knight of Grace of the Venerable Order of the Hospital of St. John of Jerusalem *(K. St. J.)*;	Board of Governors: Montreal Museum of Fine Art; Royal Victoria Hospital National Co-Chairman: The Canadian

Director:
Aledo Investment
Co. S. A.;
Allied Chemical
(*Canada*) Ltd.;
Continental
Reinsurance Corp.
(*Bermuda*) Ltd.;
DRG Ltd.;
General Motors
Corp.;
Genstar Corp.;
Metropolitan Life
Insurance Co.;
Ralston Purina
Canada Inc.;
Royal Bank of
Canada;
Sarco Canada Ltd.;
The Security
Reinsurance Corp.
Ltd.;
Shawinigan
Industries Ltd.;
Standard Brands
Inc., New York;
Trans Canada
Corporation Fund;
Textron Canada
Ltd.;
Zurich Life
Insurance Co. of
Canada

Mount
Bruno Golf;
Mount
Royal;
Royal
Montreal
Curling;
Royal
Montreal
Golf;
Saint
James's;
Seigniory;
University

Nassau:
Lyford Cay

New York:
Canadian

Ottawa:
Rideau

Toronto:
Toronto;
York

Knight of the
Order of the
Garter (*K.G.*)

Council of
Christians and Jews

Trustee:
Queen's University
(*member,
investment
committee*)

Name and Location	Position	CP and Subsidiaries Directorships and Subsidiary Titles	Other Positions and Directorships	Clubs	Awards	Professional and Community Activities
Meech, Richard C. B.A., LL.M. (*Toronto*)	Partner, law firm of Borden & Elliot	Director: Great Lakes Forest Products Ltd.	Vice-Chairman: Brown Bover Howden Inc.; Howden Group North America Inc. Vice President and Director: Textron Canada Inc. Director and Secretary: Canabam Ltd. Director: Barclay's Canada Ltd.; Budd Canada Inc.; Dresdona Industries Ltd.; Godfrey Engineering Ltd.; Howden Group America Inc.; The Personal Insurance Company of Canada; R.C. Cola Canada Ltd.; Slater Steel Industries Ltd.; Stanton Pipes Ltd.; Textron Canada Ltd.	Bermuda: Coral Beach and Tennis Colorado: Garden of the Gods; Glenmajor Angling New York: Harvard Toronto: Badminton and Racquet; Canadian; National (*first Vice President*); Toronto Golf; York	Q.C.	National Chairman: Queen's University Parent Association Member, Advisory Board: Salvation Army Member, Advisory Council: Havergal College; Ridley College Secretary: The Canadian Securities Ltd.; The Canadian Depository for Securities Ltd.; International Bar Association— Business Section; National Contingency Fund

Meneley, R.A. (*Calgary*)	Group Vice President, Petro Canada	Director: Panarctic Oils Ltd.		
Meyer, John R. (*Boston*)	Professor of Transportation, Logistics and Distribution at Harvard University; Vice-Chairman, Union Pacific Corp.	Director: AMCA International Ltd.	Director: Dun & Bradstreet; Charles River Assoc.; Union Pacific Corp. Trustee: Mutual Life Insurance Co. (*New York*)	Guggenheim Fellowship; Fellow American Academy Arts and Sciences; Fellow Econometric Society	Has served on Presidential Task Force on Transportation
Milner, Stanley A. (*Edmonton*)	President and Chief Executive Officer, Chieftain Development Co. Ltd.	Director: Canadian Pacific Ltd.; CP Air Ltd.	Director: Alberta Energy Co. Ltd.; Woodward Stores Ltd.		
Mingay, Arthur H. (*Toronto*)	Chairman and Chairman of Executive Committee, Canada Trustco Mortgage Co. and The Canada Trust Co.	Director: Algoma Steel Corp.	Director: Inglis Ltd.; Loblaw Companies Ltd.; The Mutual Life Assurance Co. of Canada; Roins Holding Ltd.; Royal Insurance Co. of Canada; Simpsons-Sears	London, Ont.: London Hunt and Country Toronto: Granite; Rosedale Golf; Toronto	Vice President and Director: The Canadian Club Trustee: The Art Gallery of Ontario Director: Ontario Arthritis Society

Name and Location	Position	cp and Subsidiaries Directorships and Subsidiary Titles	Other Positions and Directorships	Clubs	Awards	Professional and Community Activities
			Acceptance Corp.; Simpsons-Sears Ltd.; T.I. Industries Ltd.; The Western Assurance Co.			
Moore, John H. (*Lambeth, Ont.*)	Corporate Director	Director: Canadian Pacific Ltd.	Director: Bell Canada; Cadillac Fairview Corp. Ltd.; Canadian Corporate Management Co. Ltd.; Hudson's Bay Co.; London Life Insurance Co.; Northern Telecom Ltd.	London, Ont.: London; London Hunt and Country Toronto: University; York		Advisory Board: School of Business Administration University of Western Ontario; Women's Christian Association, London, Ontario Member: International Council Morgan Guaranty Trust, New York
Morrish, John Herbert B.A.Sc. (*Calgary*)	President and Chief Executive Officer, Fording Coal Ltd.	Director: Fording Coal Ltd.				Member: Coal Industry Advisory Board; International Energy Agency; Professional Engineers' Association, Ontario; University of Toronto Alumni Association

...rdull (Calgary)	President and Controller, Petro-Canada Ltd.			
Mulholland, William David A.B., M.B.A., LL.D. (Hon.) (Montreal)	Chairman and Chief Executive Officer, Bank of Montreal	Director: Canadian Pacific Ltd. Director and Chairman, Incentive and Compensation Committee and Member, Audit Committee, The Upjohn Company Vice-Chairman, Executive Committee and Member, Resources Committee Bank of Montreal Vice-Chairman, Supervisory Board, Allgemeine Deutsche Credit-Anstalt (Frankfurt) Director and Member, Finance Committee, Kimberly-Clark Corporation Director: Bank of Montreal International Ltd.; Bank of Montreal (Bahamas and Caribbean Ltd.); The Standard Life Assurance Company (Edinburgh)	Montreal: Canadian; Forest and Stream; Lake of Two Mountains Hunt; St. Denis New York: Metropolitan Quebec: Knowlton Golf Toronto: Toronto	Director: Montreal Symphony Orchestra Member: Canadian Economic Policy Committee; Council on Foreign Relations; Canadian Committee, Pacific Basin Economic Council (PBEC)

Name and Location	Position	CP and Subsidiaries Directorships and Subsidiary Titles	Other Positions and Directorships	Clubs	Awards	Professional and Community Activities
Nepveu, Paul A. B.A. (*Montreal*)	Chairman, CIP Inc. (*Canadian International Paper Inc.*); formerly Vice Chairman, Canadian Pacific Enterprises Ltd.	Director: Algoma Steel Corp. Ltd.: CIP Inc.; Canadian Pacific Enterprises Ltd.; Canadian Pacific Securities Ltd.; Cominco Ltd.		OKA Golf; St. Denis		Member: Board of Trade (*Montreal*); Chamber of Commerce (*Canadian*)
Nichol, Hon. John L. B. Com. (*Vancouver*)	President, Springfield Investment Co. Ltd.	Director: Canadian Pacific Enterprises Ltd.	Director: Alcan Aluminium Ltd.; Aluminum Co. of Canada Ltd.; Bethlehem Copper Corp. Ltd.; Crown Zellerbach Ltd.		Officer of the Order of Canada (o.c.)	Former Member, Senate of Canada Chairman: Lester B. Pearson College Pacific Member, Advisory Board: Salvation Army
Nixon, Peter M. (*Sault Ste. Marie, Ont.*)	President and Chief Operating Officer, Algoma Steel Corp.	President: Cannelton Iron Ore Co. Vice President and Director: Kremzar Gold Mines Director: AMCA International Ltd.;	Director: Ingersoll Rand Canada Inc.			Director: The Mining Association of Canada

Name	Position	Directorships	Clubs	Honours
		Cannelton Industries Inc.; CIP Inc.; Maple Meadow Mining Co.; Sault Marine Services Ltd.; Steep Rock Iron Mines Ltd.; Tilden Iron Ore Co.		
O'Brien, David (*Calgary*)	Senior Vice President, Secretary, and General Counsel, Petro-Canada	Director: Panarctic Oils Ltd.		
Ostiguy, Jean P.W. LL.D. (*Mount-Royal, Que.*)	Honorary Chairman, Richardson Greenshields of Canada Ltd.	Director: CP Air Ltd.	Montreal: Mount Royal; St. James's Toronto: Toronto	Knight of Magistral Order of Malta (*K.M.*); Knight of the Military and Hospitaller Order of St. Lazarus of Jerusalem (*K.L.J.*); Officer of the Order of Canada (*O.C.*); Numerous decorations and awards for service in	Past Chairman, Board of Trustees: National Museums of Canada Past President: Chamber of Commerce (*Montreal*); Royal Military College Club of Canada Past National President: Investment Dealers' Association of Canada
		Director: Canadian Canners Ltd.; Canadian Imperial Bank of Commerce; Ciba-Geigy Canada Ltd.; Dominion Life Assurance; Ford Motor Co. of Canada Ltd.; General Accident Assurance Co. of Canada; Kerr Addison Mines Ltd.; Procor Ltd.; Sintra Ltd.		

Name and Location	Position	CP and Subsidiaries Directorships and Subsidiary Titles	Other Positions and Directorships	Clubs	Awards	Professional and Community Activities
					World War II.; Many other awards including: Eleanor Roosevelt Humanities Award; Human Relations Award (*Canadian Council of Christians and Jews*)	
Panabaker, John H. (*Kitchener*)	Chairman and Chief Executive Officer, The Mutual Life Assurance Co. of Canada	Director: Maple Leaf Mills Ltd.	Director: Canada Trustco Mortgage Co.; The Canada Trust Co.	Kitchener: Westmount Golf and Country Toronto: National; Toronto		Past Chairman (*1978–80*) and current member of Board of Governors, McMaster University
Paré Paul B.C.L. (*Montreal*)	Chairman and Chief Executive Officer, Imasco Limited	Director: Canadian Pacific Ltd.; Canadian Pacific Enterprises Ltd.; CIP Inc.	Director: Canadian Fund Inc.; Canadian Investment Fund, Inc.; Canron Ltd.; IBM Canada…	Georgia: Augusta National Golf Club; Muirfield Village Golf Club…		Governor: Douglas Hospital Corporation, Provincial Committee of Patients; Olympic Trust of…

...qua Cacaoma;
Canada;
Royal Bank of
Canada;
The SNC Group

Montreal:
Forest and
Stream;
Montreal
Indoor
Tennis;
Mount
Royal;
Royal
Montreal
Golf

Toronto:
Toronto

Canada;
The Portage
Program for Drug
Dependencies Inc.;
St. Mary's Hospital
(*Montreal*)

Director:
Centraide (*Montreal
United Way*)

Member, Advisory
Board:
Palliative Care
Service, Royal
Victoria Hospital
(*Montreal*)

Member:
Canadian Council of
Christians and Jews;
Economic Council
of Canada;
Governor General's
First Canadian
Study Conference;
Montreal Children's
Hospital Foundation

Honorary:
Vice President, St.
John's (*Ambulance*)
Council for Quebec

Membership in:
Canadian
Association of
Paediatric Surgeons;
Foundation of the
University of
Quebec in Montreal

Board of Trustees:
The Fraser Institute

Name and Location	Position	cp and Subsidiaries Directorships and Subsidiary Titles	Other Positions and Directorships	Clubs	Awards	Professional and Community Activities
Phillips, Neil F. (*Montreal*)	Partner, law firm of Phillips and Vineberg	Director: Canadian Pacific Enterprises Ltd.	Director: Amok Ltd.; Aquitaine Canada Ltd.; Montedison Canada Ltd.; Ritz Carlton Hotel Co. of Montreal Ltd.; Royal Bank; Seru Nucleaire (*Canada*) Ltée; Stewart Smith (*Canada*) Ltd.; Uranerz Canada Ltd.		Q.C.	
Polwarth, 10th Lord, cr. 1690, Henry Alexander Hepburne-Scott, D.L., L.L.D.* D. Litt.* *Honorary (*Edinburgh*)	Member, House of Lords	Director: Canadian Pacific Ltd.	Director and Past Governor: Bank of Scotland Director: Halliburton Co.; Sun Life Assurance Co.	Brooks's; New (*Edinburgh*); Pratt's	Fellow, Royal Society of Arts (*FRSA*); Fellow, Royal Society of Edinburgh (*FRSE*); Territorial Decorations (*TD*)	Chairman: Scottish National Orchestra Society Past Chancellor: University of Aberdeen Member: Royal Company of Archers

| Pratte, Claude (*Quebec City*) | Partner, law firm of Letourneau and Stein | Director: CIP Inc.; Canadian Pacific Ltd. | President: Belleau, Auger, Ltée; Frontenac Broadcasting Co. Ltd.; Katenac Holdings Ltd.; Les Immeubles des Braves Ltée; Lepra Inc.; Placements Verpra Inc.; Sopra Investments Ltd. Vice President: R. Couillard & Assoc. Inc.; Compagnie de Radio diffusion de Shawinigan Falls Ltée; Radio Saguenay Ltée Director: Canadian Ultramar Ltd.; Inter-Québec Publicité Inc.; National Life Assurance Co. of Canada; Nordex 1978 Ltd.; Prades Inc.; Québec-Téléphone; Royal Bank of Canada; Shawinigan Industries Ltd.; | Canadian (*Montreal*); Garrison; Mount Royal; Mount Stephen | Q.C. | Member: Bar Québec; Canadian Bar Association; Canadian Lloyds Register of Shipping |

Name and Location	Position	CP and Subsidiaries Directorships and Subsidiary Titles	Other Positions and Directorships	Clubs	Awards	Professional and Community Activities
			Trans-Canada Corp. Fund; Ultramar Canada Inc.			
Rathgeb, Charles I. *(Toronto)*	Chairman, Comstock International Ltd.; Vice-Chairman, Canadair Ltd.	Director: Steep Rock Iron Mines Ltd.	Director: T.G. Bright & Co. Ltd.; Liquid Carbon Canada Ltd.; Royal Bank of Canada; Texaco Canada Inc.			Director: Olympic Trust of Canada
Reekie, Charles Douglas C.A. *(Islington, Ont.)*	President and Chief Executive Officer, CAE Industries Ltd.	Director: Canadian Pacific Enterprises Ltd.	Chairman of Board and Director: Accurcast Die Casting Ltd.; CAE Aircraft Ltd.; CAE Electronics Ltd.; CAE Fiberglass Products Division; CAE Metals Ltd.; CAE Montupet Die Cast Ltd.; Canadian Bronze Co. Ltd.; Union Screen Plate Co. Ltd.; Webster Manufacturing	Bahamas: Lyford Cay, Nassau London, Ontario: Lambton Golf and Country Montreal: Montreal Badminton and Squash; Mount Royal; Royal Montreal Golf		Member: Order of Chartered Accountants (*Ontario*)

		(London) Ltd.; Welmet Ind. Director: CAE Machinery Ltd.; Canadian Enterprises Development Corp. Ltd.; Colonia Life Insurance Co.; Northwest Ind. Ltd.	Toronto: National		
Ridder, Bernard Herman (*St. Paul, Minnesota*)	Chairman of the Board, Knight-Ridder Newspapers Inc.	Director: Great Lakes Forest Products Ltd. Director: Seattle Times	St Paul: Somerset Country St. Andrews, Scotland: Royal and Ancient Golf Washington: Burning Tree Golf	Journalism Award '*Univ. of Minnesota*'; Regents' Award	Chairman of the Board: Minnesota Vikings Football Club Chairman: University of Minnesota Foundation Member: U.S. Golf Association
Riley, Ronald Thomas B.E., M.B.A. (*Montreal*)	Vice President Corporate Development, Canadian Pacific Ltd.	Chairman and Director: Canadian Pacific International Freight Services Ltd.; Canadian Pacific Express & Transport Co. Ltd.; Château Insurance Co. Director: Argus Corp Ltd.; Dominion Stores Ltd.; Hollinger Argus Ltd.	Hillside Tennis; Mount Bruno; University		Honorary Vice President: Boy Scouts of Canada (*Quebec Provincial Council*) Board of Directors: Metropolitan YMCA

Name and Location	Position	cp and Subsidiaries Directorships and Subsidiary Titles	Other Positions and Directorships	Clubs	Awards	Professional and Community Activities
		President and Director: Cascade Pipe Line Ltd. Director: Arion Insurance Co.; CHEP Canada Inc.; CanPac Terminals Ltd.; Canadian Pacific Consulting Services Ltd.; Canadian Pacific Securities Ltd.; Provident Properties Ltd.				Director: Montreal Museum of Fine Art
Riopel, L.M. (Montreal)	General Manager Development, Canadian Pacific Enterprises Ltd.	Director: Canadian Pacific Consulting Services Ltd.; Fording Coal Ltd.				
Robison, James E. (Armonk, N.Y.)	President, Lonsdale Enterprises Inc.	Director: AMCA International Ltd.	Director: Conoco Inc.; Houbigant Inc.; Thyssen-Bornemisza N.V.	Bahamas: Lyford Cay U.S.: Greater New York; Harvard	Distinguished Flying Cross; Distinguished Service Award, Harvard Business School Association	Chamber of Commerce (U.S.); Harvard Business School Association

Rolland, Lucien Gilbert B.A., B.A. Sc. C.E. D.C.S.* *Honorary (Montreal)

President and Chief Executive Officer, Rolland Inc.

Director: Canadian Pacific Ltd.

Chairman and Director: ASEA Limited; ASEA Industries Limited; Fine Papers Ltd.; Wilson Munroe Co. Ltd.

President and Director: Dessalu Limitee; Tarascon Holdings Ltd.

Vice President and Director: Bank of Montreal

Director: Atlas Copco Canada; Bell Canada; Canadian Fund, Inc.; Canadian Investment Fund, Inc.; Donohue Inc.; Great Lakes Reinsurance Co.; Inco Ltd.; Munich Reinsurance Co. of Canada; Philips Canada Ltd.; Standard Life Assurance Co.;

Montreal: Montreal Indoor Tennis; Mount Royal; St. Denis; St. James's

Toronto: Toronto Hunt

Knight Commander of the Order of St. Gregory (K.C.G.S)

Governor: Hôpital Marie Enfant; Montreal Children's Hospital; Montreal General Hospital; Notre Dame Hospital

Honorary Vice President: Canadian Red Cross Society

Director: Montreal Symphony Orchestra

Honorary Member: University of Montreal Board of Directors

Member: Board of Trade (Montreal); Canadian Manufacturers Association; Canadian Pulp and Paper Association; Chamber of Commerce (Canadian and Province of Quebec);

Name and Location	Position	CP and Subsidiaries Directorships and Subsidiary Titles	Other Positions and Directorships	Clubs	Awards	Professional and Community Activities
			Steel Company of Canada Inc. (STELCO); UAP Inc.			Engineering Institute of Canada
Rombough, Bartlett B. (*Calgary*)	President and Chief Executive Officer, PanCanadian Petroleum Ltd.	Director: Canadian Pacific Securities Ltd.; Fording Coal Ltd.; Panarctic Oils Ltd.; PanCanadian Petroleum Ltd.				
Ross, John C. (*Lethbridge, Alta.*)	President, The Milk River Cattle Company Limited	Director: PanCanadian Petroleum Ltd.				
Ruffin, Dalton D. (*Winston-Salem, N.C.*)	Regional Vice President, Wachovia Bank & Trust Co., N.A.	Director: AMCA International Ltd.				

Name	Position	Director (CP)	Director	Clubs	Honours	Memberships
Runciman, Alexander McInnes LL.D.* *Honorary (*Winnipeg*)	Former President, United Grain Growers Limited	Director: Canadian Pacific Ltd.	Director: Great-West Life Assurance Co.; Massey-Ferguson Ltd.; Royal Bank of Canada	Manitoba; Winnipeg Winter	Hon. Col. Queen's Own Cameron Highlanders of Canada; Centennial Medal; Queen's Silver Jubilee Medal	Trustee: Victoria General Hospital Director: Canada Grains Council; C.D. Howe Research Institute; Great Lakes Waterways Development Association; Manitoba Clinic Foundation, Inc. Honorary Member: Agriculture Institute, Canada; Canada Seed Trade Association; Manitoba Institute Agriculture Life Member: Rapeseed Association; University of Manitoba Alumni Association
Rust, Thomas G. (*Vancouver*)	President and Chief Executive Officer, Crown Zellerbach Canada Ltd.	Director: Canadian Pacific Ltd.	Director: The Bank of Nova Scotia; Discovery Foundation; Discovery Parks Inc.;	Vancouver: Shaughnessy Golf and Country		Member: Canadian Pulp and Paper Association; Engineering Institute of Canada; Pulp and Paper Research Institute

Name and Location	Position	CP and Subsidiaries Directorships and Subsidiary Titles	Other Positions and Directorships	Clubs	Awards	Professional and Community Activities
			Inland Natural Gas Co. Ltd.; Quadrant Development Ltd.; Seaboard Lumber Sales Ltd.; Seaboard Shipping Co. Ltd.			
Salter, John Henry B.A.Sc. (*West Vancouver*)	Retired metallurgist. Past Executive Vice President and Chief Operating Officer, Cominco Ltd.	Director: Fording Coal Ltd.; Vestgron Mines Ltd.	Director: Day Mines Ltd.; Royal Trust Co. Advisory Board	Capilano Golf and Country; Vancouver	Order of St. John (*O.S.J.*)	Member: Canadian Institute Mining and Metallurgy; Chemical Institute Canada; Professional Engineers' Association, British Columbia
Savoie, Leonard N. B.Sc. M.B.A. (*Sault Ste. Marie, Ont.*)	President and Chief Executive Officer, Algoma Central Railway	Director: Algoma Steel Corporation, Limited	President: Algocen Mines Ltd.; Algoma Steamships Ltd. Director: All Canadian-American Investments Ltd.; Casualty Company of Canada;	Algo; Golf and Country; Railway (*Toronto*); Rotary		Member: Canadian Chamber of Commerce; Association of Professional Engineers (*Ontario*); Engineering Institute (*Canada*); Young Presidents Organization Inc.

Seaman, Daryl K. *(Calgary)*	Chairman, Bow Valley Industries Ltd.	Director: Marathon Realty Co. Ltd.	Director: Bow Valley Resource Services Ltd.; Crown Trust Co.; NOVA, An Alberta Corp.; Revelstoke Cos. Ltd.	Dominion of Canada General Insurance Co.; E-L Financial Corp. Ltd.; Empire Life Insurance Co.; Newaygo Forest Products Ltd.; Thibodeau-Finch Express Ltd.	Calgary: Calgary Petroleum; Earl Grey Golf; Ranchmen's
Shepley, James *(Washington, D.C.)*	Management Consultant. Former Chairman, Time Inc.	Director: AMCA International Ltd.			Major, United States Air Force Reserves
Sherman, Frank Howard B.Sc. *(Hamilton, Ont.)*	Chairman, President and Chief Executive Officer, Dominion Foundries & Steel Ltd. (DOFASCO)	Director: Canadian Pacific Ltd.	Director: Arnaud Railway Co.; Bank of Nova Scotia; Canron Ltd.; Crown Life Insurance Co.; Knoll Lake Minerals Ltd.;	Caledon Mountain Trout; Caughnawana Fishing and Hunting; Hamilton: The Hamilton; Hamilton	Board of Governors: Art Gallery of Hamilton; Hamilton Philharmonic Orchestra; McMaster University; Board of Trustees: Ontario Jockey Club

Name and Location	Position	CP and Subsidiaries Directorships and Subsidiary Titles	Other Positions and Directorships	Clubs	Awards	Professional and Community Activities
			National Steel Car Corp. Ltd.; Wabush Lake Railway Co. Ltd.	Golf and Country; Hamilton Thistle Montreal: St. James's Muskoka, Ontario: Muskoka Lakes Golf and Country Club Ltd.; Tamahaac Toronto: Toronto; York		National Executive Council: Canadian Manufacturers Association Director: American Iron and Steel Institute Member: Great Lakes Waterways Development Association
Sinclair, Ian D. B.A., LL.B., LL.D.° D.B.A.° *Honorary (*Oakville, Ontario*)	Chairman, Canadian Pacific Enterprises Ltd.; Vice President, Cominco Ltd. and Pan Canadian Petroleum Ltd.	Director: AMCA International Ltd.; Canadian Pacific Ltd.; CP Air Ltd.; Canadian Pacific *(Bermuda)* Ltd.; Canadian Pacific Enterprises Ltd.; Canadian Pacific Securities Ltd.; Cominco Ltd.; Great Lakes Forest Products Ltd.; Marathon	Vice President and Director: The Royal Bank Director: Canadian Fund, Inc.; Canadian Investment Fund, Inc.; Canadian Marconi Co.;	Montreal: Canadian; Canadian Railway; Mount Royal Ottawa: Rideau	Officer of the Order of Canada (*O.C.*); Q.C.	Member: Canadian Bar Association; Board of Trade (*Montreal*); Canadian Chamber of Commerce; University of Manitoba Alumni Association

			Realty Co. Ltd.; Soo Line Railroad Co.	Sun Life Assurance Co. of Canada; Union Carbide Canada Ltd.; Union Carbide Corp.	
Sloan, William (*Victoria, B.C.*)	President, Pacific Forest Products Ltd.	Director: Pacific Forest Products Ltd.	Director: Seaboard Lumber Sales Co.; Seaboard Shipping Co.		
Southern, R. Donald (*Calgary*)	President and Chief Executive Officer, ATCO Ltd.	Director: Canadian Pacific Enterprises Ltd.	Director: Canada Cement Lafarge Ltd.; Crown Zellerbach of Canada Limited; The Mercantile Bank of Canada; NOVA; Pacific Western Airlines Ltd.; Rothmans of Pall Mall Canada Ltd.; Royal Insurance Co. of Canada; Scott and Easton; United Securities Ltd.	Calgary Petroleum; Earl Gray Golf; Glencoe; Ranchmen's; University of Calgary's Chancellors	Governor: The Olympic Trust of Canada; Member: Canadian Council of the Conference Board in Canada; Charter Member: Young Presidents' Organization; Freemason; Canadian German Chamber of Commerce Inc.

Name and Location	Position	CP and Subsidiaries Directorships and Subsidiary Titles	Other Positions and Directorships	Clubs	Awards	Professional and Community Activities
Starck, Louis (*Calgary*)	President and Managing Director, GM Resources Ltd.	Director: Panarctic Oils Ltd.	Director: Alberta Gas Trunk Line Limited (NOVA)			
Stikeman, H. Heward	Senior Partner, law firm of Stikeman, Elliott, Tamaki, Mercier & Robb	Director: AMCA International Ltd.	Director: Aquila Securities Ltd.; CAE Industries Ltd.; Federal Commerce and Navigation Ltd.; Mercantile Bank of Canada; Rawson Trust (*Nassau*)	Bahamas: Lyford Cay Montreal: Mount Royal Ottawa: Rideau Toronto: Toronto	Q.C.	Former Assistant Deputy Minister of National Revenue, legal
Stinson, William W. B.A. (*Montreal*)	President, Canadian Pacific Ltd.	Director: CNCP Telecommunications; CP Air Ltd.; CP (*Bermuda*) Ltd.; Canadian Pacific Enterprises Ltd.; Canadian Pacific Express & Transport Ltd.; Canadian Pacific Steamships; Incan Ships Ltd.; Northern Alberta Railways Co.; The Shawinigan Falls Terminal Railway Co.; Toronto, Hamilton & Buffalo Railways				

Strong, G. Gordon (*Oakland, Calif.*)	Retired Publisher	Director: Great Lakes Forest Products Ltd.		
Taylor, John Daniel B.S. (*Toronto*)	President and Chief Operating Officer, Simpsons-Sears Ltd.	Director: Canadian Pacific Hotels Ltd.	President and Director: Simpsons-Sears Acceptance Co. Ltd. Director: Allstate Insurance Co. of Canada; Allstate Life Insurance Co. of Canada; DeSoto Coatings Ltd.; Rio Algom Ltd.; Simpsons-Sears Ltd.	Canadian; Granite; Toronto; Toronto Hunt; York	President and Director: Boys and Girls Clubs of Canada Director: Canadian Special Olympics Member: Council, Board of Trade, Metropolitan Toronto; Ontario Business Advisory Council
Taylor, John McGuire B.Sc. (*Calgary*)	President, Triple Five Resources Ltd. (*Former President, PanCanadian Petroleum Ltd.*)	Chairman: Panarctic Oils Ltd. Director: Corporate Foods Ltd.; Eastern Bakeries Ltd.; McGavin Foods Ltd.	Director: Canadian Liquid Air Ltd.; IC Gas Ltd.	Calgary Petroleum; Glencoe	Member: Association Professional Engineers, Geologists and Geophysicists; Institute of Mechanical Engineers

Name and Location	Position	CP and Subsidiaries Directorships and Subsidiary Titles	Other Positions and Directorships	Clubs	Awards	Professional and Community Activities
Telfer, James A. (*Toronto*)	Executive Vice President, Maple Leaf Mills Ltd.	Director: Maple Leaf Mills Ltd.				
Theis, Robert J. (*Syracuse, N.Y.*)	President, Canadian Pacific Enterprises (*U.S.*) Inc.	Director: AMCA International Ltd.; Algoma Steel Corp.; Baker Commodities Inc.; CanPac Agriproducts Ltd.; Corenco Corp.; Processed Minerals Inc.				Past President: American Restaurant China Council Member: International Foodservice Manufacturers Association; Advisory Board, Syracuse University Graduate School of Management
Thompson, John D. B. Eng., M.B.A. (*Montreal*)	President, Chief Executive Officer and Director, Roynat Inc.	Director: Canadian Pacific Hotels Ltd.	Director: J.S. Redpath Ltd.; J.S. Redpath Corp., U.S.A.	Montreal Amateur Athletic Association; Mount Royal; Royal Montreal Golf; St. James's		Director: Montreal Children's Hospital Foundation; St. Mary's Hospital Corp. Member: Board of Trade (*Montreal*); Professional Engineers' Association

Name	Position	Directorships		Clubs	Honors	Career
Trezevant, J.G. *(Irvine, Calif.)*	Executive Vice President, Field Newspaper Syndicate	Director: Great Lakes Forest Products Ltd.				
Turner, Hon. John M. M.A. B.C.L. *(Toronto)*	Partner, law firm of McMillan Binch	Director: Canadian Pacific Ltd.; Marathon Realty Ltd.	Director: Bechtel Canada Ltd.; Canadian Investment Fund Ltd.; Credit Foncier; Crown Life Insurance Co.; Holt Renfrew & Co.; MacMillan Bloedel Ltd.; Sandoz *(Canada)* Ltd.; The Seagram Co. Ltd.; Wander Ltd.	Ottawa: Cercle Universitaire d'Ottawa Montreal: Montreal Racquet; St. James's Toronto: Badminton and Racquet; Queen's Tennis; York	Q.C.; Privy Council *(P.C.)*; Rhodes Scholar	Parliamentary Career 1972–76 Last position: Federal Minister of Finance Member of the Bars of Barbados, British Columbia, England, Northwest Territories, Ontario, Quebec, Trinidad, Yukon Director: Canadian Council of Christians and Jews; Collegium St. Michael's College; Salvation Army *(Metro Toronto)*; Toronto School of Theology

Name and Location	Position	CP and Subsidiaries Directorships and Subsidiary Titles	Other Positions and Directorships	Clubs	Awards	Professional and Community Activities
Vennat, Michael (*Montreal*)	Partner, law firm of Stikeman, Elliott, Tamaki, Mercier & Robb	Director, Panarctic Oils Ltd.	Chairman: Canadian Film Development Corp. Director: Atlas Construction Inc.; Baltica-Skandinavia Insurance Company of Canada; Dumez Construction Inc.; Enheat Inc.; G.M. Gest Ltd.; Hellenic Insurance Canada Trust; Hudson Institute of Canada Inc.; J. Meloche; Richelieu Raceways Inc.			
Waddell, William H. (*Calgary*)	Senior Vice President Exploration and Production, Home Oil Company Ltd.	Director: Panarctic Oils Ltd.	Group Vice President and Director Exploration: Plains Petroleums Ltd. Group Vice President Exploration: Scurry-Rainbow Oil Ltd.			

Wahl, K.N. *(Toronto)*	President and Chief Executive Officer, Canadian Pacific Express & Transport Ltd.	Director: Canadian Pacific Consulting Services Ltd.; CanPac International Freight Services Inc.				
Ward, Walter *(Toronto)*	Former Chairman, Algoma Steel Corp.	Director: Algoma Steel Corp.; AMCA International Ltd.; Dominion Engineering Works Ltd.	Former Chairman: Canadian General Electric Co. Director: Canada Packers Ltd.; Canadian General Electric Co.; Canadian Imperial Bank of Commerce; Canadian Oxygen Ltd.; Jannock Ltd.	Kawartha Golf and Country; Peterborough; York *(Toronto)*		Board of Governors: Trent University Board of Trustees and Vice President: Art Gallery of Ontario Member: Ontario Research Foundation; Association of Professional Engineers *(Ontario)*; Canadian Electrical Manufacturers Association
White, Kenneth Alan *(Toronto)*	Chairman, President and Chief Executive Officer, Royal Trustco Ltd.	Director: Canadian Pacific Ltd.; Great Lakes Forest Products Ltd.	Chairman and Director: Commercial Union Association of Canada Ltd.; Computel Systems Ltd.; Royal Trust Corp. of Canada;	Montreal: Forest and Stream; Mount Royal; St. James's Ottawa: Rideau	Canadian Forces Decoration; Knight of the Order of St. John of Jerusalem *(K.St.J.)*	Life Governor: Douglas Hospital Honorary Chairman: St. John Ambulance *(Quebec Council)* President: Board of Trade

Name and Location	Position	cp and Subsidiaries Directorships and Subsidiary Titles	Other Positions and Directorships	Clubs	Awards	Professional and Community Activities
			The Royal Trust Co. and Royal Trust worldwide subsidiary companies Director: Canabam Ltd.; Dominion Textile Inc.; Royal Trustco Ltd.; The Steel Co. of Canada (STELCO)	Toronto: Toronto; York		*(Montreal Council)* Director: Montreal Children's Hospital; Royal Victoria Hospital; St. Mary's Hospital Foundation Member: Trust Companies Association of Canada
Williams, Marshall MacKenzie B.Eng., M.Eng. *(Calgary)*	President and Chief Executive Officer, Trans Alta Utilities Ltd.	Director: PanCanadian Petroleum Ltd.	Director: AEC Power Ltd.; Calgary Power Ltd.; Newfoundland Light and Power Co. Ltd.; Royal Trust Corp. of Canada; Royal Trustco Ltd.; Sun Life Assurance Co. of Canada Ltd. Member: Advisory Board Royal Trust *(Calgary)*	Ranchmen's		Director: Alberta Research Council; Canadian Energy Research Institute Member: Canadian Electrical Association; Chamber of Commerce *(Calgary)*; Northwest Electric Light and Power Association; Social Environment and Energy Development Studies (SEEDS)

Name	Position	Directorships	Other Position	Awards	Clubs	Memberships
Williams, Perry David (*Calgary*)	President, Westburne Petroleum & Minerals Ltd.	Director: Panarctic Oils Ltd.	Senior Vice President: Westburne International Industries Ltd.			
Wilson, William George (*West Vancouver*)	President, Cominco Ltd.	Director: Aberfoyle Ltd.; Arvik Mires Ltd.; Bethlehem Copper Corp.; Cominco Ltd.; Cominco Australian Pty. Ltd.; Hawaiian Western Steel Ltd.; Pine Point Mines Ltd.; Valley Copper Mines Ltd.; Western Canada Steel Ltd.; West Kootenay Power and Light Co. Ltd.			Vancouver	Member: Vancouver Symphony Society
Wolcott, Donald M. (*Calgary*)	Business Consultant	Director: Panarctic Oils Ltd.	Senior Vice President Production and Development: Petro-Canada Exploration			
Wolfe, Ray B.A. (*Willowdale, Ont.*)	Chairman and President, The Oshawa Group Ltd.	Director: Canadian Pacific Ltd.; Canadian Pacific Enterprises Ltd.	Chairman: IGA Canada Ltd. Director: Bank of Nova Scotia; Confederation Life Insurance Co.;	Medal of Courage (C.M.); Order of Canada (O.C.);	Primrose; Oakdale Golf; Montefiore	Governor: Mount Sinai Hospital Chairman: Canada-Israel Chamber of

Name and Location	Position	CP and Subsidiaries Directorships and Subsidiary Titles	Other Positions and Directorships	Clubs	Awards	Professional and Community Activities
			Consumers Distributing Co. Ltd.; Super-Sol Ltd.		Honorary Fellowship, Haifa University; Human Relations (*Canadian Council, Christians and Jews*); Ben Sadowski Award of Merit	Commerce President: Canadian Jewish News Honorary President: Canadian Friends of Haifa University Director: Baycrest Centre for Geriatric Care; Canadian Council Christians and Jews; Canadian Technion Society; Food Marketing Institute; Retail Council of Canada Member: Council of Trustees Institute for Research on Public Policy; Executive Committee Canadian Jewish Congress
Worden G.A. (*Burnaby, B.C.*)	Vice President Technical Services, CP Air	Director: Canadian Pacific Consulting Services Ltd.				

Yeo, Bruce E. (*Regina*)	Vice President Finance, Interprovincial Steel & Pipe Corp. Ltd.	Director: CP Air Ltd.	
Young, W. Maurice (*Vancouver*)	Chairman, Finning Tractor & Equipment Co. Ltd.	Director: Pine Point Mines Ltd.	Director: British Columbia Resources Investment Corporation; Canadian Reassurance Co.; Canadian Reinsurance Co.; Consolidated Freightways Inc.; Northern Telecom Ltd.; Safeway Stores Inc.; Toronto-Dominion Bank
Zafirian, Berj (*Toronto*)	Treasurer, Canadian Pacific Enterprises Ltd.	Director: Canadian Pacific Securities Ltd.	

Sources: Financial Post Directory of Directors; The Canadian Who's Who; Who's Who In Canada; Who's Who In America

TABLE 5 Five-Year Financial Results

	$ Millions				
	1982	1981	1980	1979	1978
Canadian Pacific Ltd.					
Revenue	12,289.5	12,336.2	9,984.5	8,177.7	6,724.5
Profit	188.3	485.6	583.1	508.1	349.7
Assets	17,273.0	16,330.2	13,038.5	11,002.4	9,255.9
Canadian Pacific Enterprises Ltd.					
Revenue	8,494.7	8,558.7	6,659.2	5,297.9	4,247.4
Profit	150.1	404.6	491.2	420.3	284.7
Assets	12,017.5	11,241.1	8,496.1	7,009.8	5,686.2

Five-Year Financial Results

| | $ Millions | | | | |
Sector	1982	1981	1980	1979	1978
CP Air					
Revenue*	880.7	827.6	698.2	555.4	474.8
Profit *(loss)*	(39.2)	(22.8)	2.8	13.1	19.9
Canadian Pacific Enterprises *(71.1% owned)*					
Revenue	8,494.7	8,558.7	6,659.2	5,297.9	4,247.4
Profit	106.0	287.0	583.1	508.1	349.8
CP Rail					
Revenue	2,147.1	2,070.9	1,773.6	1,619.0	1,428.4
Profit	117.9	127.2	121.6	108.7	75.9
CP Ships					
Revenue	269.9	336.2	338.7	255.6	177.1
Profit	(20.0)	43.8	52.3	26.3	(8.6)
CP Telecommunications					
Revenue	152.4	136.9	123.0	98.2	86.4
Profit	5.1	4.9	4.9	6.0	2.9
CP Trucks					
Revenue	291.8	291.5	243.2	211.7	208.1
Profit *(loss)*	1.5	5.5	(1.5)	(1.8)	2.1
Soo Line Railroad Co.					
Revenue	367.8	414.3	380.1	349.7	293.0
Profit	13.6	23.0	23.1	17.8	14.8

*CP Ltd. reports higher revenue figures for the airline than CP Air because it includes investment income and gain on disposal of properties, whereas CP Air confines its revenue figures strictly to money made on flight operations.

Canadian Pacific Enterprises *(Sectors)*
Five-Year Financial Results

Sector	$ Millions				
	1982	1981	1980	1979	1978
Agriproducts					
Revenue	1,137.5	1,165.2	715.6	254.8	176.9
Profit	16.6	19.9	9.6	4.9	5.8
Financial Services					
Revenue	169.5	168.2	142.2	95.8	108.3
Profit	27.4	18.8	33.2	10.1	30.8
Forest Products					
Revenue	1,654.1	1,026.6	674.9	470.4	361.2
Profit	(97.3)	16.2	45.5	47.6	18.3
Iron and Steel					
Revenue	2,680.5	3,312.4	2,382.2	2,185.3	1,854.1
Profit	(25.7)	93.6	61.2	60.2	41.3
Mines and Minerals					
Revenue	1,554.3	1,725.4	1,698.5	1,532.3	1,139.3
Profit	(13.2)	37.6	98.6	129.7	49.5

Oil and Gas					
Revenue	792.6	641.9	574.7	423.9	332.8
Profit	200.9	177.4	210.2	144.4	135.7
Real Estate					
Revenue	251.1	226.9	193.9	130.5	128.7
Profit	26.2	24.1	20.9	19.2	18.3
Other					
(Hotels, Syracuse China, Processed Minerals)					
Revenue	327.4	324.5	302.3	262.1	212.8
Profit *(loss)*	15.3	16.8	11.8	4.0	(12.2)

TABLE 6

Return on Investment

(By Rank In 1982)	1982	1981	1980 Percentage	1979	1978
Imasco Ltd.	10.2	9.0	8.2	10.0	9.5
Canadian Corporate Management Ltd.	6.9	4.9	5.6	7.1	6.6
The Molson Cos.	6.6	6.4	4.4	7.2	7.0
Burlington Northern Inc.*	4.9	4.8	4.2	4.2	2.9
csx Corp.*	4.2	4.5	3.7	3.3	1.9
Union Pacific Corp.*	3.3	5.8	6.5	7.5	5.9
International Telephone & Telegraph Corp.*	2.4	2.3	2.6	1.1	2.4
Canadian Pacific Enterprises Ltd.	1.2	3.6	5.8	5.9	5.0
Canadian Pacific Ltd.	1.1	3.0	4.4	4.6	3.8
Jannock Ltd.	(2.6)	4.3	6.6	7.9	7.3
Genstar Corp.	(3.2)	3.8	6.3	5.1	5.5
Canadian National	(3.5)	3.1	3.4	4.0	2.9

Return on Shareholders' Equity

(By Rank In 1982)	1982	1981	1980 Percentage	1979	1978
Imasco Ltd.	19.0	24.6	20.1	20.1	20.3
The Molson Cos.	17.3	16.9	12.9	18.6	18.5
International Telephone & Telegraph Corp.*	11.5	11.1	11.9	5.0	9.7
Canadian Corporate Management Ltd.	10.0	12.1	13.1	17.7	18.4
csx Corp.*	9.9	11.7	9.8	9.1	5.3
Union Pacific Corp.*	8.4	13.2	14.3	14.9	11.5
Burlington Northern Inc.*	6.3	9.7	8.7	6.8	5.6
Canadian Pacific Enterprises Ltd.	5.0	14.7	19.7	22.0	20.0
Canadian Pacific Ltd.	4.7	12.4	16.6	17.0	13.5
Canadian National	(7.8)	6.2	6.5	7.5	5.3
Jannock Ltd.	(9.0)	9.5	16.7	19.8	17.1
Genstar Corp.	(16.8)	9.9	19.7	22.3	19.4

Notes: *In United States

Burlington Northern*	*(Rail, trucking, forestry, real estate, coal)*
CSX*	*(Rail, aviation, coal, oil and gas, Greenbrier Resort)*
Canadian Corporate Management Ltd.	*(Chemicals, electronics, building supplies, greeting cards, sporting goods)*
Canadian National	*(Oil and gas, real estate, trucking, rail, telecommunications)*
Canadian Pacific	*(Transportation, telecommunications)*
Canadian Pacific Enterprises	*(Mining, forestry, hotels, oil and gas, agribusiness, real estate, steel)*
Genstar	*(Real estate, construction, financial services, marine services)*
Imasco	*(Tobacco, drug stores, fast foods, sporting goods)*
International Telephone & Telegraph*	*(Telecommunications, hotels, financial services, natural resources)*
Jannock	*(Bricks, transformers, sugar refining)*
The Molsons Cos.	*(Beer, hardware, lumber, chemicals)*
Union Pacific	*(Rail, real estate, oil and gas, coal)*

Profit Margin

(By Rank In 1982)	1982	1981	1980 Percentage	1979	1978
csx Corp.	6.9	5.6	5.0	4.6	3.1
Burlington Northern Inc.	6.7	5.5	5.5	5.4	4.5
Imasco Ltd.	5.8	5.7	6.3	5.9	4.9
Union Pacific Corp.	5.5	6.4	8.3	9.5	8.8
International Telephone & Telegraph Corp.	4.4	2.9	3.2	1.4	2.9
The Molson Cos.	3.5	3.3	2.3	3.7	3.7
Canadian Corporate Management Ltd.	1.9	2.3	2.7	3.5	3.6
Canadian Pacific Enterprises Ltd.	1.7	4.7	7.3	7.9	6.7
Canadian Pacific Ltd.	1.5	3.9	5.8	6.2	5.2
Jannock Ltd.	(1.8)	3.0	4.2	5.3	5.6
Genstar Corp.	(4.8)	5.1	6.7	9.8	7.1
Canadian National	(5.3)	4.5	5.2	6.2	4.5